The Service Society and the Consumer Vanguard

The Service Society
and the
Consumer Vanguard

Alan Gartner and Frank Riessman

Introduction by Colin Greer

HARPER & ROW, PUBLISHERS

New York, Evanston, San Francisco, London

1817

FIRST EDITION

Designed by Sidney Feinberg

Library of Congress Cataloging in Publication Data

Gartner, Alan.
  The service society and the consumer vanguard.
  Includes bibliographical references.
  1. Social service—United States. 2. Consumers—United States. 3. Welfare state. I. Riessman, Frank, 1924–   joint author. II. Title.
HV91.G35   361'.973   73–18670
ISBN 0–06–013556–5

For Audrey and Cathy,
Jonathan, Rachel, and Daniel
Robin, Janet, and Jeffrey; and for
Maya and Danny, the children of our friend
   the late George Wiley,
Who all are a part of the coming new majority

Contents

Acknowledgments

A number of the ideas presented here have been developed in earlier versions in *Elementary School Principal, Change, Liberation, Social Policy, Social Work,* and the *Teachers College Record.*

Colin Greer has been the best of friends—namely, a firm critic of our work. We are also appreciative of the efforts of Stanley Aronowitz, Roy Bennett, Barbara Ehrenreich, Herb Gans, Bert Gross, Ivan Kronenfeld, Sol Levine, S. M. Miller, Sumner Rosen, and Joan Shapiro, who have read and commented upon portions of the book. We are especially grateful to Bert Gross, who wrote in 1967, "America's Post-Industrial Revolution: A Selective Overview of a Transnational Society," a seminal study, ahead of its time, for sharing it fully with us. We would like to thank the *Social Policy* seminar where many of these ideas have been developed, and critiqued.

Gina Schachter was very helpful in digging out data, and giving valuable editorial suggestions.

Mel Freeland, Ruth Hunter, and Ethel Mingo typed, and typed, and typed, always willing to accept our tale that it was the "last draft."

To all of those mentioned, and to the staff of the New Human Services Institute and of *Social Policy,* who gave us the time to work on the book, we are grateful. Of course, for whatever shortcomings the book has, we are responsible.

Introduction

Alan Gartner and Frank Riessman's book observes two important phenomena in contemporary society: one, the expansion of human service activity; two, the potentially increased power of consumers in a society characterized, more and more, by the delivery and receipt of services. Not, of course, to say that other sectors of the economy are manifestly unimportant now; rather to suggest that a newly significant sector—with encouragingly progressive possibilities—is emerging. We must understand it better, they argue, and try to get sufficient hold on it to steer a socially salutary course. That course is not inevitable—they are aware of that, even though their excitement overloads their optimism sometimes. But it is possible, as far as they are concerned, since they cherish the promises of the sixties and refuse to read failure and disappointment. They seek instead to learn from earlier efforts and to build on gains in order to steer emerging events rather than be steered by them. Gartner and Riessman spin a fascinating web of encouraging possibilities.

In brief they see the prospect of a society characterized by the effective delivery of services and a consumer consciousness that serves at once as a demand and a force for accountability: not just accountability in delivery but accountability in what is to be delivered. The consumer as a participant in the "manufacture," so to speak, of a major sector of the economy and as a personal resource of efficiency becomes the potential heart of a new social democracy.

Hear Alan Gartner and Frank Riessman in their conclusion. Having recognized that services and the sociocultural dimensions they reflect are frequently distorted by their use as mechanisms for socializing people, and "their effectiveness is marred by professional profit and status seeking," the authors stand strongly for their view that consumers *are* becoming a central force in the emerging service society—and a potentially powerful one, too, since:

1. They are needed in the market to buy the overproduced goods;
2. They are encouraged to be continuously *dissatisfied* with last year's products;
3. They are "exploited" via high prices and taxes;
4. They have much free time in which to engage with each other and to consider their dissatisfactions and common interests;
5. They are less socialized by the traditional industrial workplace; and
6. Finally, certain consumer groups—minorities, women, and youth —are doubly alienated and angered because they are discriminated against by racism, sexism, and adultism and restricted from access to the industrial setting and the body politic.

It is the idea of possibility that is crucial to the framework of this book.

Their argument about possibility, however, is so forceful that the reader may complete the book and lose awareness of the caution and tentativeness that are included in its outlook. That would be a pity; the authors are critical observers of emerging phenomena as well as hopeful and partisan about progressive direction. So I want to remind the reader of the caution in this book by suggesting a way of understanding the balance between distortion/cooption and progressive direction, which will put the issue into historical perspective and, I trust, reinforce the critical awareness of contradictory possibilities that the authors have tried hard to marry with their personal optimism.

As Gartner and Riessman make plain, more and more college graduates (and many among those who never completed college) are entering what is now engagingly called the human-service professions—the H.E.W.–related employment sector. The number of jobs in human-service fields has been expanding at an unprecedented rate.

Someday soon, Daniel Bell points out, "the proportion of factory workers in the labor force may be as small as the proportion of farmers today."

These developments are enormously complicated, of course, but they parallel—slowly but surely—the narrowing of the industrial-production emphasis in the nation's economy. The service sector—the welfare establishment, the professions and paraprofessions of education, welfare, and health—stands not only as an expanding sector of employment but also as the focus for the ambitions and discontents of today's poor and working-class urbanites. They sense that the battle for adequacy in schools and other service agencies is also a battle for control—and thus for opportunity for those traditionally excluded—over the growing parts of the economy. The poor and the working class, or at least their spokesmen, self-designated or chosen, find themselves fighting for entry: fighting to turn the welfare establishment into a vehicle for their own independence and self-respect.

Briefly, some dimensions of the newly expanded service sector: Since World War II the United States economy has entered a new phase. Employment figures in 1950 showed that there were more service-producing than goods-producing workers. During the course of that decade there came to be more white-collar than blue-collar workers. And by the end of the decade, professional, technical, and kindred workers exceeded for the first time the number of managers, officials, and proprietors.

Within the service sector, too, there have been shifts, from industry-related services to people-based services. And what Herbert Gans called the equality revolution of the sixties, the New Deal between the Depression and World War II, and the so-called Progressive Era in the early twentieth century have all been powerful forces contributing to the growth of services.[1] Indeed our readiness to write obituaries for

1. Herbert Gans, *More Equality* (New York: Pantheon Books, 1973); S. M. Miller and Pamela Roby, *The Future of Inequality* (New York: Basic Books, 1970).

successive periods of social reform has kept us from better understanding the larger social functions served by these periods. The
obituaries are almost commonplace.

In 1958 the historian Arthur Linke asked, "What happened to the
Progressive movement in the 1920s?" Linke was concerned about the
so-called normalcy of the 1920s and the repression that seemed to
follow Progressive humanitarian concerns following World War I. Of
course, he was also reacting to the 1950s, his own time, which must
have seemed like the 1920s; the same "normalcy" and again repression after a period of social reform efforts and humanitarian zeal. In
1971 Harry Ashmore asked, "Where are the liberals?" Once again it
seemed a regenerative period—the 1960s—was to be followed by a
return to the "normalcy" of conservatism and perhaps even repression in political, social, and economic life. But perhaps we should
have been observing a new "normalcy" in process of becoming
against the backdrop of which the overtly regressive swings were
increasingly antiquated phenomena; a new normalcy characterized by
a progressive helping-service rhetoric and human service agency/pro-
fessional expansion.[2]

As these phenomena have progressed, so too have closely related
changes in the public world view, which informs institutional practices. Indeed we often forget that shifts in economic emphasis require
a new public outlook, a new conventional wisdom about personal and
social life. In this perspective, it is important to recognize a crucial
aspect of the growth in social-reform rhetoric—urban-located and
service-profession-soluble for the most part—in the decades of this
century in the way it has been teaching us to view society. Much of
the "open," "experimental," and "innovative" programming of schools
and colleges has, whatever else it was supposed to do and whatever
else it has achieved, served precisely this preparatory and reinforcing
function. So that what might be called "the sixties mood," for
example—in which applied social consciousness and social service in

2. Arthur Linke, "What Happened to the Progressive Movement in the
1920's," *American Historical Review* (July 1959); Harry Ashmore, "Where
Are the Liberals?" *Center Forum* (September 1971).

a humane, egalitarian framework are the criteria for "relevance"—
the mood so forcefully expressed at Berkeley, Columbia, and Yale,
has been filtering as a normative conventional wisdom into public
colleges and public high schools now increasingly, and for longer
periods of time than ever before, populated by working-class students, black and white. More and more since World War II (following the sudden growth of about 60 percent in service employment at
that time), the theme of service has emerged at the core of an increasingly recognizable national ideology, an ideology favoring group
cohesion, which prizes self-evaluation through introspection and
sensitivity.

My view is that these phenomena are part and parcel of a thrust
apparent quite early in the nineteenth century and reflect the awareness of continuing urban growth and agrarian decline. As I have said
elsewhere, the school is at the heart of such developments—at the
very time when the frontier is granting and then denying (via the
successive location and exhaustion of such open resources as land
itself and gold within it, opportunity for Americans on the move.[3]

As native land became less readily available, the age of the city—
the prototype of sociocultural organization predicated on the experience of limited physical space—provided the context for Turner's
view that the absence of the frontier would leave a vacuum that had
to be filled, not necessarily by real changes in social content but by
changes in the forms by which hierarchy, privilege, and opportunity
were distributed. It was in relation to the consistency of content and
the transformation of its institutional forms that the school and other
human services were crucial and became, in fact, like the frontier, a
metaphor for American society, with the school at its center: at once
a preparatory and an accrediting route in a society with jobs and
expectations becoming more and more urban and service-work-based.

Turner's superficial "democratic" celebration has tended to obfus-
cate the key point he was making: that land has been crucial to social
development; that its shrunken supply necessitated the development
of new bases for social equilibrium. Park, following Turner, saw the

3. Colin Greer, *The Great School Legend* (New York: Basic Books, 1972).

school as the institution to fill the gap; the institution to serve and support the emergent technological society. To view the school this way, it seems to me, is to recognize it as functioning much like churches in previous, land-based eras; it is to observe the growth of school significance in the mythology and reality of contemporary America and to follow its development at the center of a new creed—a creed articulated via "progressive" social consciousness and a conventional manners, which predicates people-need on professional privilege. So the "new income," as S. M. Miller dubs the expansion of human services—an aspect of status as well as of subsistence—has meant also the development of what Charles Reich once referred to as the "new property": the professional investment and profit in social-welfare (in addition to national-warfare) revenues.[4]

This is the dialectic out of which grows the service/consumer society that Gartner and Riessman talk about: altruism and self-interest are close partners and have a long-standing pact with the unfolding of historical epochs. How does a service-intensive society actually redirect and avoid strengthening the producer dominance of the "service-production system"? How does it actually redirect this expanding apparatus away from the social control, vested-interest-reinforcing functions latent in human service development from its early days?

Recall briefly the abolition and public-school movements—the beginnings of "service" with "people reform" as a major component of its thrust (as opposed to a focus on the relief of conditions) as a career—being created, fought for, and dispensed with increasing intensity during the nineteenth century via abolition, school, charity societies, asylums. All led, finally, to the establishment of new professions—professions, incidentally, around which a "marginal" population similar to previous slave and itinerant labor was a crucial part. Abolitionism was constantly concerned with the separation of freedom and equality and the need to protect the nation from those patently "unequal" while (for religious, rural, and/or economic

4. Miller and Roby, *op. cit.;* Charles Reich, "The New Property," *Yale Law Review* (April 1964), pp. 733–787.

motives) freeing them. In the long run it not only set the contours of reform in a society changing rapidly from an agrarian mercantile base to an urban industrial one, but it also indelibly identified the population around whose subject condition this would be most clearly played out in the twentieth-century "human-service" explosion.

Humanitarian reactions to nineteenth-century poverty rarely rose above a profound disrespect for the poor (almost never when it came to institutional responses), and this disrespect has continued, more or less, to pervade charitable activities in America since then, both public and private. What was new about poverty in the 1800s was its relative density in the cities and the dangers that were envisioned as a result. New York's Society for the Prevention of Pauperism announced in 1821 that "the paupers of the city are, for the most part . . . depraved and vicious, and require support because they are so." Such declarations were repeated throughout the century in Philadelphia, Boston, Baltimore, and other growing urban centers.[5] It was unanimously held that the chief causes of poverty were moral, and agencies designed to deal with poverty had also to impose strict moral standards on the poor they dealt with. Not relief but rehabilitation was the theme—the groundswell for service professions as an expanding, state-supported sector of the socioeconomy. And always, the most vigorous expectations were related to safeguarding the status quo and the rights to privilege and property.

It was out of this frame of reference that first settlement houses, then school-based service, then broad-based tax-supported human-welfare services grew—always in the context, too, of an alliance of privileged young people searching out new turf and people deprived beyond endurance against new power and new money. And so the aristocrats' alliance with the poor against the early captains of trade and industry is replicated over and over: against ethnic political patronage, for example, via "good government" pressure generated out of private do-good organizations from the Charity Society organi-

---

5. David Rothman, *The Age of Asylum* (Boston: Little, Brown, 1970); Roy Lubove, *The Professional Altruist: The Rise of Social Work as a Profession* (Cambridge, Mass.: Harvard University Press, 1965).

zation, the various progressive social and political societies of 1920
to 1950, all the way through to John Gardner's Common Cause in
very much more recent times.[6]

The kind of progressivism to be recorded in this narrative is not at
all the progressivism W. A. C. Stewart had in mind when he defined it
as an aspect of *radical* social change: namely, a series of reactions to
rigid schooling in order to liberate what has become repressed. It is
clearly much closer to the oppressor than to the oppressed. As with
schools, so, too, with broad-ranging human services.

In this perspective, it is interesting to note how the wealthy young
man's "grand tour" to Europe or around the world, the jet set, and,
most important, the easily accessible graduation or summer trip
abroad have gradually tamed the spirit of territorial expansion following the exhaustion of real frontier possibilities; how Peace Corps,
Teacher Corps, and VISTA were attempts to unite the newly exposed
nerve of social consciousness with traditional territorial outlets during
a period of transition. Volunteer do-gooding abroad, like volunteer
do-gooding in the immediately preceding "progressive" decades was,
all the good will and anomie in the world notwithstanding, a route to
what I have referred to as "domestic colonies." With new professional mandates, the "new professionals"—radical doctors, lawyers,
and teachers, for example—disdained established professional norms
and priorities and built new norms, in the context of which new
avenues and new respectability could be achieved (not inherited or
joined) through alliances with the frustrated and the dissatisfied
among those segments of the population that had been inadequately
served.[7] The growth of human services in the contemporary socioeconomy can, then, be regarded as a new frontier: as the basis, at
once, of a new conventional wisdom (a new public world view) about
personal and social life and a domain (succeeding land-based and
capital-based mobility and security) for advancement and status.

6. Peter Schrag, *The Decline of the WASP* (New York: Simon and Schuster,
1971).
7. Peter Schrag, "Common Cause: New Paths for WASP Elites," *Social
Policy* (November–December 1971), pp. 29–35.

This is not to say that statements about social improvement and humane processes are without good will and sincerity, but it is to say that there have not, according to the outcome so far, been dominant themes. Indeed, it sometimes seems as though the social rhetoric behind the successive reform thrusts that have propelled human-service expansion in this century was a public-relations campaign for the job expansion from which so many in the so-called helping professions have benefited.

But even if the social rhetoric did function in this way, that does not mean, as Gartner and Riessman show sharply, that the resulting direction (its goals and even some of its actual practices) is not toward really dealing with the problems and miseries of millions of Americans. The overriding question remains that of the balance between service and profit, of the salutary possibilities of professional altruism: Can human services be delivered in a context freed of the social-control functions and class privilege that has been characteristic of so much of their activity to date? Yes, say these authors—through the consciousness and power of the consumer in a society increasingly organized around the consumption of service products experienced by people in a personal way. Recognizing the danger that consumer rhetoric could first strengthen social-control functions by projecting a false image of accountability and manipulating populist sentiment in conservative directions, Gartner and Riessman believe in the possibility that people can free themselves from the present constraints and inadequacies of service delivery and thereby reformulate the axis of our society away from privileged hierarchy toward R. H. Tawney's vision of "human fellowship" in an egalitarian society.

COLIN GREER

The Service Society and the Consumer Vanguard

Prologue

*Individuals now talk to other individuals rather
than interact with the machines.*

*If an industrial society is defined by the
quantity of goods that mark a standard of living, the
post-industrial society is defined by the quality
of life as measured by the services and amenities
—health, education, recreation, and the arts
—which are now deemed desirable and
possible for everyone.*

—DANIEL BELL

*The established mode of production can only
sustain itself by constantly augmenting the
mass of luxury goods and services beyond
the satisfaction of vital material needs (the
fulfillment of these needs requiring an ever
smaller quantity of labor time), which means
augmenting the consumer population (mass of
purchasing power) capable of buying these goods.*

—HERBERT MARCUSE

The central problem addressed by this book is how to relate basic well-known economic trends, on the one hand, to equally clear social and cultural phenomena on the other hand. The following chart lists in outline fashion these two dimensions.

Economic dimensions	*Social and cultural phenomena*
The vastly expanded productivity without the need for a proportionate increase in the labor force (the superfluity of labor, underemployment, nonemployment, etc.).	The weakening of traditional institutions such as the family, church, workplace, and the related alienation.
The need to maintain aggregate demand, to purchase the products resulting from the enlarged productivity, leading to powerful stimulation of consumer needs.	The rise of new "leading groups" or vanguards such as women, minorities, and youth and the apparent decline of the traditional industrial worker in this role.
The enormous expansion of credit to assist in the development of consumer demand and the attendant endemic intractable inflation.	The new consumerism, consumer movements—Nader, ecology, community control, and others.
The rapidly declining percentage of agricultural workers in the labor force and the concomitant increase in service workers, students, and welfare clients.	The value syndromes of the 1960s that continue into the 1970s: personal liberation, self-determination, antihierarchy.
	The development of service consciousness—awareness regarding the human services, quality, control, and cost, the associated increase of alternative institutions, and the critique of professionalism.
	The discontent regarding work.

Economic development has moved from the agricultural to the industrial phase, and is now entering a new service phase. Prior to the advanced development of industrial productivity, based on the Third Industrial Revolution, the major emphasis of the society had necessarily to be on production-related values such as self-denial, discipline, and the like. Basic constraints were set by the forces of production and their level of development, and further constraints were set by the mode of production, by the way the productive forces were used and organized by the capitalist system.[1] While a socialist mode of production can utilize these forces in somewhat different ways, they, too, are constrained by the level of industrial development (as in China).

The service phase is predicated on advanced industrial productivity just as the industrial phase was predicated on advanced agricultural productivity. The agricultural dimensions of the society, of course, have not disappeared nor have agricultural workers. The significance of agricultural forces and ethos has, however, continued to diminish while existing alongside the expanding industrial phase. And, we think this is similarly occurring with the present-day industrial workers and ethos. That is, industrial workers and the industrial ethos exist alongside the expanding service work force and emerging service society ethos.

With the advent of advanced productivity resulting from the expansion of the forces of production, a new phase develops. This new phase is difficult to describe, particularly because of the overlap with the past and the future, and consequently, it is frequently called post-industrial and post-scarcity, but these formulations are not positive, specific descriptions. We think a more accurate description is an "emerging service-consumer society" in which service work and consumption (service and nonservice) are becoming primary, along with new service-related values. This development can take place because the forces of production have been able to meet the basic primary needs of large numbers of the population. Of course, the corporate structure (reflecting the mode of production) does not equitably distribute this new productivity but rather manipulates its

1. It is important to differentiate the *type of production* (agricultural, industrial, service) that characterizes an era from the *mode of production* (feudal, capitalist, socialist). The latter is the way the production is organized, reflecting the basic economic relationship of the society.

affluence and power to maintain control as well as relative economic stability. As it needs consumer purchasing power in order to reproduce itself, it maintains consumption by means of a heavy expansion of credit and by providing income to people unemployed in various capacities. It invests its surplus in some of the new industries in the service sectors (education, drugs) and also "contributes" to the public sector via taxes, which are used to provide services and jobs and to maintain controls.

The basic framework of the emerging service society is a political economy that includes the various economic stabilizing functions of the services and a basic contradiction wherein the human services struggle to be humane and people-serving, while being used to socialize people to the existing order and to divert dissent.

This society is characterized by enormous expansion in the production and consumption of the human services, both paid and unpaid, with the most significant expansion occurring in health, education, and welfare services and in government employment. "Each year local and state governments are adding 450,000 employees. That is an annual net increase equal to more than half the number of workers in auto plants."[2] The human services are but a part of the larger service sector, but a number of features magnify their importance.[3] First, as their work is relational in character, they affect in multiplier fashion a broad consumer population—students, clients, patients. Second, media and public attention given to the human services has led to considerable "service consciousness." Third, in addition to those services offered in a formal setting by members of the work force, there are similar services provided outside of such settings in alternative institutions, by the self-help movement, the women's movement, and others.

Another basic characteristic of the service society is the tremen-

2. "Boosting Urban Efficiency," *Business Week,* 2312 (January 5, 1974), p. 37.
3. In addition, various other services share some of the characteristics of the human services. For example, the interpersonal and consumer-focused dimensions are also seen in sales, advertising, and many personal services.

dous new significance of the consumer and the fact that the services are "consumer-intensive"; that is, their productivity is uniquely dependent on consumer involvement. Victor Fuchs points out that service activity frequently tends to involve the consumer in the production of the service.[4] For example, the bank customer fills out a deposit slip as part of the production of the banking service, the supermarket customer carries the goods from the shelves to the checkout counter as part of the production of the retail trade service, and so forth.

This special consumer role is of even greater importance in those services of primary interest to us. Indeed, it is just this greater consumer role that makes services such as education and health so interesting. The patient—in terms of history given to the doctor and the willingness to follow the prescribed regimen—is a factor in the production of his or her own good health. In the same way, students contribute to their own learning (the service product) when they are interested in the materials, work hard, seek out additional material, and generally engage themselves in the education process. How to use and design this consumer-based source of productivity is a central concern of this book.

In addition, the role of the consumer takes on special force because under neocapitalism consumers are typically exploited at the point of consumption (through high prices and taxes), encouraged constantly to be dissatisfied with the products they are overstimulated to purchase—a dissatisfaction bordering on alienation that may spread into many areas, including what we call "consumer politics."

Consumers are less integrated into the work system, more socialized by the consumer role and associated leisure and education. They are thus more open to a general awareness that traditional industrial values such as self-denial, hierarchy, and competition are less relevant. It is noteworthy that the current consciousness regarding ecological constraints could perhaps occur only in an advanced

4. Victor Fuchs, *The Service Economy* (New York: Columbia University Press, 1968).

(consumer-service) society where one could begin to think for the first time about the limiting of productivity and traditional industrial growth.

The consumer potential is perhaps the clearest "crack in the system," representing an opening, a point of potential change. Consumers have special significance because of the large amount of open, unbounded time that they possess and their necessary market role as purchasers of goods and services; and particular consumer groups—women, blacks and other minorities, youth—have special significance based on their status and power deprivation. These groups, which we consider the "consumer vanguard," are not simply poor—some are even affluent. This has important implications for discussions of redistribution, for low-income people are not the majority in our country and, thus, are not likely to be a sufficient constituency for redistributive policies.

A major contradiction of our times is that the affluence, or rather the high productivity of the economy, allows for large numbers of people—both poor and nonpoor—to occupy cultural frameworks removed from the mainstream, not to be as well socialized by the traditional institutions and values, especially in relation to competition, acquisition, and other traditional work values. These groups (e.g., women, youth, minorities), plus a portion of the affluents, are a potential majority, and although they want societal change (according to all the public opinion polls), the kind of changes desired varies from group to group, and from time to time. Thus, in terms of redistribution, some want redistribution of income, wealth, and power, some want a redefinition of roles, demanding greater social equality and respect.[5] Recasting what was once simply a materially expressed problem suggests the possibility of new alliances and new concepts of

5. Perhaps a full employment program that guaranteed everyone a decent job (based on human service job creation in the public sector) could be redistributive strategy that might have wide appeal to the new majority groups and their affluent allies. This would be particularly so if the jobs were paid for from a reduction of military expenditures and an increase in corporation taxes, that cannot be permitted to be passed on to the consumer.

social well-being—including unprecedented segments of the population in its promises.

Moreover, the women, the young, and the minorities—the groups especially deprived of power and status—are much less frequently employed in the industrial sectors than are their counterparts—white, older males. As there is less need for rapid expansion of labor in the industrial sector and the combination of big labor and big industry have maintained relatively high wages there, these groups, for the most part, have been kept out of the industrial areas via a combination of sexism, racism, and adultism.

These same groups, when they are employed, work mainly in the service areas at the lower levels. Women are librarians, teachers, social workers, nurses—the demi-professions; blacks and minorities are hospital workers, technicians, teacher aides, domestics; and the young, in addition to being in the two groups above, work at the lower levels in the human services (e.g., case aides), in the secondary labor market at odd jobs while going to school (waiters and waitresses), and so on.

In this connection, it is noteworthy that the consumer vanguard developed, especially in the sixties, a series of value syndromes related to quality of life, personal liberation, and participation, but was little concerned with economic issues, unlike the protesters of the thirties.

PERSPECTIVE ON THE SIXTIES

It was in the sixties that the agricultural revolution was most fully realized. The number of farms, the amount of farmland, and the number of farm workers all declined, while agricultural productivity rose. This increase in productivity led to a great decrease in the number of people working on the land, with a concomitant increase in the number of people going to school, living in urban centers.

The sixties was the period in which there was the most rapid expansion of public assistance in history, and a similar increase in the

	Agricultural Workers	College Undergraduates
1960	7,057,000	3,227,000
1970	4,523,000	7,0202,000

U. S. Bureau of the Census, *Statistical Abstract of the United States, 1972,* 93rd ed. (Washington, D.C.: U. S. Government Printing Office, 1972), Tables 384, 202.

number of people going to school in higher education. It is, of course, true that there are a number of other factors involved in the expansion of the college population: the sharp increase in college-age population (there was a ten-year increase in the fourteen-to-twenty-four-year-old age group, which was greater than the growth in this population segment during the entire first half of the century[6]); escape from the draft; a new emphasis on credentials. Nevertheless, the convergence in the sixties of these other factors with the agricultural revolution is an extremely important context in which to understand the relational revolution of that decade.

The sixties are extremely important to understand in conceptualizing the service society thesis because that period highlighted some important precursors of future developments.[7] Consciousness expanded, a new consumerism appeared, including new interest in the services, and aspirations for an improved quality of life appeared along with a behavioral, cultural, and sexual revolution but no politi-

6. "In every other decade of this century, the proportion of persons 14–24 relative to those 25–64 has declined, and it will decline again in the succeeding decades of this century, but in this decade, the proportion (and the absolute numbers) increased enormously." *Youth: Transition to Adulthood,* Report of the Panel on Youth of the President's Science Advisory Committee, Office of Science and Technology, Executive Office of the President (Washington, D.C.: U.S. Government Printing Office, 1973), p. xvii.

The number of those fourteen to twenty-four grew by 52 percent between 1960 and 1970, a rise more than twice as large as in any other previous decade in the twentieth century. *Ibid.,* Table 1.

7. The "triple revolution" theorists of the sixties accurately reflected the new productivity of advanced capitalism, but incorrectly assumed that this productivity would be distributed via a vastly reduced work time and increased leisure. The work week has not declined, and leisure has increased in a peculiar unplanned way with more people receiving education, old age benefits, welfare, and the like.

cal or economic revolution. This is one reason why the sixties remain incomplete and why some of the vanguard groups of that period are at least temporarily quiescent in the current ebb era. But in the present period, where there is a strong tendency to reject, simplistically, the sixties for their failures, for the expectations raised but unrealized, it is important to maintain perspective and to recognize that the source of the many powerful cultural and institutional changes that are creeping into our everyday lives actually began to appear in that era of protest.

There is perhaps no better place to see the working out of the basic contradictions of our society than with regard to the consumerism that is an essential part of the service society. The negative aspect is easy to perceive—the commercialism, the waste reflected in gadgets and trivia, the hucksterism. On the positive side, there is the involvement of the consumer in scrutinizing, evaluating, and questioning all areas of life from the environment, to education, to automobiles, and to some extent, even to politics, as in the concern about the representativeness of political conventions. We shall argue that the consumer is also extremely important in the very production of the services and thus is a force of production. Moreover, particular groups in the society, in their consumer roles, have raised important questions with regard to basic rights, personal liberation, the quality of living, and so on. These groups—women, youth, and the minorities—we call the deprived or disadvantaged consumers whom we see in many ways as vanguard forces for change. (In Chapter 3 we develop a theory as to why the consumer and the consumer role is so essential in modern society.) We believe that despite the temporary quiescence of some of these leading forces, their desire for change remains salient and they continue to reflect the most advanced ideas of the society. Currently, this is illustrated best, of course, in the women's movement and perhaps a bit less clearly by young factory workers and the new black coalition politics. Public opinion polls also indicate that even when they are politically inactive, the desire for change is still greatest among these groups. They seem to question most of the old values, the competitiveness, the traditional structures.

We think that the fact that their members work most often in the service fields and are very much concerned with service issues is an extremely important part of their potential.

THE LIMITS OF THE SIXTIES

While the consumer- and service-oriented values that emerged in the sixties represent important beachheads and in many ways are invading the consciousness of large numbers of Americans, they are by no means profoundly affecting our political and economic system. Moreover, their impact remains sharply circumscribed so long as the basic relations of production and the traditional political structure are intact. The political and economic parameters set fundamental constraints on the counterculture, the behavioral revolution, and all the movements of the sixties. True, these movements and their value reflections are in some ways in conflict, not only with traditional values, but with the profit system and the political structure. But it is a conflict which in many ways is muted, and the tremendous resilience of the society allows it to accept the new strains in many forms; some are encapsulated and isolated, others are commercialized and vulgarized; some exist side by side with the traditional values, almost as parallel systems. It may well be that as long as the capitalist economy can continue to develop the forces of production, the revolutionary potential of the consumer-service culture will probably surface only when there is a convergence of the economic difficulties of the society with the new consciousness.

There are a number of other objective elements limiting the development of the service society. One of the major ones is the separation of the new vanguards—the minorities, women, and youth—from each other. Each of these groups has its own dynamics of change and its own agenda, and this fragmentation has been a powerful force in preventing the appearance of a new majority and a changed social system.

There are also limits to the consumer role and consumer politics. While consumers seem to be a leading force in raising new demands, as consumers they do not appear to have enough power to move toward deeper societal transformation. Consumer groups are not only disconnected from each other but also tend to be overly focused on issues of the day and the locale, and do not possess sufficient organization qua consumers. They develop "movements" rather than form organizations and, unfortunately, movements are more transitory and labile. They resort to boycotts and street tactics, rather than to strikes and political action. They are too often concerned with local rather than national issues and rarely see the connection between the two. Some consumers are perhaps overly involved with issues of style and everyday life and may see culture as politics. They frequently eschew electoral politics, political conventions, and political organizations. Unless and until consumer politics is united with parliamentary politics and worker organization, the consumer force is likely to be limited. An example of such a union is the effort of the women's movement among faculty and students at Columbia University to join forces with university maintenance and clerical employees. Apparently, the effort is not simply to win rights for these workers at Columbia but to bring into the international union the new feminist concerns.[8]

These are some of the objective factors that have limited the value explosion of the sixties and the deepening of the service society. But there were subjective factors as well. Caplow notes that this era of protest was characterized powerfully by relational issues—"practically all non-economic status relationships were challenged and extensively modified"[9]—while basic economic issues were not addressed as they had been in the thirties and this was perhaps a fundamental subjective issue.

Much of the criticism of the sixties had been appropriately directed at professionalism, its mystique and its elitism. But the relationship of professionalism and the professional elite to the larger structure of the society and the welfare state was not sharply or fully dealt with.

---

8. *New York Times,* September 29, 1973.
9. Theodore Caplow, "Toward Social Hope," *Columbia University Forum* (Winter 1973), p. 7.

Thus, while professionalism has been somewhat reduced in the present period, the basic power of the professionals remains essentially intact. They have recovered from the onslaught of the sixties, albeit somewhat sensitized by the demands of the poor, the young, the women. The professionals still control most of the human service resources and decisions, despite the new attack from taxpayers and political reactionaries. The problem is complicated, to be sure, because professionals on the one hand are service producers and their knowledge and skill and the expansion of their work are crucial for a service society; on the other hand, they have been largely captured by the liberal wing of the establishment and have organized themselves in defensive, self-interested ways, which in no way contribute toward major societal transformation. In addition, they have shown considerable resistance to any significant redistribution that would be necessary for an ecologically balanced authentic service society.

There are other subjective problems as well: the consumer-service forces have not been able to solve the problem of scale, of large organization. Frequently, organization is equated with bureaucracy and hierarchy, and the baby is thrown out with the bath water. There is a strong tendency to romanticize small-scale organization, reminiscent of the one-room schoolhouse, the family doctor, and the cottage industry traditions of the service field. The problems of size and scale have not been addressed although there has been much interest in decentralization, local school boards, neighborhood service centers, and the like. In the extreme, neo-anarchism has emerged with the commune as the model along with loosely organized, vague decentralized units as the political form.

Some novel theories of social change have erupted, largely based on contagion and imitation, not without some effect at the level of everyday life and local institutions. But the emphasis has necessarily been behavioral rather than organizational. Life styles are emulated—clothes, hair, music, drugs, sex, encounters, alternative schools —but political life goes on as before, perhaps with some interesting exceptions such as the Democratic party convention in 1972, which was much more participatory and reflected the significance of the growing new consumer forces.

Theories of change, apart from being based on contagion, were also apocalyptic, looking toward an instant and complete revolutionary transformation. Tired of incrementalism, disillusioned with socialism, the new radicals saw the period as a revolutionary epoch, in which the changes in values and everyday life, along with the weakening of traditional institutions, would lead to a falling away of the system, and political and economic transformation spearheaded by contagion and revolution by example would hold sway. In many ways this can lead (and often has led) to a tremendous personalism, privatism, hedonism, and downright self-indulgence, as well as localism. In addition, inappropriate models from abroad were introduced. Disappointment with the Soviet model led to tremendous interest in the Cuban and Chinese forms. A revolutionary humanism replaced the dictates of socialist economics. In essence, however, no dialectic theory of change appropriate to a strong capitalist society emerged. Reforms that might be transformed into radical change were not considered—quantity into quality was denied, and only incrementalism remained as an alternative to be appropriately dismissed. All changes that were won were debunked because of the compromises that ensued; structural reform was denied as a possibility.

What was needed most was a real analysis of the system, rather than rhetoric and slogans about capitalism in general. The emphasis was one-sidedly localistic—student participation, community organization—and too many of the demands of the various one-issue movements were for a piece of the action rather than a change of the system; and ultimately, there were too many demands for pieces of the action which couldn't be delivered without reorganization of the system; and potential allies had been made enemies and scapegoats in the splintering process.

Finally, the media functioned brilliantly to program, then exaggerate and divert, and finally ignore the movements of the sixties. There is, it would seem, a media curve in which new "sexy" movements are given a great deal of attention only to be succeeded by a backlash that becomes the new "hot" topic. We can expect precisely that pattern now in relation to the women's movement.

But in the earliest stages, the media did provide an opening, emphasizing the excitement of community control, the demands of the youth, the militancy of welfare rights and Black Power. The exaggeration of the strength of these movements is at first useful in drawing constituents, although the danger is that they may begin to believe their own headlines and think that they are stronger than they actually are, and therefore not attempt to persuade people but permit them instead to be overpowered by the media message.

The media also play up certain aspects of the movement that are particularly violent and attention-getting. They magnify a superficial polarization and accept handy scapegoats. The activists of the sixties permitted themselves to be diverted, coopted, divided—programmed by the media. The media used them; they didn't use the media.

But finally, the media are fickle and yesterday's excitement is no longer today's news.

It is in the context of the basic limitations of the system and the limitations in attempting to change it, including lack of clarity about the nature of progress and change, that the service society movements of the sixties are inaccurately now seen as failures.

OUR PERSPECTIVE

We shall attempt to keep separate description, prediction, and action recommendations. The first six chapters of the book are largely concerned with our description of the emerging service society and the contradictions that beset it. For the most part, we make few predictions except in the final chapter of the book. We believe that human service practice is an essential ingredient of the development of an advanced service society and that this practice needs to be much more consumer-centered in some highly specific ways, and so we are concerned with consumer-oriented training, management, and policy. In the last analysis, however, such a society cannot emerge without overcoming the contradictions imposed on it by the profit system.

The most important characteristic about the service society we shall describe is that it is fraught with contradictions. Within it there are many forward-looking themes that surfaced in the sixties, relating to participation, commonality, the expansion of consciousness, and the like. But the profit-oriented system that frames the service society poses fundamental contradictions that constantly encumber the emerging values, leaving them fragmentary, ambiguous, unfulfilled, strikingly uneven in development. Thus, it is often difficult to disentangle the progressive emerging forces from the overall context that constantly distorts, manipulates, coopts, or isolates them. The ambiguity is furthered by the overlap of the old society (with its central groups—the traditional working and middle classes) and the new service sectors, which include the service workers and consumers. The new service-based ethos rarely appears in pure form—its potential is always clouded by its context. Never was this more apparent than in the sixties, the period in which new values and movements erupted and the new potential majority of minorities, young, women, and educated affluents, began to crystallize. While we shall attempt to show that the value syndromes of the sixties are by no means destroyed and in many ways have been institutionalized, there is, of course, no question that they remain incomplete at best and backlashed at worst.

One last note of ambiguity: it has been very difficult for us to decide whether to call the emerging society a service society or a consumer society. The future world will be both, and both will be unfulfilled unless production is organized to reflect people rather than profits, participation rather than power.

The book is written for the emerging progressive new majority, particularly those most concerned with the human services.

1   An Overview: Profile of the Service Society

> Most of the [service] industries are manned [*sic*] by white-collar workers, most are labor intensive, most deal with the consumer, and nearly all of them produce an intangible product.
>
>   —Victor Fuchs, *The Service Economy*

AN OVERVIEW

Various appellations have been used to describe America after World War II. For example, such terms as "post-scarcity" and "post-industrial" seek to capture the essence of changes occurring in the economic and social life of the country. Other observers have used the words "service economy" or "human-service society," labels that more nearly capture the essence of our concerns.

The measurement criteria for labeling an era are hardly standardized, but one can note a variety of developments that make a case for the "service" label. These include: (1) the growing percentage of the work force engaged in such work; (2) the increasing amount of such services (paid and unpaid) delivered in terms of both numbers of recipients and the amount they consume; (3) the importance of such services in terms of their affording access to other benefits (for example, the role of education, or of at least the credential-granting role of educational institutions, in providing access to employment and thence to income); and (4) the attention given by the public and the media to the human service institutions, their employers, and their consumers.

At the simplest level, the easiest way to characterize the emerging service society is in terms of the number of people employed in providing services in proportion to those engaged in goods production. The problem is that a diverse range of industries are classified as service production; for example, finance, insurance, real estate, personal services, retail and wholesale trade, transportation, and communications, as well as health, education, and welfare services. While there are common elements, there are crucial differences, too.

In a variety of ways, services have been a neglected area of concern. Traditional economists, from Aristotle to Adam Smith to Karl Marx, have denigrated them. Standard formulations of economic sectors have relegated them to a category of "leftovers." Following Marx, present-day socialist countries continue to see them as "nonproductive."

Our view, of course, differs sharply. At the simplest level, a sector that in the aggregate generates nearly half the country's gross national product (despite an accounting system that serves to minimize services, see end of this chapter, "A Note on GNP") and that employs more workers than any other sector cannot be treated as a residual area;[1] it is simply too important.

In order to see better the central role of the services, we need a clearer definition. Service sector definitions vary as to what they include, particularly as regards transportation, public utilities, and communications; some authors include them,[2] others exclude them,[3] still others, such as Simon Kuznets, include them in earlier studies but not in more recent ones.[4] From our point of view, the exclusion of

1. Colin Clark, *The Conditions of Economic Progress* (London: Macmillan, 1940).

2. Gur Oter, *The Service Industries in a Developing Economy* (New York: Praeger, 1967).

3. Maurice Lengelle, *The Growing Importance of the Service Sector in Member Countries* (Paris: Organization for Economic Cooperation and Development, 1966).

4. Simon Kuznets, "Quantitative Aspects of the Economic Growth of Nations; III, Industrial Distribution of Income and Labor Force by States, United States, 1919–21 to 1955," *Economic Development and Cultural Change* (July 1958); Kuznets, *Modern Economic Growth* (New Haven: Yale University Press, 1965).

those activities which, in effect, are simply supportive of goods production, namely, transportation, public utilities, and communications (excluding broadcasting and the media), is appropriate. Similarly, for our purposes, we can exclude those services, such as wholesale trade, commercial banking, and advertising, which service business not individual consumers.

Fuchs' working description of service "industries" captures much of our structure. He states that it can be said that "most of the industries in it are manned [sic] by white-collar workers, that most of the industries are labor intensive, that most deal with the consumer, and that nearly all of them produce an intangible product."[5] In effect, Fuchs is suggesting four characteristics of services—their work force composition, labor intensivity, closeness to the consumer, and lack of a tangible product. The first two of these, the issues of the composition of the service work force (and its heavily female component makes the term "manned" both sexist and erroneous) and the "labor intensive" character of service work are discussed below (Chapter 5, "A Note on the Work Force," and Chapter 8). Indeed, for our purposes, these two features are not the central characteristics of the services. Rather, the qualities of "closeness" to the consumer and intangibility are key. Sidney Fine's categorization of work as involving people-to-people, or people-to-data, or people-to-things relationships captures in its people-to-people formulation our meaning. One can see this best in the human services, where to these characteristics we add that of their beneficial intent (a quality, of course, aspired to although not always achieved). Indeed, for us, the epitomes of the services are those which are most fully beneficial, have the least tangible character, and are closest to the consumer.[6] Counseling, tutoring, and health education are examples of what we mean; each of them involves a one-to-one interpersonal relationship,

5. Victor Fuchs, *The Service Economy* (Columbia University Press, 1969), p. 16.
6. It is activities such as these where the potential power of consumer intensivity is greatest (see Chapter 8).

they do not necessarily produce a tangible product or necessarily involve any physical object between server and served, and they are directly beneficial in purpose.

While those services that are least tangible, closest to the consumer, and most beneficial in purpose are the quintessence of what we are describing, one can see variations along the axes of each of these core characteristics. For example, the selling of services for profit may continue to include the characteristics of intangibility and closeness to the consumer but the quality of benefit is affected by the intrusion of the profit motive. Likewise, the qualities of closeness and intangibility are lessened when the service is provided through the intermediary function of a machine, such as a teaching machine. While the arena where the three quintessential characteristics of the human services are present is small, the far larger area where interpersonal and relational activities occur (much of retail trade, personal services, the visual media) vastly extends the areas of person-to-person service and what we call service consciousness.

However, we need to distinguish between the phenomenon of service work evidenced by the growing number of workers employed in the service sector and the corollary service-society ethos that we consider important. That ethos includes new values and institutions, a special role for the consumer, new leading groups or vanguards, and a political economy that embodies a unique relationship to the state.

Although there is value in thinking of the services as a whole—if only to note the broad shifts in the economy—a more refined grouping is necessary to our interest in the human services.

Since 1940, when the civilian work force was evenly divided between those in goods-producing and those in services-producing work (prior to 1940 the work force was predominantly in the goods-producing sector), increasing percentages and numbers of workers are to be found in services-producing jobs. The shifting ratio of the work force, from 51 : 49 goods- to service-producing in 1950, became 36 : 64 in 1968, and will be, it is estimated, 32 : 68 by 1980.

Civilian Labor Force (in Millions)*

	Total	Goods- producing workers	Services- producing workers
1940	49.3	25.6	24.5
1947	51.7	26.3	25.4
1968	80.7	28.9	51.8

* This trend is continuing with a projected ratio in 1980 of 32 goods-producing to 68 services-producing workers.

Within the service sector total there are hidden shifts, as Daniel Bell points out:

The word "services" disguises different things, and in the transformation of industrial to post-industrial society there are several different stages. First, in the very development of industry there is a necessary expansion of transportation and of public utilities as auxiliary services for the movement of goods and the increasing use of energy . . . Second, in the mass consumption of distribution (wholesale and retail) and finance, real estate and insurance. . . . [A] third sector, that of personal services, begins to grow—restaurants, hotels, auto services, travel, entertainment, sports. . . . Finally the claims for more services and the inadequacy of the market in meeting people's needs for a decent environment as well as for better health and education lead to the growth of government, particularly at the state and local level, where such needs have to be met.[7]

The human service sector is different from the industrial sector in ways that are vitally important to the character and quality of the service sector. These services are ostensibly initiated to produce benefits for the recipient; they are explicitly relational and interpersonal, creating a multiplier effect (that is, they produce an impact far beyond the numbers employed).

It is the common characteristics of the human service occupations that are the most interesting. Perhaps the best way to examine these characteristics is to juxtapose the human service occupations, which

7. Daniel Bell, *The Coming of the Post-Industrial Society: A Venture in Social Forecasting* (New York: Basic Books, 1973), pp. 127 ff.

**Distribution of Employment Within the Services-Producing
Sector, 1870–1971**

	1870	1900	1920	1940	1947	1971
Transportation and utilities	20%	23%	27%	17%	16%	9%
Trade, finance, real estate, insurance	28	30	31	36	42	39
Personal services	48	42	36	40	20	25
Government	4	5	6	7	22	26

are largely in the public sector, against the private goods-producing sector. At one level, these differences can best be seen in terms of the nature of the relationship of the sector's products to the consumers. In the human services, consumers have a right to the service and a right to participate in decisions affecting the service; there is a public concern for the quality of the service; and, increasingly, the quality of that service is not a function of an individual's ability to pay. For example, the right to an education, long recognized, is now being expanded to include the handicapped; consumer roles have been accelerated in a wide range of human service programs; and a new concept of state responsibility for equality of educational services is being developed. Part of this relates, of course, to the fact that those who deliver the service are supported through public funds (even when they are not directly public employees), but even when this is not the case, there is some sense of the rights of the service consumer.

For the workers, the central feature of the work is serving people. However poorly it is fulfilled, there is an ethos of service and commitment in this work. Whatever the many failures of human service workers to live up to proclamations of service to others, it can hardly be gainsaid that the attitude of a teacher toward a student is qualitatively different from that of a production-line worker toward an engine mount. Nonetheless, Greer's reminder of the gap between rhetoric and reality is a valuable caution: "We are seriously diverted from analyzing how we are really doing and what we might be doing to solve our social problems by our persistent and erroneous desire to regard the expansion of the human service professions as synonymous with the social progress our social rhetoric talks about."[8]

A central difference between goods-producing and services-producing activities is the way they are measured in national accounts, especially the gross national product. Unlike the measurement of goods, for which the market price can be established, in the services sector the value is assessed in terms of the cost of labor. Thus, the value added to the GNP as a result of the work of a school or hospital is the sum of its salaries. (See end of chapter, "A Note on GNP," for a further discussion of these points.) This approach not only uses a measure that is at best more appropriate to the diminishing goods-producing sector, but there is built into it a bias against reports of services productivity. The standard measures for improved productivity in the goods-producing sector—increased investments, improved technology, reorganization, and faster work rates—have less application in the services, particularly the consumer-intensive human services. (We will develop this point in Chapter 8.)

As the number of human service workers has increased, the number of those served by these activities has also grown. Although growth has occurred in other human service fields, it is most dramatically evident in higher education. As Seymour Harris points out, "Since 1870 the rate of growth of enrollment in institutions of higher education has greatly exceeded the growth rate of the entire population, but the proportion that enrolled students represented of the population aged eighteen to twenty-four grew even more rapidly."[9]

Thus, while enrollment in relation to population increased sixteen times between 1869–70 and 1963, enrollment in relation to population aged eighteen to twenty-one and eighteen to twenty-four increased twenty-two and nineteen times, respectively. In actual numbers, college enrollment grew from .05 million in 1870 to 1.3 million in 1940 to 6.8 million in 1970; from fewer than 1 percent of

8. Colin Greer, "Human Services on the Road to Social Progress," *New York Times,* July 20, 1972.

9. Seymour E. Harris, *A Statistical Portrait of Higher Education.* Report to the Carnegie Commission on Higher Education (New York: McGraw-Hill, 1972), p. 411.

those eighteen to twenty-one in 1870, to 14 percent in 1940, to 47 percent of that age group in 1970.[10] (With the end of the draft, there has been a slight drop in the number of young men attending college.)

While not so dramatic as the growth in college attendance, the percentage of all age groups enrolled in school has increased. Between 1947 and 1966, the percentage of those enrolled in school, ages five to thirty-four, rose from 42 to 60 percent, with the greatest gains among five-year-olds (53 to 72 percent), sixteen- and seventeen-year-olds (67 to 88 percent), and eighteen- and nineteen-year-olds (24 to 47 percent).[11]

And this growth has not been restricted to those enrolled in formal education. Moses has developed the concept of the "learning force," that is, all those involved in organized learning activities both at the "core" (elementary, secondary, and higher education) and on the "periphery" (business or government programs, antipoverty agencies, adult education, and correspondence and TV courses). He found 101 million people in the learning force in 1965, estimated 124 million for 1970, and projected a figure of 146 million by 1976.[12] In this connection, Bertram Gross estimates that the real teaching force is over six million, rather than the usual estimate of two million teachers in the formal education structure.[13]

Increased educational services affect and relate to access to job and income benefits in ways that are not always clear or rational. Whether appropriate or not—and Berg's work[14] is but the latest of many studies to question the appropriateness—longer periods of time spent in educational institutions do lead to a greater access to jobs and thus income. Even Jencks, who is so dubious of the effect of educa-

10. *Ibid.*
11. *Ibid.*
12. Stanley Moses, "The Learning Force: A More Comprehensive Frame for Educational Policy," Syracuse University Publications in Continuing Education (Syracuse: Syracuse University, 1971).
13. Personal communication.
14. Ivar Berg, *Education and Jobs: The Great Training Robbery* (New York: Praeger, 1970). See also S. M. Miller and Frank Riessman, *Social Class and Social Policy* (New York: Basic Books, 1968), chapter 5.

tion, offers evidence of the increased job opportunities available to diploma or degree holders.[15]

Not only is there an increasing number of persons delivering and receiving these human services,[16] but the character of the services

15. Christopher Jencks, *et al.*, *Inequality: A Reassessment of the Effects of Family and Schooling in America* (New York: Basic Books, 1972).

16. A one-day census of people subject to institutional care in California, in 1969, found that they exceeded 7 million—a total nearly as large as the state's entire civilian labor force that year. Further, the number of persons employed by those institutions exceeded six hundred thousand. These already sizable figures do not include those served by other, and less formal institutions or those who render services in these institutions or on a less than full-time paid basis in the listed institutions.

Subject Population, 1 Day Census in 1969, California*

Institution	Number of Subjects	
Adult felons		
Prisons	23,018	
Parole	13,027	
Adult Probation	102,042	
City and County Jails	27,918	
Youth Authority Wards		
Detention	5,908	
Parole	14,778	
Juvenile Probation, active	94,724	
Juvenile Hall	4,182	
TOTAL, Law Enforcement		285,597
Cash Grant Recipients	1,540,571	
Certified, Medical Assistance only	212,593	
General Home Relief	83,012	
TOTAL, Social Welfare		1,836,176
Mentally Ill		
Resident and on visit	16,116	
Extramural care	5,406	
Mentally Retarded		
Resident and on visit	12,545	
Extramural care	11,591	
Tuberculosis	232	
General, long-term, other special	6,491	
General, short-term, other special	51,087	
TOTAL, Hospitals		103,468
Kindergarten through grade 12		
Public	4,645,000	
Nonpublic	407,800	
TOTAL, Schools		5,052,800
GRAND TOTAL		7,278,041

* Octavio I. Romano, "Institutions in Modern Society: Caretakers and Subjects," *Science*, CLXXXIII (February 22, 1974), Table 1.

appears to be undergoing significant change as well. A primary change is in the increased consumer orientation of the services.

THE CONSUMER DYNAMIC

In the service society there are two basic dynamics, the consumer dynamic and the service dynamic, each of which has its own properties. The convergence of the two dynamics has great importance in producing the service-society ethos, the value syndromes, and the interpersonal revolution that emerged in the sixties and continue into the seventies.

In an advanced capitalist society the need for maintaining aggregate demand leads to a tremendous emphasis on stimulating consumer dissatisfaction. In order to stimulate the market demand so necessary to use up the enormous productivity of the Third Industrial Revolution, there develops a huge emphasis on buying—buying new products, new gadgets, this year's car, dress, TV. We are constantly stimulated to be dissatisfied with the old: new needs are awakened or manufactured, expectations and horizons are raised. We are told not to save, and easy credit terms are provided. Buy the new product, inflate the ego, feel better about ourselves, win approval, get the girl (or boy). Last year's suit, car, and TV set are dull, inappropriate, out of style. Don't be satisfied with them: expect more. This deep compelling theme is not only fertile ground for constantly expanded product expectations, but it also transfers easily to the self and the interpersonal. We become dissatisfied with *ourselves,* with our relationships. They must be expanded and developed. We look inward to improve the quality of our inner life and expand our inner consciousness, just as in reflecting consumerism we look outward to the quality of our consumer goods and the environment.

THE SERVICE DYNAMIC

Services essentially have to do with people and people interactions, and it is this simple dimension that subtly but pervasively affects major value themes of our era. The themes of our day are deeply concerned with self and relationship dimensions—expression; inner life, growth, and development; ego expansion of consciousness; sex; participation; encounters; confrontation. The services (and the human services are the most pristine form of the services) are characterized by individualization. Thus, the great reaction in our society today against the impersonal, the cold, the formal, the bureaucratic, rule-oriented action that is not flexible, individual, specific, personal.

This is not only reflected in everyday life and the media, but was most characteristic of the "era of protest," the political revolt of the sixties in which, as Caplow points out, practically all noneconomic *status relationships* were challenged and modified: the relationships between whites and blacks, parents and children, teachers and pupils. This was truly a *relational revolution*.

The basic themes of the sixties—built around the behavioral revolution, the counterculture, and the sexual revolution—all were very much concerned with interpersonal issues—personal liberation, individual rights, identity, self-actualization, participation, egalitarian, antihierarchical relationships.

The "equality" revolution of the sixties was really a revolution about relationships; it was not concerned with a basic economic restructuring of the society, nor with any of the economic issues that characterized the thirties. It was a concern with rights, entitlements, and identity. The vastly expanding service structure provided the context for this new revolution. The revolutions of the sixties were concerned with relationships and personal freedom. They reflected the service work world and the consumer leisure life. Dissatisfaction and higher expectations spread to all kinds of institutions, including the family, school, church, government, and workplace.

The convergence of the consumer dynamic with the service dynamic occurs around the fact that the consumer, who is constantly encouraged to demand more, to be dissatisfied, begins to generalize these feelings to services and to self.[17] This is greatly reinforced by

17. The convergence of the two themes, of course, is seen most easily in the TV ads in which we are encouraged to buy a product in order to improve our self-image and win greater recognition and thus feel good. Not only the

the open, unbounded time characteristic of the consumer role which allows considerably increased interest in the self, interpersonal relationships, and the quality of life.

It is the consumer vanguard groups in particular that provide an important nexus bringing the two dynamics closer together.

This occurs for the following reasons:

1. When they are employed, women, youth, and minorities work most often in the service fields, particularly at the lower levels.

2. They spend considerable time in consumer roles (in the home, school, and on welfare) outside of the labor force.

3. Their dissatisfaction and alienation is even greater than that of the average consumer because of their lessened power, and the fact that they have less access to high-status jobs—both in the industrial and professional sectors. Sexism, racism, and adultism have combined to disparage them in their work and consumer roles.

To some extent it is the very strength of neocapitalism that provides the point of motion, the crack in the system, the opening. It is the enormous productivity which leads to the need to sell the products, to increase the dissatisfactions of large numbers of consumers, many of whom are not needed for much of their lifetime in the work force and are permitted protracted education and early retirement.

CONTRAST WITH THE "POST-INDUSTRIAL SOCIETY"

No discussion of a service society could take place meaningfully without placing it in relation to Daniel Bell's post-industrial formulations and elucidating our differences and agreements with him.

Bell, like Marx, views emerging economic forces as crucial determinants of the character of society in the present and the future. The

---

advertisements but the TV stories work in a similar manner and are deeply concerned with relationships, ego, growth, not simply with material status, goods, and the old conformity. Ultimately, when one gets fed up with the simple materialism of products, acquisition, and the related competitiveness, there is more concern for the inner life, for inner peace, for alternate states of consciousness, for drug-expanded awareness, for Eastern quiescence.

main new force that Bell centers upon in *The Coming of the Post-Industrial Society*[18] is knowledge: the occupational groups that possess it, the scientists and engineers, are his key occupational groups—the vanguard, so to speak.

But Bell fails to accent the interrelationship of the forces and relations of production. He sees chiefly a one-way relationship whereby the forces of production and their new representatives, the engineers and scientists, are primary. He fails to see the interaction of the existing capitalist relations of production and the derivative corporate state. Bell gives scant attention to the neocapitalist dimensions of contemporary society in which, to some extent, the state is used for vastly expanded profits by multinational corporations, and where the work remains highly bureaucratized and hierarchical with the technicians and engineers and knowledge workers by no means free of these conditions.

We differ from Bell in another very important respect. He stresses the post-industrial similarities of advanced productive societies such as both the United States and the Soviet Union, but ignores the significance of the way this production is organized differently and the consequences that flow from that fact. The dynamics of the service society that we shall describe are unique to an advanced neocapitalist economy and its needs, and thus are sharply different from both the Soviet Union and China. Moreover, socialist societies, as they reach a more advanced stage of productivity, will not have a consumer-service society such as is emerging in the United States even though there will be considerable production of both services and consumer goods and an increasing consumer emphasis. They will not, however, necessarily have continually to stimulate their consumers in order to maintain demand.

Our major criticism is directed at what Bell overlooks in the emerging forces of production, particularly in regard to the "services." At some points Bell does flirt with the idea of the key role of the services, indeed, in one of his earlier papers, he goes a long way

18. Daniel Bell, *The Coming of the Post-Industrial Society* (New York: Basic Books, 1973).

toward characterizing the post-industrial society by its human service components.

A post-industrial society is based on services. Hence it is a game between persons.

Individuals now talk to other individuals rather than interact with the machines; and this is the fundamental fact of work in the post-industrial society.

If an industrial society is defined by the quantity of goods that mark a standard of living, the post-industrial society is defined by the quality of life as measured by the services and amenities ─ health, education, recreation, and the arts—which are now deemed desirable and possible for everyone.[19]

It is interesting to speculate as to why Bell did not develop further the significance of these services, particularly the human services. He reverted instead to the scientist and engineer—the more conservative groups—as models rather than the service practitioner, the psychologist, the teacher.

Were Bell to turn more fully to the services, he would recognize that a major force of production in the expansion of the services, in addition to the rapidly growing professional sector, is the consumer.

The strategic role of the consumer in the services has a populist potential quite contrary to the elitist potential of Bell's favored engineers and scientists. So, too, the "soft" services (health, education, social services, recreation) are far more likely to be public in character than is the work of the engineers. This public character again offers the opportunity for an increased popular role in the society.

The tremendous significance of consumers at this point in history is related, then, both to their unique role in capitalist economics and their special role in regard to the development of the services. (See Chapter 8.) This convergence gives the consumer a primacy hitherto unheard of in any society and perhaps gave rise to the "consumer politics" heritage of the 1960s.

19. Daniel Bell, "Labor in the Post-Industrial Society," *Dissent,* XIX, 1 (Winter 1972).

Bell sees the counterculture of the sixties as a disjunction that was largely regressive. He makes no attempt to seek out the structural basis for the new values arising, for example, from the feminist movement, the youth movement, the environmental movement, the Nader movement, the consumer movement, those of blacks and other minorities. (See Chapter 4.) If one looks at the structural factors related to the new service work, at the expanding service consumption, and at the tremendous new significance of the consumer in an increasingly service society, one would see that what might seem to be a disjuncture from a post-industrial perspective is, in fact, not that at all. Rather, the movements and values of the 1960s are quite related to the new role of the consumer in society—the consumer as a special force of production in the development of the services, and the consumer as economically exploited, given attention to, and encouraged to be dissatisfied.

In the table below we distinguish both our agreements and disagreements with Bell's analysis by referring to his summary of the differences between industrial and post-industrial society and by adding to his comparison characteristics of what we call the emerging service society. The first two columns, "Industrial" and "Post-Industrial," and the topic headings are adapted from Bell's Table 1–1, "General Schema of Social Change."[20] while the last column, "Service Society," is ours.

As one can readily see, there is considerable overlap between Bell's formulation and ours. In essence, it seems to us that he stops short of major developments that are occurring. We are suggesting that the functions that Bell focuses upon are those of a neocapitalist system in whose womb a new service society is growing. The new service society is not developing in a vacuum; it is emerging in a neocapitalist industrial context.

It is this dialectic interaction that Bell fails to take into account. In his formulation, the action is largely going one way from the technical structure to the relations of production to the state. But the state may

20. *Ibid.,* p. 117.

	Industrial	Postindustrial	Service society
Regions	Western Europe Soviet Union Japan	United States	United States
Economic sector	Secondary	Tertiary, quaternary, and quinary	Quinary Health, education, and government
Occupational slope	Semi-skilled workers Engineers	Professional and technical Scientists	Human-service professionals (education, health, social services)
Technology	Energy	Information	Relational
Design	People/fabricated nature	People/ideas	People/people
Axial principle	Economic growth	Theoretical knowledge	Consumer values

not primarily reflect the knowledge people or be "the executive committee of the ruling class," or represent the people; it may represent all three as a battleground for new dimensions of the class struggle.

THREE "SOCIETIES" COEXISTING

We believe that it is possible to formulate the concomitant and overlapping existence of three strata within our overall society. On the one hand, there is the old industrial sector composed largely of upper-working-class and middle-class people, many of whom live in middle America and whose cultural traditions emphasize authority, respect, puritanism, old-style individualism, nationalism, security, and so on. Many of these values are under powerful attack; they do not represent the new frontier and the groups holding them are in many ways defensive. The old values that they espouse are not essential for the development of the society. They are largely anachronistic but the people holding them are real, the institutions they represent have not died, and they still have considerable political power, particularly in alliance with other groups.

Then there is the neo-industrial group referred to by Bell and the post-industrialists. These are the higher-level technicians, managers, engineers, scientists, and research specialists, who are critical for the development of advanced modern capitalism. For the most part, they have been well coopted for capitalist goals of productivity, accumulation, profit, expansion, growth, power. They are an educated elite; while they to some extent have some tension with the traditional capitalist forms that Bell and Galbraith and others imply are somewhat restrictive, they nevertheless have been well rewarded by the system, in no way feel disenfranchised or deprived—a necessary characteristic of any vanguard. To some extent they have developed a whole series of new values and cultures, particularly around rational administration, management, organization, merit, credentials, efficiency, creativity, relative autonomy, and a wide variety of educationally related values—for example, broadmindedness, openness, flexibility, imagination, autonomy, growth. While for the most part they reject both the counterculturalists and the old-style traditionalists, they have something in common with each group. Their educational elitism and far-reaching knowledge allow them to be contemptuous of the traditional, narrow, security-bound middle classes, but their attachment to the system and the related goals of efficiency, advancement, power, and status are inconsistent with the counterculture and the new consumer-oriented movements of the deprived that demand more far-reaching social change, equality, the end of meritocracy, a new humanism.

The third group, we believe, derives from the consumer-service base that is emerging in our society, from the new importance of the consumer that we discuss more fully in Chapter 3, and the significance of the services, particularly the human services. The groups involved here are by no means homogeneous—they include the women, students, minorities, service workers, some of the educated affluents, particularly those involved in or related to the professions but less involved in industry, management, research, engineering, and science.

It must be remembered that all three groups are enveloped by the basic neocapitalist frame and this conditions their roles, functions, and values. While there may be important strains or tensions deriving from some of the developing groups, they nevertheless are basically *contained* by the overall system and its present power. Unless this is thoroughly understood there will be a strong tendency to exaggerate the progressive system-changing potential arising from the new groups, the new values, the new forces of production, the counterculturalists, the liberationists, and so on. The fulfillment of their visions can occur only with new basic relations of production in some kind of new participatory democratic socialist society that exists nowhere as a model—although some small precursors may be emerging. This is one of the reasons why we think it is important to illustrate carefully this new emerging segment of our society. Even more important, however, is the fact that our orientation is directed toward an activist change in a radical direction away from both old capitalism and neocapitalism; and, therefore, we look for cracks in the system, points of motion or change. It is the service and consumer vanguards that we think are important in this respect, and this book will attempt to outline their origins within the overall capitalist system, the tensions they produce, and the limits set upon them by the profit system frame. It is extremely important, nevertheless, not to exaggerate the power of these emerging forces, to recognize that they are being continually utilized for neocapitalist purposes and that they are essentially unfulfilled.

THE HUMAN SERVICES AS THE FRONTIER

Recall that in our definition there are two outstanding characteristics of the human services: one is that these services are intended to produce benefit or well-being for the recipient either affectively or cognitively; and, two, the character of these services is essentially relational, interpersonal, a "hands on" approach. Therefore, we see human services as being interpersonal in process and beneficial potentially in end or intent, although, of course, this does not necessarily occur in practice.

In essence, the service society derives its character not only from the tremendous expansion of paid and unpaid service work and service consumption but from the powerful multiplier impacts deriving from its very relational character, its labor intensivity (it uses more labor per unit of production), the special significance of education, the role of the media,[21] and the fact that large numbers of its workers directly impact on many other people. Nor should its role in the political economy of the nation be underestimated. It is no wonder, then, that the basic values of our time—which are increasingly invading the older industrial segments of the society, the older middle class and traditional working class—are service values having to do with humanization of work, for example, the improved quality of life and the environment, the expansion of consciousness, the reduction of hierarchy, bureaucracy, authority, and centralization, and the development of self. The service society has, in addition to its highly significant service work force, a very large consuming nonwork force; that is, a large number of people who do not provide paid labor for a large portion of their lives—including students, women, welfare recipients. The service society, because of its enormous productivity and the special need it has to keep people off the labor force or not counted in the labor force while at the same time requiring their consumption, can afford this tremendously significant large segment of consuming nonworkers. When these groups do work, they largely work in the service areas and they spend considerable portions of their time consuming services such as education and providing unpaid services such as day care and community services.

The human services, and their effectiveness, are important, thus, because of their use in contemporary advanced capitalist society, the large (and increasing) fiscal resources involved with consequences both for the state and consumers, the large (and increasing) number of persons (both paid and unpaid) providing services, and the even larger number receiving services. And their importance is likely to

21. Comparing coverage in the *New York Times* for an average day in 1972 with the same day ten years earlier, there was an increase of 11 percent in stories about human services issues, and an increase of 48 percent over 1952.

increase in a world coming to recognize the scarcity of energy resources and finite raw materials, and, most of all, because it is in the arena of the human services both where the struggles of the service society are being fought and where the new service-society ethos is being spawned.

In all the current discussion about growth, one basic confusion stands out above all others: one type of growth, namely industrial growth, is equated with total economic growth. A part is confused with the whole. Practically all of the debaters, whatever their viewpoint, seem to accept the notion that industrial growth (which is resource-depleting and capital-intensive) is equivalent with total economic growth.

But the fact of the matter is that we may be able to have enormous growth in the development of health services, education, recreation, art, culture, research, mental health—what can be called the "people services" or "human services"—while at the same time contracting industrial production, which is rapidly ripping off the resources and energy of the earth. These human service activities are labor- and consumer-intensive rather than capital- and resource-intensive, and, unlike in the past, we are long on human capital and short on all other resources.

In other words, it is not *all* growth that must be limited. Emile Benoit states the issue well.

What is needed instead is *selective* growth. We can look forward to a continued rise in per capita incomes and real welfare if there is a shift: (1) from goods production to services and leisure; (2) from status displaying goods to goods yielding mainly intrinsic satisfactions; (3) from resource wasteful and polluting goods to resource conserving and pollution combating goods; (4) from population growth to population decline; (5) from braking expenditures on higher education and research and development to maximum achievable expansion of this sector, plus a reallocation of resources to give new emphasis to environmental problems.

The advantage of services over goods is that they absorb little or no scarce raw materials and create little or no pollution. Most services, of course, have to be provided by some physical mechanisms, and do require the production of some *complementary* goods: hospitals, offices, and medical equipment for health services, classrooms, offices, laboratories, etc., for education and research and so forth. But the relative strain on the environment over the long run is far lower than for the sale and consumption of goods, which not only require the construction of facilities and equipment but which use these facilities and equipment for the further transformation of raw materials into products which will be used up and discarded.[22]

To achieve a human service society will require a major shift toward the development of genuinely significant large-scale alternative life styles. This is not a new primitivism, a regression to an earlier stage of development, a communal life style, a deinstitutionalization, or a return to the past based upon scarcity and a low level of technology. Rather, what is proposed is that we organize our resources very carefully to produce a high level of culture and aesthetics and new qualities of living that are not based upon a "thing" culture, waste, and built-up demand for things that exhaust the world's resources and pollute the atmosphere.

The British scientists' "Blueprint for Survival" clearly documents that continuous industrial growth is leading to unemployment and the underutilization of people; by contrast, growth of human services will lead to the fullest utilization of people. In addition, if the human resources are used efficiently and meaningfully, we can have a greatly improved quality of life.

I envision a society in which $800 billion of human services are produced with 120 million jobs, eliminating 50 million jobs in goods production (10 million in automobile-related industries alone). There can be no unemployment in an ecologically balanced economy. Unemployment cannot be permitted because of the needs of a world with scarce resources, because the insecurity that unemployment brings contributes to unecological hoarding impulses and because enforced idleness contributes to unecological, antisocial behavior. But only work compatible with nature can be tolerated in the future. This means that all activity that does not contribute to quality of life or that contributes at too great a cost in

22. Emile Benoit, "What Society for Spaceship Earth?," *Social Policy*, IV, 3 (November–December 1973).

natural resources must be abolished. More and more, manpower must be employed in health, education, welfare (particularly in activities that would enable people to cope with their environment), leisure, conservation and resource development.[23]

The ecological utopia does not call for a lack of growth but rather a shift in growth from the traditional industrial area to the human services, or people-serving, sphere with a concomitant marked reduction of unemployment.

GROWTH AND PROFITS

There is an implication, however, in the concern about stabilizing industrial growth that is not usually referred to directly by the ecologists or their detractors. The heart of capitalism is the expansion of industry and profit derived therefrom; the new environment-conserving perspective runs right into the teeth of this drive. While capital can be and is invested in the human service industries, such as education and hospitals, these are potentially under public control and need not be produced for profit. Schools need not be built *for profits;* nor hospitals either. There is no compelling drive which parallels the profit motive of industrial capital. In this sense, the perspective for increased investment in the human services may, under certain conditions, be more congenial to socialist nations, although the Soviet Union shows no such proclivity and traditional Marxism looks toward infinite industrial expansion. China, on the other hand, has been far less concerned with standard industrial growth than the Soviets, and more directed toward the people-serving, people-staffed services. The human service world view obviously demands enormous people-oriented planning and rational control—characteristics that are anathema to capitalism.

It is noteworthy that the advocates of continued industrial growth who appear to support some ecological perspective center their arguments on pollution rather than the drying up of resources. Thus, they

23. Arthur Pearl and Stephanie Pearl, "Toward an Ecological Theory of Value," *Social Policy,* II, 1 (May–June 1971).

argue that we will need continued industrial growth in order to obtain the necessary funds to clean up the atmosphere. Moreover, since they favor business expansion, they propose new products such as pollution-free cars. They fail to recognize that many pollution problems would diminish rapidly if industrial growth were sharply curtailed and we moved to different forms of living that were less dependent upon the automobile, for example. The human services, incidentally, produce far less pollution as well as less environmental impoverishment.

The new society calls for a new quality of life, but by no means does it imply a lowered standard of living. It will require a shift in preferences, life styles, work, and leisure. It will require new training and education for new kinds of work for many more people and the obsolescence of many of the skills employed in the resource-depleting, earth-impoverishing industries. In addition, the problem of redistribution of income in a society in which the standard consumer goods are not expanding will have to be dealt with intelligently and with planning. The vast expansion of the human services will allow for a tremendous redistribution of them to the disadvantaged, underserved groups in the population.

Thus far, outside of segments of the youth and some intellectuals, there are no clear-cut constituencies for the ecological viewpoint, other than the media. (The underserved and unemployed may be an important new constituency.) It is still a cry in the wilderness, a demand for a future ideal, a consciousness raiser. To attract support, an ecological strategy must demand recognition that growth and an improved quality of life are not being surrendered, but rather that the sectors of the society in which growth takes place are to be shifted. A new vision will have to be developed regarding what the good society is to be like—nonhierarchical, participatory, decentralized. New definitions of efficiency and productivity will have to emerge. The main themes will probably be redistribution, participation, quality of life— and service may be the keynote.

A Note on GNP

The data that emphasize the growth of the services area are all the more impressive given the "anti-services bias . . . embedded in the concepts used by our statistical agencies."[1] This antiservice bias is not new. Adam Smith's view was that the labor of "the sovereign . . . with all the officers of both justice and war . . . churchmen, lawyers, physicians, men of letters of all kinds, players, buffoons, musicians, opera singers, dancers was unproductive of any value."[2] Marx fully accepted this view of Smith's, and this antiservice bias is even stronger among communist countries.

It is paradoxical that just as GNP became accepted as a measure of national productivity, shifts in the economy have made it a less valuable tool. As it measures the value of products at their market price, it must use surrogates for those activities such as human services which generally have no market price. Instead of the absent market price, the salaries of the service producers is used. Thus, for example, the contribution of education to GNP, aside from the goods it purchases,[3] is in terms of the salaries paid to teachers. This is doubly misleading.

1. Bertram M. Gross, "America's Post-Industrial Revolution: A Selective Overview of a Transnational Society," unpublished manuscript (1967), p. 7-3.
2. Adam Smith, *The Wealth of Nations* (New York: Modern Library, 1937), p. 315.
3. This is not a negligible amount. For example, in 1971, $57.7 billion of the $139.2 billion (41%) cost of the purchases of state and local government was in the form of purchases from private industry.

More or less pay to the teacher seems to have little effect upon pupil learning, and thus it is misleading to imply growth in education as a result of rising salaries for teachers. More important is the fact that measuring education in terms of teacher salary ignores the multiple effects of education—in addition to teacher income, there is the potential gain in pupil knowledge, in increased skills at present and for the future, in terms of effect upon children, peers, community, etc.[4]

The GNP measure conduces toward emphasis upon production, especially of the capital-intensive nature. Thus, for example, the deleterious consequences of productive activities are not counted; or, in a certain sense, they are counted twice—that is, the environment-polluting consequences of manufacturing are not subtracted from the

Gross National Product, 1965 (Billions)

	Official	Reformulation by Kendrick*	Reformulation by Gross
Households			
Personal services	—	$ 144	$ 260
Capital	—	71	71
Productivity gain	—	—	24
Total households	—	215	355
Volunteers	—	14	25
Government and other non-price sectors			
Personal services	$174	174	174
Capital	—	48	48
Productivity gain	—	—	23
Total	174	222	245
Price sectors			
Reported	507	507	507
Unreported	—	42	68
Total	507	549	575
TOTAL	$681	$1000	$1200

* John W. Kendrick, "Studies in the National Income Accounts," *Contributions to Economic Knowledge Through Research,* 47th Annual Report, June 1967.

4. Editor's Note to Robert Lekachman, "Humanizing GNP," *Social Policy,* II, 3 (September–October 1971), p. 34.

GNP resulting from industrial activity. Indeed, when resources (human and capital) are spent to "clean up" the waste, that, too, is counted an addition to the GNP.

Gross[5] has continued efforts by Kendrick to recalculate GNP. Note that more than two-thirds of the increase in GNP recalculated by Kendrick and over 85 percent of the increase recalculated by Gross is in the services sector.

It is in the costs of household services where Gross' estimates most go beyond those of Kendrick. (The "official" GNP simply ignores the housework that had been done by paid household help and is now done, increasingly, by women who also hold paying jobs.) Gross[6] estimates, for 1965, the following:

Personal Services in the GNP, 1965 (Billions)

Home maintenance		$100
Child care		45
Other personal care		60
Transportation		30
To work	$14	
Shopping	10	
Children	6	
Procurement		15
General management		10
Total	$30	$260

A final flaw in GNP is that it skews our perspective by encouraging capital-intensive activities compared with those which are labor-intensive. Not only does this encourage wastefulness of material resources but it leads us to believe that as services are less amenable to capital-intensive activities, productivity increases are inherently less likely there, and are more inflationary. Further, as will be discussed in later chapters, it leads us to seek productivity gains in the services in the same way we do in goods production, rather than

5. Gross, *op. cit.*, p. 8–6.
6. *Ibid.*, p. 8–8.

looking to the unique feature of services where the consumer is a factor in production.

The flaws in GNP, both as to its misuse as an overall measure of well-being and its inadequacies within the more limited area of national production, have not gone uncommented upon. We have already noted the recalculations of Kendrick and Gross. James Tobin and William Nordhause, both of Yale University, have since 1970 been developing a Measure of Economic Development (MED). In it, they concentrate on personal consumption, a reflection of the increasing centrality of the consumer in present-day life. Thus, they exclude what they call "necessary overhead costs of a complex industrial nation-state" (e.g., national defense, police and fire protection, road maintenance), include the value of leisure time and unpaid "non-market" work (e.g., household chores), and deduct the cost of "disamenities" (e.g., congestion, litter, pollution).[7]

7. *New York Times,* July 29, 1973.

2 Political Economy

It is no accident that [the] Soviet kind of revolution could never take place in the West. Here, the capitalist system has not only attained many of the goals which, in the underdeveloped countries, have been the driving power of the modern revolutions, but capitalism has also succeeded, through the constant development of income, the complexity of the instruments of mediation, the international organization of exploitation, to offer to the majority of the population a possibility of survival, and, frequently, a partial solution of immediate problems.

—Lucio Magri, "Parlement ou Conseils"

In a sense, the service society conceptualization we present is an attempt to explain and integrate social phenomena that seem to characterize the present era by connecting them to basic large-scale changes at the economic level. The phenomena include the facts that:

1. The industrial worker does not appear to be a leading force for social change as he was in the thirties or as he was portrayed in a traditional Marxist analysis.

2. The groups that seem to be playing a leading role, raising important new demands, are the women, the youth, the minorities, the educated affluents.

3. The major movements of our time seem to be related to consumer-oriented issues—the environment, the quality of life, participation, decentralization, inflation, and taxation. Moreover, the move-

ments of the sixties—ecology, Nader, community control, welfare rights—were related to consumer issues, and frequently to service issues such as education. Sometimes, it would appear that a school strike is more decisive than an automobile strike, at least in the consciousness of people.

4. There has been an expansion of the recognition of rights of all groups—handicapped children, prisoners, women, welfare recipients, homosexuals, tenants, students.

5. Traditional institutions and the norms and customs connected with them have been seriously challenged—the family, the school, the church, the government, and most recently the workplace. A behavioral revolution and a sexual revolution, accompanied by considerable alienation, disorientation, dislocation, seems to have taken place.

6. A new service consciousness appears to have erupted with large numbers of the population concerned on an everyday basis with institutions related to mental health, health, day care, drugs, ranging even so far as the development of services to assist people in facing death. The interest in these services includes concern about their cost, quality, and control.

7. A new dimension of politics seems to have emerged, which emphasizes less electoral politics and traditional organization building, with more accent on movements, boycotts, publicity, legal actions, consciousness raising, parent groups, tenant groups, and buying groups, and the issues seem more service- and community-oriented—accountability, prices and taxes, decentralization.

8. There seems to be a great deal of alienation, not only in the society in general, but particularly among teachers and government employees, who feel that their talents and training go unutilized and suffer bureaucratic restrictions from above.

9. Finally, the period of the last ten years has been marked by considerable unevenness of motion, of progress. There are many significant new demands about the quality of life, human relationships, equality, personal liberation, growth, participation, and much increased acceptance of countercultural traits of dress, style, and new forms of behavior; there is more openness and informality in every-

day life and perhaps in local institutions and much consciousness raising. But, on the whole, few if any large-scale economic and political changes have taken place in the society. In many ways most of the developments seem unintegrated into the major structures of the society—in a sense unfulfilled, incomplete, more rhetoric than reality. Sometimes it seems as though the old institutions are dying and new ones have not yet formed to take their place, except on a small scale or in the minds of people, or in small, isolated alternative institutions, but not built into the economic and political fabric of the society.

All of these things are taking place alongside a partial resurgence of capitalism following the Great Depression of the thirties. Modern capitalism seems to have acquired considerable skill in managing relative economic stability, a fairly high standard of living for numbers of people, the reduction of major wars (which in the past were very destructive to various capitalist states), the continuance of the development of the forces of production with a hitherto unheard of level of productivity that permits great numbers of people to remain outside the labor force, to be nonemployed so to speak, to say nothing of new forms such as multinational corporations possessing tremendous transnational power. In essence, neocapitalism has not been stagnating; it has been accumulating capital, profits, and power and it has delivered the goods and services to numbers of people.

It is just because of this neocapitalist dimension or frame that the new progressive potentials go unfulfilled. But the task is also to explain the origin, the sources, the roots of these new developments which do not seem to stem from working-class consciousness or the revolutionary consciousness anticipated by Marx deriving from the industrial working class. We want to propose that it is service workers and consumers and the conditions of both their work and nonwork lives that are much more crucial in the development of the new values, the new ideology that particularly emerged in the sixties via the counterculture, the behavioral revolution, the environment movement, and the emphasis on personal liberation. The vanguards of these movements are not the old industrial workers, but the new service workers and consumers and particularly the women, youth, and minorities who work more often in the service sectors and are essentially deprived of economic and political power both as consumers and producers. It is important to note that the bulk of the service workers in the human service fields such as education and health are employed not at the top levels, as physicians and administrators, but as allied health workers and teachers. (See table below.) Most of the workers in these fields are not highly paid, but are in many ways bureaucratized and controlled.

Employment in Elementary and Secondary Schools, 1970*

Total	4,189,957
Administrators	170,263

* 1970 Census, Table 8, "Detailed Occupation of Employed Persons by Industry and Sex."

Employment in All Health Industries, 1970*

Total	4,246,187
Physicians	280,929

* Ibid.

SOURCES OF MOTION UNDER NEOCAPITALISM

In light of the fact that neocapitalism appears to be relatively successful in achieving a degree of economic stabilization and the reduction of large-scale wars, the question naturally arises as to where, if anywhere, are the sources of change, the contradictions, the forces of motion, the cracks in the system that might lead to a new, more egalitarian, participatory society. This is a basic question for all radicals as well as a number of reformers who perhaps might be called radical reformers.

Many different kinds of answers are offered. Some argue that economic contradictions have moved to a new level reflected by the pervasive inflation (and stagflation), the instability of the dollar, the loss of international outlets for investment.[1] These analyses are largely at the economic level and while recognizing the power and resilience of the capitalist system, particularly the American system, nevertheless assert that inevitable contradictions at a new level will emerge and that there will be increasing conflicts between the United States and the European and Japanese systems.

The struggle will take place, it is argued, around issues of trade, competition for the world market, and like factors, all of which will be reflected ultimately in a United States economy that will deliver less goods at higher prices to the American people, perhaps along with an increasing number of recessions of somewhat greater depth. Hence, the basic class conflicts between the capitalist and the large number of workers will be exacerbated. Some, such as Paul Sweezy, believe that the difficulties will appear in the developing world that will resist unequal trade and the robbing of their basic resources.[2] These views essentially look for new expressions of the basic economic contradictions of capitalism. In general, they hold that these economic difficulties will in some way be reflected at the political level, but they are not particularly concerned about the superstructure, the cultural levels, the values.

James O'Connor, another modern Marxist, sees increasing difficulties developing in the United States around a fiscal crisis in the public sector, with the major capitalist groups struggling against workers and consumers to socialize their costs both in the areas of research and in the supplying of services.[3] The increasing cost of

1. Roy Bennett, "The Renaissance of Socialism," *Social Policy,* IV, 4 (January–February 1974).

2. Paul Sweezy, "Marx and the Proletariat," *Monthly Review* (December 1967), pp. 25–42.

3. James O'Connor, *The Fiscal Crisis of the State* (New York: St. Martin's Press, 1973). See also Frances Piven, "The Urban Crisis: Who Got What and Why," in Robert Paul Wolff, ed., *1984 Revisited* (New York: Knopf, 1973), pp. 165–201.

these services deriving from wage increases won by unions accelerates the conflict. The problem is compounded by taxpayers' resistance to paying increased taxes for service expansion or even service maintenance under certain circumstances.[4]

Another contradiction relates to the fact that as the likelihood of large-scale war is reduced and a detente begins to emerge, there is likely to be increased questioning as to why such a high defense budget is maintained. Capitalists, of course, prefer defense expenditures because these are much less under popular control due to presumed needs for secrecy. As the military sector is largely capital-intensive and profits are permitted to be very high, there should naturally be some redistribution as public funds are moved out of that sector into the more labor-intensive service areas that are potentially under greater popular control.

Within the framework of a system that has achieved a fair amount of economic stability and can furnish the goods and services to large segments of the population, there has arisen considerable interest in sources of motion that might appear in the superstructure, at the cultural levels, in the social and secondary institutions. This view is most prominently expressed by Stanley Aronowitz in *False Promises*. Aronowitz sees the cultural areas (and child and adolescent play) as potential zones of freedom.

> We may say that mass culture contains a contradiction between the ideological need for stability, equilibrium, and integration, on the one hand, and a latent need for creativity and innovation, on the other. The former calls for the degradation of the artist and the intellectual into a mere functionary; the latter demands that he or she retain a degree of independence and a capacity for critical thinking. Thus, even though the

---

4. As the fiscal crisis becomes more pronounced, a number of backlash reactions take place, some of which are people being pushed off welfare, paraprofessionals being used to take the place of professionals, second-class college education being provided for large numbers of people, welfare recipients being required to work in public service jobs at extremely low (or no) wages, work-study programs being used as a form of getting labor at low wages, large numbers of people being given credentials that are of decreasing worth. David Deitch, "Inflate and Rule: The New Capitalist Strategy," *The Nation* (November 12, 1973), pp. 496–500.

work of artists or film-makers may remain strongly tied to the norms of the dominant consensus and the system of class domination, it also may to some extent contain a critique of reality.

Such critical content is, to some degree, presented in Bogdanovich's *The Last Picture Show.* The quality of life in Bogdanovich's small town in mass society is far from the idyllic sweetness of Thornton Wilder's *Our Town* or even the crass, bourgeois comfort of *Peyton Place.* Even the film *Superfly,* which in many ways attempts to parrot white films of the same genre, retains an understanding of the Black underworld figure as a person seeking to find autonomy and self-determination in a world that is monopolized by white businessmen.[5]

Similarly, the post-scarcity theorists such as Reich, Roszak, Bookchin, all responding in somewhat different ways to the countercultural ethos of the sixties, expect motion to derive from an expanding awareness of the possibilities of new qualities of living based on abundance. A vision is projected of a humanistic post-scarcity society that is highly cooperative, communal, and participatory and no longer needs the values of competitive capitalism, values related to acquisition, materialism, puritanism, self-denial, and so on. This group of thinkers accents not only the positive countercultural features but also the alienation, the rejection of traditional authority-building institutions such as the family, schools, and churches. In essence, these arguments hold that it is not the economic contradictions or the failure to continue to develop the forces of production that will lead to the downfall of the system, but rather, strangely enough, it is the very success in these economic areas that has unleashed new forces of motion at the cultural levels, in everyday life, and in local institutions. The strategy, then, is to continue to develop consciousness at these levels preparatory for a "long march" through all the institutions rather than emphasizing emerging economic contradictions.

There are other views as well; some suggest that division among the elites is crucial with the "Cowboy-Eastern" conflict being a

5. Stanley Aronowitz, *False Promises* (New York: McGraw-Hill, 1973), pp. 119–120.

primary illustration. Others believe the environmental and energy crises will provide fundamental difficulties to the expansion of growth in the private and industrial sectors and this will be influential in producing strain.

THE ACHILLES' HEEL

The Achilles' heel of neocapitalism is its very strength. Capitalism has not failed to develop the forces of production. These have in fact developed very rapidly in the last decade, limited now perhaps by the energy crisis. Relative stability has been achieved; that is, there are no major depressions or large wars. Endemic inflation, recessions, unemployment, and resource depletion are the economic problems of modern capitalism—at least they are the manifest problems. Beneath them a much deeper problem exists related to the very fact that productivity has expanded enormously without a proportionate increase in the labor force. This fact has produced some basic problems for the system, which are constant and enduring, and in some surprising ways provide the opening for major transformations in the society stemming from the new movements, the new vanguards, and the fact that much change is taking place at the cultural or superstructural level, rather than at the political level. (Until the two levels converge there is unlikely to be any full-scale radical change.)

The first basic problem faced by the system is its need to sell the products emanating from the new superproductivity. Hence, tremendous emphasis must be placed upon the consumer and the maintenance of large-scale consumer demand. At the simplest level there is a need for a large number of consumers with money to buy, and a desire to buy, and so we have the tremendous development of advertising and sales (whose own employees become part of that consumer market) and in a more direct fashion are very much concerned with stimulating consumer purchases. It is highly functional for the system to support a consumer market, even if these consumers are not employed; and a tremendously advanced productive system can afford a large degree of nonemployment among those people receiving education, welfare, social security, unemployment insurance, and so on.

But consumers must not only be persuaded to buy, they must have the wherewithal to do it, and thus we have a tremendous inflationary credit expansion where large numbers of consumers are persuaded to buy things on time and to borrow. Naturally, there is also a great deal of pressure to stimulate consumers to buy new products that hitherto didn't exist at all, to create needs, if indeed they are needs, and in particular to build in obsolescence and to create demand for this year's product because it is new and different and presumably better than last year's product. The system is further buttressed by the huge expansion of employment in the service sectors, in government, in the human services, all of which contribute to aggregate consumer demand.

This whole problem of advanced capitalism does not exist at all as a *necessity* in a socialist society. In a socialist society the increase of productivity need not lead to the constant stimulation of consumer demand to buy the products in order for the system to reproduce itself. This is not to say that a socialist society will automatically or necessarily use its surplus (the production which is not used for direct and immediate consumption) for positive people-oriented goals. That surplus can be used for military investment, for the expansion of a special elite in a society, for police and control functions, for example. The point is that there is no economic need to stimulate consumer demand to purchase the expanding productivity. This productivity could be used to increase the production of consumer goods, which might be provided to the consumer at even lower prices, thus increasing the standard of living of the country and/or it could be used to reduce the number of hours worked per year. The surplus could be used to expand production further, or to distribute it differently. The answers to these questions are not preordained by economic socialism; they are fundamentally political questions related to the nature of the control of the society. It is in this way that we think the post-industrial analysis of Bell and others breaks down because it fails to consider how the forces of production are used differently in different social systems, dependent basically on the relations of production: that is, whether they are capitalist or socialist. The expansion of the forces of production in neocapitalism produces a totally different set of problems, problems which characterize the emerging service society we are describing.

Clearly the forces of production do not determine the relations of production; unlike the technocrats we do not think they do, but the new forces must be reckoned with—they do provide a pressure, a constraint, a tension, a crack in the system, an opening for change. *In the dialectic between the forces and the relation of production, it is the forces that are the moving, growing dimension,* ultimately requiring a response by the productive relations and the political structure. The ongoing contradiction between the growing, changing forces and the old relations of production is reflected daily in the service society that is emerging on a neocapitalist base.

The second major problem faced by the expansion of the forces of production in the context of capitalist relations of production relates to problems of nonemployment. In the abstract, the capitalist system has the option of using the advanced productivity in a number of different ways. (These options, incidentally, are considerably greater in a socialist society that is not conditioned by the need for profit, selling goods, and maintaining consumer demand.) One of the most obvious options is, of course, the reduction of the work week. This is made possible by the fact that the increased quantity of goods produced by the same number of employees could lead to a shorter work week for all. The expansion of production could be distributed in part through the shorter work week, and in part through lower prices, thus increasing the standard of living in the society and reducing what Marx called absolute impoverishment. There is no question that in the last seventy years absolute impoverishment has been reduced in advanced capitalist societies, and this has resulted from the expansion of productivity. But it is noteworthy that the average weekly hours worked have not been reduced markedly from 1930 to the present, while from 1850 to 1930 the average weekly hours for all industry was reduced from 70 hours in 1850 to 61 in 1900, to 46 in 1930.[6]

It would be interesting to conjecture what would occur if the 40-hour week were reduced to 35 or 30 hours. Unemployment and even much of nonemployment would disappear; that is, there would be a need for a much larger labor force that would of necessity have to include more minorities, women, young and old people, than is currently the practice. There would be much less need for welfare, unemployment insurance, and protracted education serving to keep people off the labor market. Moreover, the general wage level would probably be increased not only in the primary sector, which is highly organized, but to some extent in the secondary sector, which could no longer have a big reserve army of nonemployed workers to draw upon. There would be a shift in bargaining power away from the employer to the employee, and the various divisions of the labor market would not hold as easily.

While the reduction of the 40-hour week could lead to the maintenance of consumer buying power, it would probably reduce profits and shift the balance of power between the employer and the employee in the direction of the employee. Most strikingly, it would reduce the segmented labor market, wherein those employed in manufacturing are relatively well paid, are mostly white, male, and

6.	Average weekly hours				
	1850	1900	1930	1945	1960
All industries	60	61	46	47	41
Nonagricultural	65.5	57	44	45.5	40

What is most significant, however, is the statutory or legal maintenance of the 40-hour week and the fact that it does not appear to have declined, in fact, in manufacturing over the past thirty years. It is noteworthy, however, that there is a considerable increase in part-time "irregular" work especially by women and in the service industries. Some areas, especially clerical, and certain building trades (e.g., unionized electrical workers) have lower hours. While the work week is stable, if one includes the number of holidays, longer vacations, and number of sick days, the length of the work year is reduced. Clyde E. Dankert *et al.,* eds., *Hours of Work* (New York: Harper & Row, 1965).

between the ages of twenty-five and fifty, while a disproportionate number of more poorly paid young people, old people, women, and minorities are employed in the poorly paid secondary labor market or are maintained off the labor market, in the home, college, or welfare line. (It is admittedly not entirely clear to us why the work week reduced so markedly in the first part of the twentieth century and did not continue to reduce as productivity has expanded since the 1930s.)

But in a socialist society it is economically unnecessary to maintain a constant hourly work week when production expands. The surplus could be used, and we emphasize *could,* for decreasing the number of hours of work per week or per year, without worry about affecting wage levels, consumer demand, or the unity or division of the labor force.

THE SERVICES AS A POINT OF MOTION

There are a number of reasons why we see the services, particularly the human services, as the new frontier, the place where the action is and is likely to be, an emerging source of potential motion producing tension for change, albeit always limited by the basic profit frame in which the service society is emerging.

1. The environmental crisis makes the development of the services far more important for the economy as they are not energy-reducing and not polluting. Vast growth can continue in the service sectors while it will ultimately have to be constrained in the industrial areas because of a diminution of energy resources.

2. The groups that are reflecting the new, more advanced values of the society (the minorities, the women, and the youth, and to some extent the educated affluents) have expressed considerable interest in service issues—for example, welfare rights, community control in the sixties, and currently the concern about how the services discriminate against them in the case of women and blacks. In addition, young people are very much interested in working in the human service

fields. These groups have been the prime movers in raising issues concerning accountability, relevance, and vitality in the services, have called attention to the limits and failures of these services, and along with the affluent educated have been much concerned with developing alternate service styles—encounters, community schools, hot lines, feminine counseling, vaginal politics. In essence, service is a major agenda for all of them, although in different ways for each.

3. An advanced society, with increasing income for large numbers of people, must increasingly move toward the consumption of services and consumer durables. Christian Engels in the latter half of the nineteenth century noted that the proportion of money devoted to food begins to drop as national incomes rise. An increasing proportion is devoted first for durables (clothing, housing, automobiles, and then for luxury items such as recreation and personal services). Bell notes that then "the claims to a good life which a society has promised become centered on the two areas fundamental to that life—health and education."[7] The whole quality-of-life concept is very much related to the expansion of services.

4. The human services, because of their basic intent (benefits for people) and mechanism for achieving this objective (relations among people), have important positive intrinsic potential. A corollary is that since services are intended to serve large numbers of people, they are not there simply for the profit of owners. They have an implicit, not-for-profit dimension. To the extent that services are closer to the consumer by definition, or more consumer-related, this is a constraint against elite tendencies, bureaucratic removal, and the like.

5. The battle for the public sector, increasingly the area of main concern in neocapitalism, is largely a battle for who pays for these services, who will get them, and how good they are to be. Is the money to come from the taxes of working- and middle-class people or from the corporations and the reduction of the military sector?

6. The multiplier impact of the services, particularly education but also counseling, health, and recreation, gives them a potential power

7. Daniel Bell, "Labor in the Post-Industrial Society," *Dissent,* XIX, 1 (Winter 1972), p. 166.

far beyond the actual numbers employed in these areas and the percentage of the gross national product produced—although in both cases these are large and growing. Workers functioning as teachers, counselors, social workers, play a very important role in the influence they have on many other people—students, patients, clients. The media have a similar effect and much of the relational ethos in the human service areas affects other fields such as personal services and sales. Since education is required for access to large numbers of white-collar positions in our education-intensive society, as well as to jobs in the knowledge sectors, the indirect effects are multiple. (We will turn to the special issues related to education in Chapter 6.)

7. Because the service fields are expanding so rapidly with large numbers of people at the lower rungs, there is likely to be an over-supply of these workers, and to the extent that they are organized they will contribute to the general crisis in the public sector. They may in some cases demand governmental creation of more such service positions, thus redistributing resources away from the private and military sectors. This public sector, and particularly the service activities of the public sector, are more under the potential control of the populace than are the defense industries.

8. As efforts are made at cost-cutting in the services, and they are increasingly industrialized and hierarchized, there develops consider-able resistance because the service workers appropriately feel that their training and skills go underutilized. To the extent that they are paid poorly, kept at the bottom of the ladder, this further contributes to their resistance.

9. In an advanced society the recognition of tremendous service needs, as well as the rights of people to have these needs met, expands considerably. Thus, today, there is a recognition of the need of educationally handicapped children and mentally troubled people for services as rights; similarly, the right to higher education. Large new needs, such as needs of the dying for special services, to say nothing of dealing with the problems of the living arising from drugs, alcoholism, the large number of chronic illnesses, the needs for family

planning and day care are all recognized now as basic needs and rights in the society.

ON THE OTHER HAND

For each of these positive potential aspects of the services there is, on the other hand, a contradiction stemming in one way or other from the basic neocapitalist frame in which the services are used— sometimes for direct profit, sometimes for the socialization and control of people, sometimes for the support of a large professional structure, and so on. The development of the human services within the capitalist social system produces many contradictions apart from the basic limitations imposed by the competition for resources at the national level and the constraints set by the military economy.

The great concern for gadgets, technology, and various machine-oriented approaches in human service work, which are the products of private industry, has had a distorting effect on the impact of education in the United States. Similar distortions, operating in different forms, can be found in the medical-industrial complex in which drug manufacturers and increasingly insurance companies play a major role.

And, of course, the role of monopolistic professional associations has had a powerful effect through the use of credentialism and professionalism. The way the health professionals function in the Medicaid and Medicare programs illustrates the limiting effects on the human services of the various professional monopolies.

Add to all this, of course, the basic cultural ethos that affects all the services—the competitiveness, the rat race, the pretentiousness, the lack of vitality, the concern for form rather than content.

It is clear, then, that we are not presenting the growth of the human services as some unalloyed progressive force in the development of our society. In fact, we have only scratched the surface of the various ways in which the corporate structure distorts both the human services and the human service workers. (See Chapter 8.)

Similarly, it would be a great mistake to believe that everyone involved in the human services is concerned with a progressive humanization of them. The interests of publishing companies and drug companies, for example, are not the same as the interests of parents, patients, paraprofessionals. The human services themselves are distorted by the basic framework of the society—profit, racism, and sexism. Unless the potentially progressive forces in the human services are disentangled from the forces that constrict them, there will not be developed a positive people-serving society.

To be more specific: while the services may have intrinsic people-benefiting qualities, they also have been highly bureaucratized and are in many ways sexist and racist both within the service fields themselves and between the service provider and the service consumer. While the services should serve the needs of large numbers of people, they are typically inefficient—not reaching people and in other cases reaching them poorly and ineffectively. Again, while the services have much redistributive potential, the ripping off of this potential by highly paid service providers was a major concern during the sixties. On the one hand, the professional service giver and the consumer have much in common in relation to the expansion of the services, but they also have considerable conflict, particularly to the extent that the service provider mystifies the service and makes the consumer more dependent and is concerned with his own benefit and advancement rather than the needs of the consumer. In some ways the services have a potentially positive image but this is marred not only by their inefficiency, bureaucracy, status orientation, and monopolistic control, but also by the fact that a powerful tradition exists to the effect that services are essentially nonproductive and exist at the expense of productive labor, labor that produces profits and goods.

While education as a major service has many potentially positive qualities and multiplier effects, it also socializes people to the prevailing system and norms, produces an exaggerated need for credentials, and contributes to the white meritocracy. While the vanguard groups and large numbers of people are very much concerned about the quality of services and the cost of them, this agenda can easily remain very narrow and localist, preventing major changes in large institutions of the society. Attention can be diverted away from the primary economic sources of power and deflected to the secondary institutions, such as schools and health institutions, leaving the primary sources of power at the political and economic levels untouched. Unless large numbers of taxpayers who are nonservice providers can come to see the quality of services as being very important, there will be considerable resistance to the expansion of these services. To the extent that consumer durables are powerfully advertised and demand overstimulated for them, to that extent the services will suffer in competition.

It is clear, then, that the services reflect the basic contradictions of society and any strategy in the service area must consider these contradictions and must develop a perspective of action to deal with them.

POLITICAL STRATEGY

The basic relationship of capitalist institutions to the service society has to be recognized fully in order to understand the special problems of contradictions that beset the development of the services. The fact is that while there is a great deal of concern about the services, their effectiveness nevertheless remains powerfully constrained, subject to the pressures and pulls of various interest groups, only dimly responding to consumer needs. This means that there must be a *battle for the services,* a battle between forces emerging within the service society and its leading groups on the one hand, and the constraints set by the industrial capitalist context on the other. Failure to recognize that this underlying battle is taking place leads to exaggerated formulations, so that some people talk about the redevelopment of the services as though these were taking place in a vacuum where the only concerns were the benefiting of people, while others, noting the ways in which the services function in the society, argue that the human service institutions are only mechanisms for the maintenance of the corporate state. We would like to suggest that there is an important truth in both formulations; understanding one without the other produces a one-sided distortion, either mechanical radicalism or naïve liberalism, and fails to provide the perspective necessary for engaging in the struggle for the service society which would include an understanding of the progressive potential of the service forces, a potential that is frequently immanent, unactualized.

THE LIBERAL WELFARE STATE VIEW AND THE RADICAL CRITIQUE

The liberal view held by most professionals in the service fields regards the expansion of public services as an automatic good in and of itself. Services are needed, the argument goes, and they can be provided by employing the underemployed—professional and nonprofessional. More recently, this liberal perspective has come to recognize, at least to some extent, the inadequacy of existing service delivery and to call for the reorganization and restructuring of the services in order to improve their quality and effectiveness along with continuing the call for additional services. The broader social context and its hierarchical, competitive foundation are overlooked, however.

On the other hand, at least one group of radical critics eschews the public sector entirely, feeling that it is essentially a diversion from the necessary exposure of the increased concentration of capital and power in the private sector. Other radicals regard the public sector as the "weak link" in the status quo and strive to expand expenditures there in order to "strain the system," at the same time that they attempt to expose the "real" functions and limitations of the services themselves.

All three viewpoints—the liberal and the two radical perspectives—are insufficient bases for action. The liberal perspective, which emphasizes the need for more services, overlooks the ways these services can be used against people and must fail because it will draw only narrow support (mostly from the professional establishment), while at the same time antagonizing even sympathetic taxpayers who do not want to pay for services that do not serve.

That radical perspective that wishes to ignore the services fails to understand that these services—and the emerging service state (in which service consumption and service employment are no longer secondary)—are the battleground of neocapitalism; they are, so to speak, where the action is. Increasing percentages of the work force are employed in providing these services; and an ever larger percentage of the gross national product is devoted to public services. Education, health, leisure, mental health, and day care, for example, are increasingly seen as basic necessities of life by right.

But there is another, perhaps even more important reason why the public sector cannot be ignored. The relative and perhaps temporary economic restabilization of modern capitalism means that major social developments likely to occur on the domestic scene in the United States will continue, for the most part, to take place in the social and cultural institutions. It is because of capitalism's relative economic stability that the focus shifts to the level of culture and consciousness, albeit in an uneven fashion. The underlying economic structure and power relations remain relatively intact so services such as health and education become an important agenda for action.

Moreover, if the public sector is ignored, the various dangers that are projected—cooptation, diversion, and the like—will be magnified in the absence of serious counterforces, and the agenda will be handed over to the establishment forces.

The radical wing that strives to use the public services largely to strain the system and ultimately to bring it down cannot be effective unless it has the support of a broad constituency. This support can be obtained from those who have some commitment to the expansion and improvement of the services in question; but it cannot be obtained by cynically using the services. Straining the system without a constituency genuinely committed to some of these demands is likely to lead only to backlash. Unfortunately, this was too well illustrated in the response to the welfare rights strategy, which also was concerned with straining the system but projected no vision of social change that could involve large new constituencies other than welfare recipients. The demand for authentic human services must involve not only the recipient, the taxpayer, the consumer, but also the service giver, who may come from the ever-growing sector of under-employed and poor Americans as well as from the traditional professional sources.

THE BATTLE FOR THE SERVICES

In order to understand this basic battle or dialectic more fully it may be useful to spell out, to some degree, each side of the dialectic.

The service sector fulfills many important functions for neocapitalism: purchasing power for employees to buy the highly expanded goods production; employment for workers displaced in agriculture and industry and for the growing labor force; pacification and control of various dissenting groups in the population; investment sources for unused surplus capital; the general regeneration and relegitimization of the system; and the development of a huge stratum of service providers whose benefits depend primarily on the welfare state's distribution of services and who are thus loyal to it.

While the service society functions in the manifold ways we have suggested to buttress, reinforce, and legitimate capitalist society and the profit system, there are nonetheless intrinsic characteristics of the services that are antithetical to industrial capitalism. It is important to consider both sides of the dialectic, particularly if one wants to understand the limitations, distortions, and unfulfilled character of the human services as they are organized in our society: the fact that the services are not developed in a planned way in relation to people's needs; that they are powerfully overly professionalized; that they do what they're supposed to only imperfectly, that is, that schools teach only imperfectly, health services do not adequately provide health, etc.; that they make the consumers dependent and mystify them and do not offer the services in a humane fashion; that they are frequently racist and sexist.

THE COUNTERFORCE

Despite this lack of fulfillment or incompleteness of the services, they, nevertheless, by their very existence, produce a major strain on the industrial system. They draw away surplus profits via taxes in the direction of services rather than the expansion of the private sector. As they function mainly through the public sector, they are potentially under greater control of the public, the people, the consumer, the voter, a control which began to be actualized in the 1960s.

Within all of the uses of the human services and the public sector, there are the seeds of strain, motion, much of which expresses itself through the consuming groups who have been raising new issues in new forms—for example, the environmental movement, consumerism, the women's movement.

Service providers, including professionals and students (future providers), have in many ways resisted the pressures on them emanating from the attempts to bureaucratize and industrialize them and their fields. André Gorz points out that the expectations of the professionals and technicians, deriving in part from their training and traditions, have been badly disappointed in the actual workplace where their skills typically go underutilized and bureaucratic structures limit and overcontrol them.

. . . technicians, engineers, students, researchers discover that they are wage earners like the others, paid for a piece of work which is "good" only to the degree that it is profitable in the short run. They discover that long-range research, creative work on original problems, and the love of workmanship are incompatible with the criteria of capitalist profitability. . . . They discover that they are ruled by the law of capital not only in their work but in all spheres of their life, because those who hold power over big industry also hold power over the State, the society, the region, the city, the university—over each individual's future. . . .

. . . once a certain level of culture has been reached, the need for autonomy, the need to develop one's abilities freely and to give a purpose to one's life is experienced with the same intensity as an unsatisfied physiological necessity.

The impossibility of living which appeared to the proletarians of the last century as the impossibility of reproducing their labor power becomes for the workers of scientific or cultural industries the impossibility of putting their creative abilities to work.

The industry of the second half of the twentieth century increasingly tends to take men from the universities and colleges, men who have been able to acquire the ability to do creative or independent work; who have curiosity, the ability to synthesize, to analyze, to invent, and to assimilate, an ability which spins in a vacuum and runs the risk of perishing for lack of an opportunity to be usefully put to work.[8]

This is most striking with regard to government employees and teachers perhaps, both groups having expressed considerable alienation and dissatisfaction. In essence, they want to serve, they have been prepared to do so, and the very nature of service practice requires a good deal of freedom, flexibility, and mutual interaction with a consumer. It is not a process that is easily industrialized, rationalized, "Taylorized"; rather, it is one that requires individualization and sensitivity and discretion. This is not only true of the human service work process itself, but has also been part of the training of the service providers. Teachers are trained to teach children and would like to individualize as much as possible. Large, overcrowded classes and highly controlling rules from above are anathema to them. Their tradition is the one-room schoolhouse, and that tradition plus their training and the basic nature of the human service process is counter to the way business and industry are run; this produces a basic strain between the human service workers and the traditional profit sectors of the society—a strain that is contagious, affecting not only other service workers but, increasingly, industrial workers, who begin to demand more participation and increased humanization of the work process. (See Chapter 5.)

Nevertheless, the basic vested interest of large portions of the service providers, the professionals, and the government employees limits any large-scale wholehearted attack on the system in which they function. Rather, they gripe, organize for their own benefits, salaries, working conditions, and the like, and keep alive at the level of rhetoric the concern for serving and commitment while remaining fundamentally alienated.

8. André Gorz, *Strategy for Labor: A Radical Proposal* (Boston: Beacon Press, 1967), pp. 104–106.

The service providers, however, as one of their vested interests, do have the requirement that the services be expanded, that there be more jobs, and that more money be spent on these services. Quite apart from the question of need of the recipients, this demand does increasingly expand the service sector of the society and to some extent draws a portion of the surplus from the profit sector. However, these constraints are not terribly severe as long as these resources are utilized for purposes consistent with the profit sector, that is, for producing a socialized work force, a satisfied population, and a professional constituency that supports the welfare state. Nonetheless, under certain conditions, the continued expansion of this huge public sector, potentially under greater public control than the profit sector, functions as something of a strain on the system.

THE CONSUMER FORCE

The consuming sectors provide still another form of pressure or strain on the system depending upon their degree of strength, consciousness, and organization. At the simplest level, to the degree that they demand the expansion of services, whether as parents or welfare recipients, their pressure serves in a redistributive direction affecting the overall profit or surplus. To the extent that these services actually serve—that is, health benefits, for example, that really improve health, day care centers that really develop children—they produce added nonmonetary income for the consumer. Until the 1960s, this was pretty much the major effect of the service consumer. But with the 1960s came demands about the *quality* of these services and controls by the consumer regarding their character and direction. This is an extremely important demand, one that goes right into the teeth of the battle for the human services. Because if these expanded services cannot as easily be used to control, pacify, and socialize people, then their benefits for the establishment are significantly reduced and the potential service society benefits enhanced.

In the first stages this does not ordinarily or necessarily result in a markedly improved quality of service, because much of the agenda is taken up with the struggle to shift control. Out of this struggle not only may the quality of the services be improved and a much greater consumer involvement be obtained, but the power of the traditional sectors to utilize services for the maintenance of the profit system is potentially curtailable. This is the heartland of the battle for the human services. We are in the midst of just such a period where the issue is largely over control and where service quality has not yet been drastically improved as a result of the shifting balance of power. But the demands of the 1960s for consumer involvement, greater participation, and the general expansion of service awareness are critical elements in the battle.

BATTLE DIALECTICS

For the most part, the initial response of the profit sector to the expansion of the services is resistance. It resists the encroachment on resources and on decision-making prerogatives. In the American situation, this has usually taken two forms, reflecting the two wings within the establishment, the liberal and conservative elites. The conservative group usually offers an all-out resistance to any expansion of governmental services, while the liberal wing, frequently coalescing with the professional stratum, advocates expansion to a limited degree, but without surrendering control to either service workers or service consumers. The liberal group sees services being extended to more and more groups in the society, but does not see these groups controlling either the services or the society. In essence, it is a progressive elitism, a top down formulation. Surrendering control of the services is antithetical to a status quo profit system. Nevertheless, and this is extremely important, when the services have been expanded, as a result of demand from consumers and workers in combination with the liberal elite, the profit system and the state may adjust to this new situation and even find ways of benefiting from it. Thus, as we have noted above, the expansion of the services can be used to quell resistance and dissent, to provide employment, markets, and system equilibrium via the consumer purchasing power that is created.

Moreover, a system that can provide these benefits is relegitimated and revitalized. The services can be utilized in manifold ways to serve various functions for the system: educational services can be utilized to socialize people in accepting the status quo, authority, hierarchy. Welfare services may be utilized to cool the discontent of unemployed workers and their families as well as to provide the consumer purchasing power that assists the system to maintain its economic equilibrium. Family planning services can be utilized to reduce the population of the poor and the minorities, and so on.

The battle for the services takes place not only over how much service is to be provided, but how it is to be provided, for what purposes, and with what degree of consumer control. No one victory for consumers is sufficient. What the system could not give yesterday, it gives today, perhaps under pressure; it can do so because of its resources and strength, and then the battle must move to a new stage. This is the essence of change. As each concession is wrested from the establishment, the latter in turn makes adjustments so that what initially may have seemed like an enormous victory frequently may be turned to the advantage of the very groups that resisted the expansion of the services in the first place. In some cases, the services are only diluted: we get school buildings instead of education; hospitals instead of health; day care centers instead of day care; professionals get higher salaries, but services are not expanded. In addition, of course, the establishment wins an important ally, the professional constituency. In other cases, portions of capital are invested in the education industry, or the day care industry, or the drug industry; and a medical-industrial empire is built up with big insurance firms acquiring capital to invest. In other cases, social work and mental health ideologies may be encouraged to convince people that their problems are essentially internal and individual and that blame should be turned away from the external system. Sometimes small benefits are provided, rather than the big ones that are needed.

But the result is not a foregone conclusion at any one point in time and the process continues. The 1930s saw a large expansion of services, entirely under professional control; the 1960s not only expanded the services, but introduced a new quality, the importance of consumer involvement. This demand, too, while initially resisted, has eventually been accepted and diluted but not removed or annihilated. Unless we understand this back and forth dialectic process, we will surrender either to cynical hopelessness or utopian demands for an apocalyptic, instant and complete revolution in which all benefits are won once and for all, something which has not occurred even remotely in any revolutionary context.

It is important to realize what is won, even when it is diluted and even when it has functions for the "other side." For example, the winning of the right to abortion in the United States is a powerful and significant victory for human rights, for women, and a tremendous expansion of health services. This is true despite the fact that it also functions as population control of poor and minority groups, a function that may be useful to the corporate state. Similarly, access to higher education on the part of the minorities via open enrollment is a highly significant opening, even though the education they receive may be tremendously limited, more technical than educational, and allow for the cooptation of portions of the minority groups. This dialectic character is the essence of most change that benefits, to varying degrees, both the change advocate and the system. The degree of compromise is open to struggle and the process goes on to the next stage. Most of the demands of the 1960s have actually been institutionalized in the 1970s, albeit without their cutting edge; nevertheless, the fact that they are accepted as a part of the system can provide a new plateau, a new staging ground, for the next set of demands.

It is important to understand that while all services in one way or another can be manipulated to serve some establishment functions, and this should be carefully and precisely exposed, services can provide very specific benefits for large portions of the population.

Thus, expanding health services can lead to decreases in the infant mortality differential that exists between blacks and whites, as well as to employment for people who are underemployed in the private sector. Services also may be developed to reduce the drug addiction and alcoholism that debilitate people and prevent their involvement both in capitalist endeavors and in social change.

Services for the old, for the physically and mentally handicapped, obviously have intrinsic value. Some services provide people with information about their rights, for example, their legal rights. Education, while it may be utilized to socialize children to various bureaucratic values, may also provide access to literacy and information, and at times seems to produce some rather radical constituencies at the college and high school levels. Services like day care, while they can be manipulated to force people off welfare, may represent significant gains for children and their parents.

The need for services is immense, the quality of life to be achieved by their adequate provision is unprecedented. Finally, one of the most important things to be gained from the expansion of quality services is the chance to do productive work rather than either unsatisfying work or enforced leisure. Granted, the opportunity to do fully productive work is always limited by the bureaucratic structures in which the work takes place; nevertheless, there are some intrinsically valuable satisfactions to be realized by providing needed services well, and particularly by providing such services for one's own community.

If, for instance, day care centers were under the combined control of day care workers and the community, mothers and fathers might be able to work at preventive health service jobs, delivering services that were useful to the community. This work is potentially de-alienating and meaningful. But to be thoroughly meaningful, the parents should participate in determining the character of the health work they do; and they should participate in determining the character of the day care centers that take care of their children. Furthermore, if the massive expansion of services can be paid for by the taxes of large-scale corporations and wealthy individuals rather than by the taxes of workers and middle-class people, then it might be really possible to move toward a redistribution of income, services, and power in our society.

But in order to achieve any of these objectives, which to varying degrees are system-straining and perhaps system-transforming,[9] it will be necessary to develop the widest and fullest public consciousness about the potential of the services as well as the factors in our society that limit this potential. We need to clarify the relationship between the emerging human service society and the rising demands for alternative human life styles emanating from the women, the minorities, the young, the committed professionals, and the advocates of an ecologically balanced world.

While it remains important for radicals to emphasize the significant concentrations of wealth and power that are taking place in the private sector, and promote consciousness by exposure, it is not sufficient simply to expose. It is going to be necessary to fight for a positive public service program based on positive visions for future developments.

DANGERS

Naturally every strategy has its dangers as well as its possibilities; the "more is better" view may remain dominant, and the liberal wing of the establishment may attempt more fully to direct the public sector toward a whole new area of managed state capitalism. Large-scale investment in the human services may take place in the context of tremendously expanded but manipulated public employment at low wages powerfully bureaucratized from above, with the costs of the public sector passed along to the consumer and the worker. The essential function of the public sector would then be to stabilize the private sector and maintain the latter's primacy with little redistribu-

9. A strategy for achieving system-transforming reforms is outlined by Gar Alperowitz in an unpublished paper entitled "Preliminary Notes: Toward an Alternative Program of Political Economy for a Pluralist American Commonwealth." He calls for specific reforms: (1) which may be attainable, but (2) which lead to larger demands, and (3) which help illuminate the limits of the present system, and, finally, (4) which can be coupled with positive alternatives that point toward a new system (p. 35).

tion taking place. Even though capitalist groups usually have resisted the expansion of the public sector, they may still turn around and use it to socialize their costs (for the health and training of workers, etc.). This could be advanced by splitting the professionals and the poor, the unions and the community, the welfare recipients and the workers, the service givers and the service receivers, the youth and the blacks, the women and the men.

It is not clear whether the professionals, their agencies, institutions, and unions cooperate with the new workers drawn from the poor, and the communities that are being served. While a new perspective is emerging among many professionals in the large, expanded educated sector, there are dangers here as well. In particular, the professionals have a life style that emphasizes great consumption of education, culture, and leisure. While this brings with it many new concerns about human relations, freedom, expression, sensitivity (the "new enlightenment"), it also carries with it a strong vested interest in maintaining the standard of living necessary for this life style, and may resist any significant redistribution that would hurt it (cost-free liberalism). Thus, the new radical ethic, while it has important anticapitalist overtones, is in no way socialistic or redistributive. Frequently it appears quite labile, subject to fluctuations in the economy, in the media, in the availability of professional jobs.

It is clear, of course, that every service benefit also benefits the existing system. It relegitimates the system and deals with social problems that are disturbing to it. Thus, family planning reduces the birth rate; the reduction of drug addiction may reduce crime and the fear of crime; day care may be used to push people off welfare; providing service jobs can produce buying power and hide unemployment. For every benefit to the people there are also some benefits to the system. We have no real choice here—the benefits are necessary and the system may have the power and resources to provide them and to relegitimate itself. The crucial questions against which service expansion and activity must be tested are: Who pays for the benefits? How good are the benefits? Do they lead to redistribution of income, services, and power and to the projection of a vision of a new kind of society? How much control do the service recipients and the service workers have over these services?

Our belief is that the public sector is a major battleground for change in our society and cannot be ignored by people seriously committed to structural change. It is an area in which significant benefits can be achieved for large numbers of poor people—benefits related to health, housing, day care, and so on. Services badly needed in these areas, while they may also serve establishment interests, are in part clearly beneficial to disadvantaged groups and offer a number of opportunities for redistribution: redistribution of income via jobs in these areas (and a concomitant full employment policy); redistribution of services to include those now poorly served; and redistribution of national priorities toward people-serving activities (social investment) and away from the military and private sector control.

3 The Emergence of Consumer Power

There is a questioning all over the world, by colonialized peoples, by minorities, by women, of an order of life in which others—teachers, administrators, social workers, members of other classes and races, and of the other sex—care for them, no matter how well-intentioned the care might be.

—Margaret Mead

In the last decade there has been an upsurge of consumer power expressed in manifold ways: the consumer protection movement spearheaded by Ralph Nader and the environmentalists; the demands for community control and the involvement of consumers on community boards; the great expansion of the *rights* of all groups—welfare recipients, handicapped children, tenants, prisoners, women, homosexuals; the meat, lettuce, and grape boycotts; the expansion of student participation; the Alinsky-stimulated citizen actions, and countless others. Accountability, quality of life, and participation have become important phrases in our everyday life. One of the central aspects of the service society relates to this expanded role and power of the consumer and the related consumer values.

The significance of consumers at this point in history is related both to their unique role in capitalist economics and their role in regard to the development of the services. This convergence gives the consumer a primacy hitherto unheard of in any society.

THE CONSUMER AS THE "WEAK LINK"

What are the social origins of the new consumer thrust? The role of the consumer is perhaps best understood in relation to certain special conditions of neocapitalism. A major change in the forces of production has taken place over the last thirty years, bringing a vastly expanded productivity without the need for a proportionately expanded labor force. Moreover, the agricultural revolution has led to a greatly decreased need for farm labor. Our emerging service society is predicated on the expanded productivity of industrial production; just as the industrial society was based upon the expansion of agricultural productivity. This new productivity has resulted from the harnessing of new sources of power (the Third Industrial Revolution) together with new computerized techniques for the management of information and new organizational techniques for the management of people. But monopolistic industry has not used the new productivity to produce goods at lower prices; instead, it maintains high prices, producing a basic inflationary push (particularly insofar as it is able to pay relatively high wages as well). Large segments of the labor force are employed in monopolistic industry and are relatively well paid; thus, the combination of big capital and big labor robs the unorganized worker and the consumer.

The state has become the instrument for dealing with the problems generated by the new productivity. Two basic problems had to be dealt with: the maintaining of purchasing power and the masking of increased unemployment and underemployment. Both problems have been met by keeping large numbers of people out of the official labor market (in colleges, on welfare, in training programs, on unemployment insurance, pensions, and social security), largely in consumer roles.

The service society is based upon a highly advanced productivity in the industrial sector that allows large numbers of people, for great portions of their lives, to remain outside the work force. These people are essentially hidden, not counted in the labor force, frequently disparaged. They are "dispensable" people, to use Jean Baker Miller's phrase,[1] as far as production is concerned, but they are not dispensable as consumers. Their purchasing power is essential for the maintenance of economic equilibrium, for limiting depressions and recessions.

Moreover, since John Maynard Keynes, a major form of exploitation has taken place through the price structure, through constantly rising prices, endemic inflation, and a regressive tax structure, all of which shift the impact of exploitation toward the consumer.[2] The consumer becomes the point of exploitation. To some extent, the consumer may be the "weak link" in the neocapitalist structure— robbed in the marketplace on the one hand and less well integrated by the traditional industrial structures on the other—and therefore perhaps more open to different value influences, particularly in the increasingly important consumer role.

Ernest Mandel makes an interesting point regarding the role of consumption and its relation to alienation.

Alienation is no longer purely economic but has become social and psychological in nature. For what is the motivation of a system for constantly extending needs beyond the limits of what is rational? It is to create, purposefully and deliberately, permanent and meretricious dissatisfactions in human beings. Capitalism would cease to exist if people were fully and healthily satisfied. The system must provoke continued artificial dissatisfaction in human beings because without that dissatisfaction the sales of new gadgets which are more and more divorced from genuine human needs cannot be increased.[3]

Perhaps these dissatisfactions are a source of both consumerism and alienation, two extremely important features of the emerging service society. Thus, consumers are continually stimulated to be dissatisfied with last year's product and credit is expanded at exorbitant rates,

1. Jean Baker Miller, "On Women: New Political Directions for Women," *Social Policy,* II, 2 (July–August 1971), pp. 32 ff.

2. Robert Lekachman, *Inflation* (New York: Random House, 1973).

3. Ernest Mandel and George Novak, *The Marxist Theory of Alienation* (New York: Pathfinder Press, 1970), p. 21.

particularly for certain population groups.[4] Consumers for good portions of their lives are not needed in the industrial work force; they may be less socialized by and freer of the constraints imposed by working in a typical hierarchical, bureaucratic, industrial setting.

In addition to the general forces affecting consumption, there are particular groups of consumers—the young, the women, and the minorities—who are especially deprived of power and status, and, in addition, are much less frequently employed in the industrial sectors than are their counterparts—white, older males. As there is less need for rapid expansion of labor in the industrial sector and the combination of big labor and big industry have maintained relatively high wages there, these deprived groups, for the most part, have been kept out of the industrial areas via a combination of sexism, racism, and adultism. Together with the general disparagement of these groups, of course, come some small gains: protracted education, support in the home, welfare benefits. These are benefits which can be well afforded by an affluent economy, and to that extent they limit the resistance of these groups, but beginning in the sixties, increasing resistance has emerged from these consumers and largely in their consumer roles.

We begin to see, then, the very special role of the consumer in relation to his/her place in the profit system. This converges with and is greatly enhanced by the special role of the consumer in relationship to the services, particularly the human services. Before turning to some of the special roles of consumers with regard to the services, let us look first to developments regarding consumers in general.

The current rash of consumer activities in response to sharply rising food prices is but the most recent manifestation of consumer-based activities which have been growing rapidly in the past decade. In the public sphere, whereas in 1960 no state had a consumer affairs office, by 1970 thirty-three did, and by 1973, all fifty had such

4. Since World War II, consumer debt has jumped 1600 percent—now $400 billion. Most of this debt is owed by lower-income people. The poorest 60 percent of the population, while receiving 32 percent of the income, owe 85 percent of this debt. Marc Weiss and Martin Geller, "The Rise and Fall of the Cold War Consensus," in Judith Carnoy and Marc Weiss, *A House Divided: Radical Perspectives on Social Problems* (Boston: Little, Brown, 1973), p. 56.

offices, as did 110 cities and 25 counties.[5] In 1970, the ten most common complaints received by these state offices were in regard to automobiles, advertising, appliances, credit, nondelivery of merchandise, magazines, home improvements, franchise dealers, warranties and guarantees, and sales tactics.[6] Nationally, consumer protection laws, often bitterly fought by manufacturers and frequently weakened by legislative compromise and administrative regulations, have been passed in considerable number.[7] This federal action has been mirrored at the state level both in legislation passed and administrative actions taken. Of particular interest are not only those activities designed to protect consumers but those that do so by involving them, *viz.,* the 1971 Rhode Island law making consumer representatives an official party to the negotiations between hospitals and Blue Cross in setting rates, and the various activities by the State of Pennsylvania Insurance Commissioner, Herbert Dennenberg, in making available to consumers information heretofore unavailable or inaccessible (for example, comparisons of insurance company services and charges, hospital rates). A major public weapon has been class action suits by consumers, now permitted by the laws of five states and Puerto Rico, with bills permitting such suits pending in twenty-six additional states.

There are many and varied indices of increased public concern with and activities in consumer affairs.

5. George E. Berkley, *The Administrative Revolution* (Englewood Cliffs, N.J.: Prentice-Hall, 1972); Office of Consumer Affairs, *Directory of State, County and City Government Consumer Offices* (Washington, D.C.: U.S. Government Printing Office, 1973); "Buying Guide Issue," *Consumer Reports,* XXXVII, 12 (December 1972).

6. Office of Consumer Affairs, *State Consumer Action, Summary '71* (Washington, D.C.: U.S. Government Printing Office, 1971).

7. Among the major laws in the last years of the 1960s are the Fair Packaging and Labeling Act (1966), the Child Protection Action (1966, amended in 1969), the Traffic Safety Act (1966), the Flammable Fabrics Act (1967), the Wholesale Meat Act, the Consumer Credit Protection Act (1968), the Interstate Land Sales Full Disclosure Act (1968), the Wholesale Poultry Products Act (1968), the Radiation Control for Health and Safety Act (1969), the Poison Prevention Packaging Act (1970).

—Subscriptions to *Consumer Reports,* the key consumer magazine, which in its first thirty years, 1936 to 1966, grew to some 800,000, leaped in the following five years, 1966 to 1971, from 800,000 to over 2,200,000.

—Public Interest Research Groups (PIRGs), college-campus-based groups mobilizing student and professional (lawyer) resources to work on local consumer issues, are active at 138 colleges, in 19 states and the District of Columbia, with over 400,000 dues-paying members.[8]

—The Consumer Federation of America, launched by Consumers Union and 55 other organizations by 1968, by 1971 had over 200 member organizations.

—Membership in consumer credit unions more than doubled over the course of the 1960s.[9] And in a blend of the consumer action and the feminist movement, in 1973, the Feminist Federal Credit Union was chartered by the Federal Credit League. The group, the first of its kind, is open to members of the Detroit Women's Liberation Collective and three Detroit-area chapters of the National Organization for Women.

CONSUMER-INTENSIVE SERVICES

Let us now turn to specific consumer roles with regard to the services. A basic characteristic of services is, as Victor Fuchs points out, that they tend frequently to involve the "consumer" in the "production" of the service.[10] For example, the bank customer fills out a deposit slip as part of the production of the banking service; the supermarket customer selects and carries his or her goods from the shelves to the checkout counter as part of the production of the retail trade service.

8. *New York Times,* September 5, 1973.
9. *The Credit Union Yearbook* (Madison, Wis.: Credit Union National Association, 1957), and David Hamilton, *The Consumer in Our Economy* (Boston: Houghton Mifflin, 1972).
10. Victor Fuchs, *The Service Economy* (New York: Columbia University Press, 1968).

This unique consumer role is of greatest importance in the human services. Not only is the student, for example, a consumer of the service, that is, learning, but also he/she is a factor in the production of it. Similarly, the patient is a factor in the production of his or her own good health. The consumer here is a force of production and the human services are not only labor-intensive, but may also be called consumer-intensive.

Traditional notions argue that productivity in human service work cannot be increased sharply because it is not amenable to capital-intensive inputs and, as it is labor-intensive work, inputs are costly and potentially inflationary. The point, however, is that human service work is consumer-intensive and that the key to increasing productivity in this sector lies in effectively engaging and mobilizing the consumer. (We will return to this issue of the consumer's role in increasing the productivity of the human services in subsequent chapters.)

While much of the potential power of consumers in the service sphere relates to their importance in relation to service production, it should be noted, in addition, that the services by their very nature are relational, and in the relationship the service is produced near the consumer—in contrast, for example, to the more distant relationship of automobile production and consumption. These factors give added importance to the consumer role.

The convergence of the consumer's special role in service production and his/her importance in the economy as a whole provides an important key for understanding the consumer's potential political power.

The economic power of the consumer began to be converted into political power in the sixties with the rise of a considerable number of consumer-related movements—community control and welfare rights, to give two examples.[11]

11. The new consumerism as expressed via the consumer movements earlier described, as well as the environmentalist movement, are by no means restricted to the service spheres, but rather embrace all production spheres, public and private. Major values of the day such as the concern for the quality of life clearly derive their power from consumer concerns (see Chapter 4).

SERVICE CONSCIOUSNESS

Beginning with the black and youth movements of the sixties and continuing with the women's movement and the taxpayers' revolt of the seventies, the human services in our society have been under powerful consumer attack. They have been variously portrayed as inhuman, ineffective, insensitive to the consumer, unaccountable, not relevant, and lacking in vitality. A rapid rise of what might be called "service consciousness" has taken place among consumers; services are carefully scrutinized and evaluated by the user, the community, the public, not merely by the professionals and their peers, or the agencies and their executives. The days of professional and agency total autonomy may be numbered, and while "peer review" is an important aspect of accountability, it is insufficient in the eyes of the consuming public.

In the 1960s, the questions raised by blacks regarding the services led to demands for community control, the employment of neighborhood residents, new forms of work-study, and an open enrollment that might provide workers who were more effective and thereby produce service work that was more relevant.

The youth movement was also very much concerned with the lack of relevance and vitality of the services they were receiving, particularly education, and the services they were prepared to offer, such as medicine and law, and they began to develop various forms of alternative institutions, such as free schools, halfway houses, and hot lines.[12] In the seventies, the women added their voices with particular concern for the ways in which various services discriminated against women. They are particularly critical of the health and mental health institutions and have countered with feminine counselors and the like.

In the first stages of service consciousness, or what we call the

12. It is interesting to note that various public consumer affairs agencies have responded to the new consumer activities with the installation of "hot lines," a services innovation of the new consumer involvement in the services. Office of Consumer Affairs, *loc. cit.*

battle for the services, the professional rather than the establishment was the main target.

As Margaret Mead has noted, "There is a questioning all over the world, by colonialized peoples, by minorities, by women, of an order of life in which others—teachers, administrators, social workers, members of other classes and races, and of the other sex—care for them, no matter how well-intentioned the care might be."[13] It may be premature, however, to declare that the era of professional control is over. Indeed, Daniel Bell says that the conflict between professional and consumer is the post-industrial service sector's equivalent to the industrial era's conflict between capitalist and labor. Whatever the formulation, there is no question as to the powerful role of service providers, particularly as they have become increasingly organized. Nonetheless, there are varied signs of greater—if not preeminent—consumer roles.

The new consumer role (or, more accurately, roles) is seen most sharply in relation to those consumers who are poor, or minority group members, or both. The services have largely failed to meet the needs of these groups, and race and class tensions between them and servers, along with antipoverty and related programs, have encouraged new consumer roles. Indeed, it is in the effort of such groups to gain for themselves a significant measure of control of antipoverty and model cities programs, public schools, and welfare and health services that we can see the most dramatic efforts of service consumers.

While consumer control has rarely been achieved, there has been a heightened sense of accountability, along with efforts of various sorts to make the services more responsive.

—This emphasis on accountability has affected the modes of governance of human service programs. Community advisory boards have been established in every human service field.
—New forms of payment have been developed, such as performance contracting and voucher systems, in order to capture some of the presumed power of the service buyer.

13. *New York Times,* Jan. 12, 1974, p. 51.

—Certification systems based on competency or performance have been developed in order to identify more closely what the practitioner is able to do.

—Methods of work analysis (job or functional task analysis) and methods of management and budgeting (such as PPBS) are also designed to clarify the work done and to bring it under greater scrutiny and control.

These various devices have not only been used to increase accountability to consumers but a number of them have clear cost-cutting and management-control dimensions as well. However, singly and as a group, they have served to weaken, if not break, the professional monopoly.

The idea of service as a right has been increasingly developing. Long true in elementary and secondary education, this right to services has expanded—in one degree or another—to include postsecondary education, health care, and legal services. Recently, various groups that had been excluded from those entitled to such care, such as the handicapped and the mentally ill, have gained the right to services through legal action.[14] And in the decisions in several school financing cases, there is the development of the idea that the consumer has a right to equal services. In sum, a broad variety of services are coming to be seen as public rights, and these services, it is being argued, are to be provided in such a manner that there are no second-class recipients.

Another feature of the consumer orientation of the services is the increased involvement of the consumer as a service giver. Of course, the growing number of people employed as human service practitioners are themselves, on occasion, service receivers. In addition to this sequential pattern, a growing number of people are simultane-

14. A new journal, *Mental Retardation and the Law,* catalogues legal activities seeking greater access to services by the handicapped, mentally ill, and imprisoned. The field of the legal rights of the mentally ill has expanded sufficiently to warrant four different three-day conferences for lawyers around the country.

ously playing the role of both consumer and server.[15] This includes those in mental health and drug programs who, in the "helper therapy mode,"[16] are serving others as they participate in their own "cure." Another aspect of this phenomenon is the development of learning through teaching programs.[17] Even in medicine, there is increased attention to the role the patient can play in both illness prevention and recovery. The biofeedback technique is a growing field;[18] doctors are giving readings (and tape cassettes) to patients regarding their illnesses, and thus training them in self-help.

In the human services, it is asserted that consumers have a right to participate in decisions affecting the service; there is a public concern for the quality of the service, and, increasingly, the quality of that service, it is argued, should not be a function of an individual's ability to pay.

Part of this relates, of course, to the fact that those who deliver the service are supported through public funds (even when they are not directly public employees), but even when this is not the case, there is some sense of the rights of the service consumer.

THE ALTERNATIVE INSTITUTIONS

One of the most important expressions of consumer revolt in the sixties took place around the alternative institution or, more accurately, the alternative ways of providing services—alternatives to the standard professional ways that were felt to be failing. One study suggests that The Diggers, a countercultural group in San Francisco, was the first of these groups, offering free food, a crash pad (itself a new service), and services.[19]

15. Alan Gartner, "Consumers as Deliverers of Services," *Social Work,* XVI, 4 (October 1971), pp. 28–32.

16. Frank Riessman, "The 'Helper-Therapy' Principle," *Social Work,* X, 2 (April 1965), pp. 14–25.

17. Alan Gartner, Mary Conway Kohler, and Frank Riessman, *Children Teach Children: Learning by Teaching* (New York: Harper & Row, 1971).

18. Gerald Jonas, *Visceral Learning: Toward a Science of Self-Control* (New York: Viking, 1973).

19. Ted Clark and Dennis T. Jaffe, *Toward a Radical Therapy* (New York: Gordon & Breach, 1973), p. 122.

These efforts were concerned with providing services in new ways —less professional, less hierarchical, less expensive, involving advocacy and the concern for social change, emphasizing consumer responsiveness and accessibility.

In education, the more child-centered free schools have had an impact serving numbers of affluent people, but more important they have begun to influence the traditional educational structure through the emphasis on alternative programs, open classrooms, and the like. In the mental health field, encounter groups, sensitivity training, and growth centers have contributed to a new psychotherapy going beyond traditional mental health approaches. The development of the "human potential" groups illustrates this phenomenon.

Human Potential Movement Groups[20]

T-groups	Gestalt groups
sensitivity training groups	bio-energetic groups
recovery groups	Weight Watchers
Alcoholics Anonymous	integrity groups
survival groups	theater games
Synanon	graphic groups
nude encounter groups	massage experiences
human interaction groups	truth groups
sensory awareness groups	psychological karate
marathons	personal growth labs
psychodrama	human potential groups
sociodrama	confrontation groups
transactional analysis	self-management groups
inquiry groups	primal therapy groups
conflict-management labs	humanistic "psychotherapy"
life-planning labs	Kraftig Gefuhl
psychosynthesis	Zen
meditation	Tai Chi
movement groups	yoga
alternate life-style labs	

20. Frederick Massarik, *New Perspectives on Encounter Groups* (San Francisco: Jossey-Bass, 1972).

Young people have been involved in service giving and service receiving in the area of tutoring and in a great variety of youth-serving endeavors—runaway houses, crash pads, free clinics, book-stores, educational reform projects, cooperatives, hot lines, vocational and educational clearing houses, peer counseling groups.

Switchboards centralize and disseminate clear, concrete information on such topics as drugs, pregnancy, venereal disease, and the availability of such basics as food, shelter, clothing or jobs. They also create a body of knowledge concerning the handling of bad drug trips; this has led to a decline in bad trips as a significant problem, even while drug use itself increases. Rather than turning the care of bad drug trips into a specialized skill, crisis centers experimented with techniques and passed them on to large numbers of volunteers. The eventual result is that most young people are aware of how to intervene in bad-trip situations, thereby decreasing the need for such a special service. Most crisis centers now report fewer bad-trip interventions.[21]

Illustrative of the effect of alternative institutions upon "mainstream" organizations is a *New York Times* report on the encounter movement.

Having largely discarded its more extreme and coercive aspects along with extravagant assertions of instant personal redemption, the encounter concept has quietly found an accepted place in such established institutions as schools, churches, industry and even the military and sports.[22]

And William Schutz, of Esalen, captured the development when he noted that while encounter may be passé in New York and California, "in Athens, Ga., and Rock Island, Ill., it's like four and five years ago—for the overwhelming majority of Americans, encounter is just beginning."[23]

CONSUMER POLITICS

It is noteworthy that most of the changes we have described seem to stem from groups largely in their consumer roles—from students

21. *Ibid.,* p. 124.
22. *New York Times,* January 13, 1974.
23. *Ibid.*

rather than youth in general; from welfare recipients rather than union members; from service receivers rather than professional service givers; from consciousness-raising women's groups rather than from female factory workers. While the values and issues that these groups raise may contagiously affect other segments of the population, the initial thrust seems clearly to have been coming from groups not integrated into worker roles, groups on the periphery of industrial society.[24]

Out of this has emerged a consumer politics with new tactics, forms, issues, ethos, and style. It is a politics which, in many ways, is in marked contrast to worker tactics, e.g., strikes and parliamentary politics (see table below). This new consumer politics is reflected in many ways: the use of boycotts and consumer protests, the demands for accountability and relevance, the emphasis on local community issues, Naderism, the concern over style, culture, and everyday life, the tremendous disturbance over inflation, the new demands such as the voucher system in education, the tenants' movement, the consciousness-raising groups, the demands for decentralization and community boards, the revolts of prisoners and patients and high school and junior high school students, and on and on. Significant, also, has been the demand for improvement of services, itself a powerful consumer demand.

Of course, both women and minority groups have entered the political arena with increasing strength in the past few years. While attention has been given to the increased representation of women at the 1972 Democratic Convention (up from 13 percent in 1968 to 40 percent in 1972), representation of women rose at the Republican Convention as well (up from 17 to 29 percent). And in 1972, there was a 28 percent gain in female state legislators.[25]

In 1974 there are 107 black mayors, compared with 82 in 1973. One black senator has held office in both 1973 and 1972; 16 black

24. The very nature of the consumer role with its more "unbounded," open time is important.

25. Jo Freeman, "The New Feminism," *The Nation*, CCXVIII, 10 (March 9, 1974), p. 300.

Roles	Tactics	Types of organizations	Issues
worker	strikes work-ins and 　　sit-ins heal-ins industrial sabotage slowdowns	unions	wages working conditions supplementary benefits hours
consumer	legal actions boycotts publicity participation on 　　community 　　boards	movements consciousness-rais- 　　ing groups parent groups buying coops tenants' groups	community control accountability quality of goods and 　　services prices and taxes

representatives in the House in 1973 compared with 13 in 1972. Black state legislative officials numbered 238 (42 senators and 196 representatives) compared to 206 (37 senators and 169 representatives) total in 1972. On the local level (county, municipal, law enforcement, education), 1973 statistics show gains in each area; total figures are 2,288 black officials in 1973 and 1,954 in 1972.[26]

NEW VANGUARD AND OLD

It is interesting to contrast the revolutionary potential of the new consumer forces with the classical Marxist revolutionary vanguard— the industrial worker. Marx, in essence, argued that under capitalism the working class was the most revolutionary force for three reasons: its centrality to capitalist production (more than any previously exploited class, the working class was indispensable for production); its concentration in the factory, leading to its capacity for self-organization; and its exploitation in the strictly Marxian sense (i.e., the extraction of surplus value), which is to be distinguished from other

26. *National Roster of Black Elected Officials* (Washington, D.C.: Joint Center for Political Studies, 1972, 1973).

forms of oppression. Moreover, Marx believed that the working class was the only class that could free everyone by freeing itself, and had nothing to lose but its chains.

The modern consumer vanguard,[27] if indeed it is that, does not appear to have many of the characteristics that Marx assumed would be necessary for a revolutionary role: the new groups, while oppressed and alienated, are not necessarily exploited in the classical Marxist sense because they are frequently unemployed and thus do not produce surplus value, or they are employed in the public sphere in "nonproductive" human services work where surplus value is not created according to classical Marxist theory. They are clearly not central to industrial production, although they may be very important to consuming that production. And many of the upper-middle-class women and youth have much to lose; it is not at all certain that everyone's liberation would be accomplished through theirs.

While the new vanguard forces[28] may have powerful needs for

27. The aged are a less clear vanguard because for large portions of their lives many of them may have worked in the industrial labor force, and they may be white male, etc.; but it should be noted also that large numbers of the aged have always been poor, have worked in the secondary labor force when they worked, have been longtime nonemployed, or underemployed, and now in their open time, supported in part by social security, welfare, and the like, they are increasingly expressing their dissatisfaction with the social system.

28. The human service professionals are another significant group who have a mixed role. On the one hand, as consumers, they are needed and cheated, via inflationary prices and high taxes, and as service workers they are indispensable to an advancing service society. Moreover, they have much free time in their consumer roles and their shorter, or flexible work weeks; moreover, they are interested in service issues and self-related issues because of the very nature of their work roles, as well as their consumer situation and the long period of education and its attendant of socialization. On the other hand, they are economically relatively well off, "bought off" by the system, given considerable status and prestige, and in large part consist of white males. It is noteworthy that the societal critiques come from those professionals among the deprived groups, the women, the minorities, the young, who are more bureaucratized, less well paid off, and in the less advanced positions and the professions. These groups form a particularly important vanguard of the human services in a service society. They are the groups that demand changes in the service institutions, develop the alternative institutions, demand increasing consumer control and involvement, and are particularly concerned with the service agenda, not only because they consume the services, but because they work in them, or are preparing to work in them.

revolutionary change, they lack the power to produce it. They are not naturally organized in the workplace, although they may, by their concentration in neighborhoods and institutions, develop an affinity and a capacity for self-organization; certainly this has been apparent in the women's movement, among the students, and among the minorities in urban settings. Urban life itself produces this type of concentration. Women, blacks, and other minorities have each, because of their common identity, a potential for organization that has, of course, been demonstrated.

Although the power of these groups is weakened by the fact that they are not crucial to production, as they increasingly move into service production (and even to some extent into industrial production), they may gain strength via their worker roles. This, together with the tremendous impact of the media and of education, which extends the new demands and new consciousness to ever-increasing portions of the populace, including industrial workers, provides a significant new potential. It may very well be that the new vanguards have only a limited revolutionary potential which cannot be fully actualized until the various groups—women, youth, minorities— become members of the working classes themselves and, in turn, affect the other members of the working classes.

Finally, the special significance of consumers as a productive force in the service economy may assist us in understanding their potential.

CONCLUSION

The role of the consumer takes on special force because under neocapitalism the consumer is typically exploited at the point of consumption rather than production, encouraged to be constantly dissatisfied with the products he/she is overstimulated to purchase— a dissatisfaction bordering on alienation that may spread into many areas, including what we call "consumer politics."

While consumers seem to be a leading force in raising new demands, as consumers they do not appear to have enough consciousness to go beyond small, isolated, institutional changes and move toward deeper societal transformation. Consumer groups are too disconnected from each other, are overly focused on issues of the day, and do not possess sufficient organization and power as consumers. Workers, service and industrial, white- and blue-collar, on the other hand, have great potential power but thus far have not been in the forefront in striving for basic change.

A dialectical answer may emerge as the disadvantaged consumers —women, minorities, and youth—increasingly become a part of the labor force, particularly in the important service sector. Then, the progressive values deriving from their consumer roles may combine with the power deriving from the worker role. Revolutionary motive and revolutionary agent may unite. The danger remains, however, that some of the defensive self-interest stemming from the worker role may mute the advances of the consumer vanguards.

4   The Culture of the Service Society:
The Value Explosion of the Sixties

> During the Era of Protest [the 60's], practically all non-economic
> status relationships were challenged and extensively modified:
> the relationships between whites and Blacks, parents and chil-
> dren, teachers and pupils, policemen and citizens, officers and
> soldiers, bishops and clergy, the artist and his [sic] audience, the
> government and its citizens, and most important of all, men and
> women. As the protest movement gained momentum and took
> new forms, some of its theorists were inevitably drawn into
> challenging the legitimacy of all authority, however derived.
>
> —Theodore Caplow, "Toward Social Hope"

Since the sixties there has arisen a broad range of new values and
related movements. New words and demands have entered our consciousness and to some extent our life (alienation, personal liberation, encounter, the quality of life, male chauvinism, counterculture,
ecology, malaise, life style, growth center, self-actualization, meaningful work, participation, and more), embodied in many cases in the
various movements of the sixties and the early seventies, the student
movement, the black and minority third world movements, the
women's movement, the ecology movement, the consumer movement,
the human potential movement, and so on.

How are these various themes and movements related to changes
in our emerging service society—a society characterized by an in-

creasing proportion of people producing and consuming services, as well as reading about and thinking about services, a society in which services are important both for economic stability and social/political control?

It is possible, of course, to believe that the new values are only accidentally related to the changes in our social structure. Or, that they represent a counterrevolutionary reaction to the changes, as was earlier suggested by Brzezinski,[1] who saw the counterculture largely as a reaction similar to that of the Luddites, who were reflecting their own obsolescence by attacking the advances of the society and wished really to stop history. Or, as does Daniel Bell,[2] who writes of the disjuncture of social structure and culture in modern society—by social structure he means the post-industrial knowledge explosion and by culture he is referring to the modern counterculture emphases of the youth.[3] Or it is possible to take the views of Charles Reich[4] and Theodore Roszak,[5] who see the modern values as highly revolutionary, reflecting a moral rebellion against the bankruptcy of corporate liberalism, the establishment, or the "welfare-warfare" state where real human needs are neglected by large-scale organizations that dehumanize their members. This view is rooted in the belief that there is a new affluence (the "post-scarcity" society) which makes unnecessary the old values of repression that were linked to scarcity.

It is clear that both groups—Brzezinski, and the counterrevolutionary theorists and the new revolutionary theorists, Reich, Roszak, *et al.*—are looking at the counterculture in different ways. Reich, *et al.*, view it as highly positive, the historical vanguard, and the

1. Zbigniew Brzezinski, *Between Two Ages: America's Role in the Techno-tronic Era* (New York: Viking, 1970).

2. Daniel Bell, *The Coming of Post-Industrial Society* (New York: Basic Books, 1973).

3. Kenneth Keniston, *Youth and Dissent* (New York: Harcourt Brace Jovanovich, 1971).

4. Charles Reich, *The Greening of America: The Coming of a New Consciousness and the Rebirth of a Future* (New York: Random House, 1970).

5. Theodore Roszak, *Where the Wasteland Ends* (New York: Doubleday Anchor, 1972) and *Making of a Counter-Culture* (New York: Doubleday, 1969); Theodore Roszak, ed., *Sources* (New York: Harper & Row, 1971).

Brzezinski group sees it as counterrevolutionary, anachronistic, regressive. They see the disjuncture as temporary while the Reich group sees it as the forerunner of the future and perhaps as the predeterminer of a changed society.

The Brzezinski group stresses the major social transformation undergone as we pass from an industrial to a post-industrial, technotronic society which it views as highly rationalized, characterized by high productivity, automation, increased leisure time, rapid rates of social change, rational administration largely of a hierarchical, disciplined character. Enormously high levels of education will be required and the power will lie with those who possess educational capital. The knowledge industry will be the central motor of historical change. Basically a technical managerial approach to the solution of human problems will occur rather than one related to power and conflict, or ideology. The countercultural people see the key modern development as a "post-scarcity" society, although it is not entirely clear how this post-scarcity base, which is, of course, far from fully actualized, specifically produces all the new modern values. Further, the whole concept "post-scarcity" must be reconsidered in light of environmental and energy crises.

There is no question that both groups are pointing to aspects of change and potential change in the modern society. We would suggest, however, that a more specific analysis based upon the neocapitalist emerging service society formulation can explain more effectively not only the counterculture values of the youth, but the whole wave of new consciousness that goes far beyond the oppositional youth dimension. Moreover, we will attempt to classify not only the range of new value syndromes but the specific limits of their institutionalization. That is, while we believe that the new values are very important and have had a significant effect upon the consciousness of many groups in our society and are spreading to other groups contagiously, nevertheless, the full expression of these values in practices and institutions is limited by the power and influence of the corporate state. Despite this, however, these new developments have considerable power and cannot easily be violated, as we shall see.

VALUES AND MOVEMENTS OF THE SIXTIES

In our view major themes and values characteristic of the service society surfaced sharply in the sixties, particularly around the various movements of that period: the civil rights and Black Power movements, consumer protection, ecology, youth, free speech, peace, welfare rights, and community control movements, and the demands for rights and entitlements by large numbers of people ranging from patients, to prisoners, to homosexuals.

It is our contention that the values of the sixties are being institutionalized in everyday life, in people's life styles, in behaviors and consciousness. Institutionalization, of course, has a double edge: on the one hand, it typically is watered down and weaker, in some respects, than the value in its original more pristine mobilizing form. For example, the demand for participation and community control in the sixties had a much sharper edge than it does in the seventies. On the other hand, the very fact of institutionalization and acceptance has a strengthening feature, a feature that would be much stronger if the basic economic structure were to change.

Much of the discussion of the sixties focuses on the counterculture, and the so-called oppositional youth. Bell, Brzezinski, Kahn, *et al.,* disconnect the counterculture from the other values and movements we have mentioned above, and tend to fasten their attention on a limited range of counterculture features. We are much more interested in the larger configuration and the various value syndromes emanating from these movements. The syndromes that we shall describe below frequently overlap, the lines of difference are blurred, and in many cases it is possible to combine different value elements together to construct a different pattern.

Our intention is to demonstrate in a broad way that these value patterns are related to significant service society features. In some cases, they are derived from various vanguard groups, such as women, youth, minorities. They function in many ways to support the new service (relational) work and the requirements of that work. Finally, and more nonspecifically, they are related to the new importance of the consumer role in society and the nature of consumer time—open, unbounded, less structured. In a sense, then, our analysis suggests a convergence of many different elements in the service society. This accounts for the speed and force with which these values developed in the sixties and the fact that they are spreading further in the seventies despite the decline of the movements of the sixties and the general backlash.[6]

They are spreading particularly to the workplace, in the women's movement, to groups in the population that are typically more middle-class and traditional, in the mainstream school, in the media, in everyday life and its reflected human relations. Our analysis, then, is very different from those who see the new values largely as a disjuncture, disconnected to social structural dimensions, independent of and unrelated to social forces, and, in some cases, downright anachronistically dysfunctional.

What are the new value themes and how are they related to the emerging service society? As we sketch out the various value configurations it will be clear that there is considerable overlap among them and the boundaries that we suggest are tentative working definitions. It will also be apparent that different vanguard groups, sometimes the blacks and minorities, sometimes the youth, sometimes the women, are central for particular value syndromes. And it should be clear that we are talking of tendencies and developments, not universally held values.

Rights, Entitlements, and Personal Liberation

One of the most important syndromes, and one that affects very much the others, is the extension of rights and entitlements to a variety of groups beginning with the third world minorities and

6. It should be noted, of course, that there were other elements and events in the sixties which played a special role in the rapid propelling of some of these values, e.g., the war and the draft, the third world, the development of the "pill," and the rapid expansion of media power which gave special attention to *new* movements, *new* ideas, *new* values, *new* themes, and *new* words.

extending to students,[7] women, old people, homosexuals, children, welfare participants, prisoners, patients, and so on. In the sixties, in particular, there was a great expansion of the right of students to participate in the decisions of the university, rights for the poor, the right to information about products, the right to a fair hearing for welfare recipients, and of particular interest, various personal autonomy rights with respect to sex, family, birth control.[8] It is noteworthy that in some areas these rights are being extended in the seventies—in the rights women are demanding, the right of the educationally handicapped to education, the right of the mentally ill to rehabilitation, the right to higher education as expressed in the Higher Education Act of 1973, the right not to be discriminated against via tests, and so on. Many of these rights relate very directly to services, such as education, health, and rehabilitation.

Accountability and Relevance

The rights of the service receivers, the consumers, relate very much to a new trend with regard to professional practice and credentials. The new demand was clearly for relevance, accountability, vitality of the service, whether it be education, health, mental health, or whatever. There was a concern that services "deliver" and a new service consciousness was arising in the critique of professional practice, particularly the critique of teachers at all levels from elementary school to graduate school.

As in the case of the rights and entitlements theme, the spearhead-

7. In the past four years, according to a Harris poll, those who felt that "student demonstrators who engage in protest activities," and "Blacks who demonstrate for civil rights," did more harm than good dropped by 33 and 32 percent, respectively. *New York Post,* October 1, 1973.

8. By 1972, 71 percent of a representative sample of white adults favored birth control education programs in public high schools. This was up 10 percent over two years earlier. A majority of both men and women, Catholics and non-Catholics, favored free birth control services for teen-age girls who requested them. This percentage, overall, in 1972 was 54 percent, up from 38 in 1970. "Contraceptive Education for All Teens, and Services on Request Favored by Most Adults," *Family Planning Digest,* II, 5 (September 1973). Table 1.

ing movement was the third world minorities, particularly the blacks, and the thrust here spread out to other groups—other minorities, youth, women. This theme received much of its power from parent and community groups along with enlightened professionals, and the alternate-institution people who were looking for new kinds of human services that worked, that were humane, nonbureaucratized, not defended by tradition, secrecy, and mystique. One of the major demands was to demystify the professions, and new kinds of professionals emerged in law, medicine, journalism, and architecture, for example.[9]

Self-expression, Self-actualization, Autonomy, Individualism

Another major value theme has to do with the development of the inner life, with growth and self-expression and personal liberation, and here it overlaps with the first theme concerning rights. This syndrome is expressed in the desire for open classrooms, free schools, the reemergence of progressive education, and the desire for spontaneity, openness, informality, freedom.

New forms of psychotherapy have appeared, frequently not called that at all: growth centers, alternative states, encounters, sensitivity groups, consciousness raising. The opening up and discovery of the self along with the expanding of consciousness is primary, and so the interest in drugs spread. Anything that interfered with this development was looked at askance—tradition, control, discipline, structure, form, rationality. This trend has clearly been led by the affluent young and their parents in different forms and directions, but their personal liberation owed much to the blacks.

The wish for emotional expression spills over into many areas, including style and culture, and most clearly, sexual relations. A national study compared sexual attitudes and behaviors[10] in 1972

9. See Ronald Gross and Paul Osterman, *The New Professionals* (New York: Simon & Schuster, 1972).

10. Any survey of this sort runs the risk of those questioned reporting on their behavior in the light of what they perceive as the expected answer. However, as we are as interested in changes in attitudes as we are in behavior, this methodological problem may not be decisive.

with those reported on by Kinsey in 1947.[11] Kinsey reported that one-third of single women had intercourse by age twenty-five, while the 1972 study reports the comparable figure as over three-quarters. The authors of this study state that "premarital sex has become both acceptable and widespread; the change is especially noteworthy in females."[12] There is an increased variety in, frequency of, and, apparently, pleasure derived from sexual activities. Kinsey reported that four of ten husbands with more than grade school education had ever engaged in oral sex, while the 1972 study states that 60 percent of such men had done so in the past year alone. There is increased variety in coital techniques, as well as increased frequency of intercourse, especially among single females but also among older couples. For married couples, ages thirty-six to forty-five, Kinsey reported a median of seventy-five acts of intercourse per year, while the 1972 study reports ninety-nine, and for married couples over fifty, the respective medians are twenty-six and forty-nine. And there is a sharp rise in the percentage of times in intercourse that the partners reported they had reached orgasm; this was especially true among females.

A wide variety of social changes has occurred, including greater explicitness in, observations of, and research upon sexual activities (contrast the more open response to the far more explicit work of Masters and Johnson to that which greeted Kinsey's work); broader media attention on the stage, in movies, in print; greater acceptance of varying unconventional living arrangements;[13] legal changes regarding private sex acts among consenting adults; changes in abortion laws; increased availability of contraceptive devices. In examining attitudes, while age is a differentiating factor, the break is between

11. Morton Hunt, "Sexual Behavior in the 1970s," *Playboy,* XX, 10 (October 1973), pp. 84–88.

12. *Ibid.,* p. 86.

13. Between 1960 and 1970, the Census reports an 820 percent increase in unmarried couples living together, compared with a 10 percent increase in married couples living together. No doubt, part of this increase is a result of more openness in reporting on such arrangements. But, surely, those who so report are only a portion of those who so live together.

those under and over forty-four years of age, not at some younger level.

In summary, Hunt states that within the context of the continuing dominance of heterosexual marriage, there is greater "spontaneous and guilt-free enjoyment of a wide-range of sexual acts in the context of the emotional significance of sexual expression."[14]

The Quality of Life

Concern for the quality of life has both external and internal dimensions—externally it was directed toward ecology, the environment, and the Nader-oriented issues regarding commodities and services. Internally it was directed toward the expansion of consciousness, the use of leisure and art, and much of the inner self-expression described above. It was largely led by the affluent young and their parents.

Egalitarian–Antihierarchical Theme

A major theme has been directed at traditional hierarchical authority and discipline as found in the family, school, workplace, church.[15] There has been a sharp drop in respect for and trust in the basic institutions of society. For example, a study by the Center for Political Studies, University of Michigan, found that trust in basic governmental institutions, between 1958 and 1972, dropped among whites from 50 percent support to barely 5 percent, while among blacks the drop was from 50 percent support to nearly 50 percent estrangement. Among all age groups, support has dropped over the course of the four waves of interviews conducted between 1958 and 1972; while youth have been more estranged than older persons in each previous

14. Hunt, *op. cit.* p. 207.
15. In response to a Harris Poll, those who felt that "People who don't believe in God" did more harm than good, had dropped by 32 percent in the past four years. *New York Post,* October 1, 1973.

wave, in 1972, those aged fifty to fifty-nine, sixty to sixty-nine, and seventy and over ranked even higher than youth in estrangement.[16]

Unlike the earlier analysis of Erich Fromm,[17] which criticized irrational authority, there appears to be a tendency to attack indiscriminately all authority and discipline. A neo-anarchism has emerged with a powerful pro-humanism emphasizing the "natural man" and spontaneity; this has extended to small groups, communes, networks, and communities where the good life could be led.[18] The central enemies were bureaucracy and bigness and formality and structure. A strong Rousseauean component has been revitalized, and deep populist themes tapped.

An effort was made to build alternative institutions frequently on a nonhierarchical basis. This theme quite obviously was led much more by the affluent young, although some of its antibureaucratic overtones have important spillover into various institutions where professionals and service workers are employed. It is frequently directed at alienation and powerlessness.

The Interpersonal Psychology Theme

If physical science is the center of Brzezinski's technotronic world, and engineers and scientists at the center of Bell's post-industrial society, then psychology and the behavioral revolution are the centers of the service society. And the prophets are Maslow, Schutz, and Rogers; the key words are self-actualization, encounter, human potential, joy. The service society is a relational society and the new humanistic psychology is tremendously concerned with interpersonal relations, self-development, sensitive awareness of others, including at the nonverbal level. *Psychology Today* is a key magazine bringing

16. "Newsletter," Institute for Social Research, University of Michigan, I, 18 (Spring–Summer 1973), pp. 4 ff.
17. Erich Fromm, *Escape from Freedom* (New York: Holt, Rinehart and Winston, 1941).
18. See Murray Bookchin, "On Spontaneity and Organization," *Liberation,* (March 1972), pp. 5–17.

the behavioral revolution message to vast numbers of people (897,000 subscribers as of October 1, 1973) who are concerned about sexual expression and many of the new values mentioned above. The expansion of psychological knowledge into everyday life is very impressive. This theme is led by affluent adult professionals.

Work and Play

Work and leisure or play are frequently blurred in the new work theme. Self-expression is crucial to both, as is a nonhierarchical orientation. This is perhaps best expressed in the free school movement. Systematic, disciplined hard work is looked upon askance. Work, rather, is to be self-actualizing, joyful, nonhierarchically organized, an expression of self, and should be as free and autonomous as possible. Other dimensions of the new work syndrome emphasize that it should be meaningful, useful, community-serving, participatory, satisfying, and nonbureaucratic. This theme is perhaps led from two different directions: on the one hand there are the affluent adults and the young with their alternative institutions, and on the other are the third world minorities who are increasingly opposed to dead-end, boring, meaningless work. In addition, there are the professionals who feel that their training, skills, and self go unutilized in highly bureaucratized work structures.

The Service Advocacy Theme

The sixties saw a great deal of concern about human service, helping, serving, particularly by the young who were concerned about working in the ghetto, helping the poor in direct nonprofessional ways. This is also reflected in the development of new professionals where young people, students, and the like are selecting and recasting professional work in an uncareerist, serving manner.[19]

19. See Ronald Gross and Paul Osterman, *loc. cit.*

The Anticonformity, Antiacquisition, Anticareer Theme

A powerful theme developed initially among the young, spread via various alternative therapeutic institutions to adults who increasingly wanted to reject the acquisitive life, the rat race, conformity, competition, manipulation, and even in some cases material values. A new humanism has appeared concerned with enjoying life and people and leisure and art and inner experience and nature and living for oneself, rather than conforming for success. This dovetails with the antihierarchical, the self-development, and the quality of life themes.

The old culture, when forced to choose, tends to give preference to property rights over personal rights, technological requirements over human needs, competition over cooperation, violence over sexuality, concentration over distribution, the producer over the consumer, means over ends, secrecy over personal openness, social forms over personal expression, striving over gratification, Oedipal love over communal love, and so on. The counterculture tends to reverse all these priorities.[20]

The Identity, Self-determination Theme

The Black Power movement which spearheaded "Black Is Beautiful" is illustrative of this identity theme. Reversing the traditional racism and the more modern environmentalism which in one way or the other represented blacks as inferior, the new theme went beyond a vague cultural pluralism and argued instead that blacks had a unique identity which was, indeed, very positive and healthy. This identity was based upon deep traditions—African and others—and emerged from a long history of struggle against oppressive majorities and their oppressive culture. The theme was reflected at both the political and cultural levels—with the accenting of physical and cultural characteristics, the demand for Black Studies programs, in the political rejection of alliances with a preference to go it alone at least as a first stage. The emphasis was on group identity and self-determination and

20. Philip Slater, *The Pursuit of Loneliness* (Boston: Beacon Press, 1970), p. 100.

there was a strong rejection of potential contamination by other, nonblack groups.

The theme, of course, spread rapidly to other minorities such as Chicanos, Puerto Ricans, and Native Americans, and more recently has been expressed in the women's movement with its desire for the woman's identity, self-determination, and personal liberation. The theme leads to a powerful attack on discriminatory ideology that, whatever its presumed objective, winds up putting down in one form or other the group in question, whether it be the IQ of blacks or the sexuality of women. The particular significance of this theme is that it does not attempt to "explain" inadequacy but essentially denies presumed inadequacy and reinterprets the phenomena.

THE NEXUS

We come now to the key question: What is the relationship of these various value patterns to the emerging service society?

At the simplest level of occupational determinism, one could argue, of course, that a good number of the new values are directly reflective of and useful to the new service occupations.

Obviously in a relational, interpersonal society, humanistic psychology and the whole syndrome related to it is likely to come to the fore. The need for sensitivity to others, great awareness of oneself, are not only useful in relation to the human service work, they have wide applicability in sales, advertising, personal services, and the like.

Another key syndrome relates to the need for creativity, self-actualization, and development. These are characteristics which are much in demand, not only in the professions and the human services but also in the knowledge sectors.

But it is difficult to control and manipulate creativity on a hierarchical basis. The creative person needs lots of freedom, room to grow and express himself rather than traditional restriction, boundaries, and controls. Permissiveness in child rearing and the revival of progressive education are in many ways consonant with the development of the new creativity that is so needed in the service occupations, as well as in the knowledge sector and in the expanded leisure life. The new occupations require more autonomy, use of the self, and again, one of the rallying cries in the professions is the fact that the emerging bureaucracies have stifled the creativity that the service workers have been trained to bring to their jobs and expect of their jobs. André Gorz has been among the most prominent theoreticians to point out this powerful source of alienation at the workplace for educated labor.[21] He notes that workers in scientific and cultural industries experience the impossibility of putting their creative abilities to work and thus tend to rebel against the bureaucracy, a rebellion which, incidentally, may be more fully expressed by their children, who are presumably being prepared for similar labor by educational institutions. The anticipatory socialization of the children requires a good deal of openness, creativity, and informality but this is received in the traditional, rigid, test-bound, grade-oriented, authoritarian school.

While some of the new values can be partially explained by their suitability to the new work structures and work lives of service workers, a more generalized, nonspecific mode of explanation is necessary to understand fully the many value dimensions. In essence, we are talking not only about service occupations or even service sectors; we are talking about an emerging service society. And the service society is characterized by features that go beyond the characteristics of specific service occupations. And so, our interpretation must be much more on the nonspecific, indirect effect of the new emerging values and their relation to the various aspects of the service society. Nevertheless, the specific occupations and their socialization and anticipatory socialization functions are not irrelevant.

Much of the thrust of the new values comes from the various groups we have mentioned, not so much in their service work roles, but in their consumer roles. Thus, it is particularly important to understand the special role of a consumer in the service society

21. André Gorz, *Strategy for Labor* (Boston: Beacon Press, 1967).

because the values put forward by the third world minorities, students, and women cannot entirely be explained in terms of their noninvolvement in the industrial sectors, but must be particularly understood in the light of their roles as consumers and potential service workers.

CONCLUSION

It is fashionable to believe that the values and movements that emerged in the sixties are lost, wiped out, violated, or rejected. There is some superficial basis for this view in that the cutting edge of the movements and their related values are no longer center stage. The counterculture, welfare rights, the youth movement, community control, Black Power, seem thoroughly distant. The blacks are quiet, the youth are back at school, and the counterculture has become spiritual. A new privatism prevails, sometimes masked as personal liberation. Still, the consumer movement and Nader go on; the environmental movement in some ways is stronger than ever; the women's movement is still on the rise and has won many victories; there are more blacks in elected office than ever before in American history; the mainstream school system is adopting alternative open-classroom types of practice; consumer participation on boards continues high; schools have been highly sensitized, as are other institutions, to community pressure; open enrollment remains, if not strong; the encounter movement is spreading; more people are involved in growth and development activities than ever before; and the acceptance in everyday life of countercultural values and ethos is truly amazing—for example, the use and acceptance of marijuana, new sex customs, abortion, rock, zen, liberated speech.

What all this means, it seems to us, is that the basic motion of the sixties and the service society (and the consumer values) has not been lost. Some of the values are vulgarized, commercialized, and watered down. But others have been institutionalized, accepted in consciousness and everyday life. They have deeply affected human relations and some have contagiously spread to new areas, including the workplace.

The consumer role that is becoming increasingly dominant in modern life is characterized by much more unbounded time in which the individual as agent feels freer to make choices, to do one's own thing, to live one's life style. He/she can be less concerned with organization, hierarchy, tradition. The consumer role permits more interest in growth, self-development, expression, liberation, personal rights, the environment, nature. In some cases this leads to a tremendous privatism, personalism, and hedonism, while in others, consumers' demands for accountability of services and quality of goods attracts them to Nader, the environmental movement, participation in school activities.

The consumer is seen in many roles: as taxpayer, student, volunteer, woman-at-home (housewife), community board member, parent, patient, client, customer, media viewer, welfare recipient, unemployed worker, and pollee (to be polled). In a sense, of course, everyone—worker, taxpayer, voter—is a consumer and much more time is spent in the consumer role in our society. But the worker-consumer in the traditional industrial structure is much constrained by rules and the pressures of organization. The consumer as student, welfare recipient, woman-at-home, while they all surely have pressures, are less constrained by the rules and requirements of organized work. These groups, in addition, are also largely politically disenfranchised—they're in some sense "unnecessary people," in Jean Miller's terminology,[22] dispensable as far as production is concerned (although very necessary as consumers). They are, in turn, less integrated in the production and work processes, less socialized by these processes, and more open to new trends, feelings, and ideas derived from neighbors, peers, the media, consciousness-raising groups, and so on. In Chapter 3 we have indicated various other dimensions of the consumer role, which gives it special significance in the current era—the fact that consumers are constantly overstimulated to pur-

22. Jean Baker Miller, "On Women: New Political Directions for Women," *Social Policy*, II, 2 (July–August 1971).

chase goods with highly expanded credit, their rising expectations and potential dissatisfaction and alienation, and the fact that the inflationary economy typically cheats them at the point of consumption. They are extremely important for the stabilization of the economy, not as worker-producers, but as consumer-buyers of overpriced, overadvertised products.

It is clear, then, that the value configurations we have been describing are overdetermined, in part by the consumer culture, in part by the intrinsic human potentiality and character of human service work (a kind of occupational determinism), and in part by the groups in our society who are most involved in service work and in disenfranchised consumer roles—the women, the youth, and the minorities—the consumer vanguards, so to speak.

5   Is There a New Work Ethic?

> We are challenging, in effect, whether human beings exist for the sake of production and profit, or whether we are engaged in production for the sake of human beings.
>
> —Leonard Woodcock, *New York Times,* September 23, 1973

Considerable attention has been given in the last few years to a "new work ethic." This alleged new development is characterized by a presumed desire of workers, both blue- and white-collar, to humanize work—to reduce the boredom, routinization, and fragmentation of the work process, to make work more meaningful, and to remove the traditional industrial discipline with its hierarchical overtones and lack of autonomy for the individual worker. The essence of the new conceptualization is that work is to partake of a positive quality of life and must not be merely a means of acquiring income that will be consumed someplace else. There is little question that this scenario has been given considerable attention by the media, and by some academics and industrialists.

In addition, a number of major publications have supported the new work ethic thesis, for example, the report on *Work in America* by a Special HEW Task Force and the Sheppard and Herrick book, *Where Have All the Robots Gone?*[1] To some extent, these reports

---

1. *Work in America: Report of a Special Task Force to the Secretary of Health, Education, and Welfare* (Cambridge, Mass.: MIT Press, 1973); Harold

have stressed the extremes, that is, the group from 10 to 20 percent of the work force that indicates a definite dissatisfaction with the nature of their work. Moreover, the groups expressing this dissatisfaction are disproportionately found among the young and those with more education. But the survey findings have varied little in the last decade in the amount of dissatisfaction reported,[2] with the great majority continuing to say they are *relatively* satisfied. An important question here is the *intensity* of satisfaction or dissatisfaction but, unfortunately, there seems to be little data dealing with this question.

Turning to more behavioral indicators, the argument, of course, has been made that there is an increase in absenteeism, labor turnover, strikes, industrial shortage, decreases in productivity, and poor morale at the workplace. But as Harold Wool points out in a very instructive essay, the aggregate statistical data on a national level are not very supportive, particularly with regard to strikes, labor turnover, and productivity, when one looks at these rates over a twenty-year period.[3] There is a small increase in absenteeism from 3.3 percent in 1967 to 3.6 percent in 1972. However, the other data, particularly in the auto industry, which has received major attention as an arena of worker discontent, show a sharp increase in absenteeism. For example, it has increased at General Motors from 2.5 percent in 1961 to 5.3 percent in 1970.

Moreover, annual turnover in the automobile industry has cost General Motors at least $79 million per year, according to a company bulletin,[4] with Chrysler hiring "44,000 workers in a single year just to maintain a work force of 100,000."[5]

L. Sheppard and Neil Q. Herrick, *Where Have All the Robots Gone?* (New York: The Free Press, 1972). See also, "Worker Alienation," 1972, Hearings before the Senate Subcommittee on Employment, Manpower and Poverty, July 25 and 26, 1972.

2. Harold Wool, "What's Wrong with Work in America?—A Review Essay," *Monthly Labor Review,* XCVI, 3 (March 1973), pp. 39–43.

3. *Ibid.,* p. 41.

4. Daniel Zwerdling, "Beyond Boredom—A Look at What's New on the Assembly Line," *Washington Monthly,* V, 5 & 6 (July–August 1973), p. 82.

5. Doug Fraser, UAW Vice President, cited in Franklin Wallick, "Enriching Jobs—Or Bosses?," *Newsletter of the Democratic Left,* I, 3 (May 1973), p. 7.

The crucial question is what type of phenomena underlies the new work ethic conceptualization. That is, what specific experience is being referred to by the work ethic interpretation—an interpretation that, incidentally, has been challenged by many as an enormous exaggeration that is not characteristic of the main sectors of industry. Some union officials, including UAW's Leonard Woodcock, emphasize not boredom or monotony as causes of worker discontent, but issues around the organization of work, especially a plant management which the workers see as brutal and oppressive.[6] Other union officials, as well as other commentators, emphasize the continuing concerns with "bread and butter" issues, both as inflation saps workers' buying power and rising living standards increase workers' sense of an adequate living standard.[7]

Wages, fringe benefits, hours—the traditional concerns of workers —continue to be essential matters of concern. Indeed, some of those who argue against "new" workers' concerns point to the continuation of such traditional concerns among workers. And there are data to support such a view. A study covering seventeen factories throughout the country encompassing 2,535 sewing machine operators found that among both "highly dissatisfied workers" and "less satisfied workers" their top preference of what they wanted in connection with their jobs was more job security, pay equal to other plants, more or different fringe benefits.[8] And William Winpisinger, Machinists' Union vice-president, points out that "worker job satisfaction dropped in the late 1960s and early 1970s when worker income—in relation to inflation and taxation and purchasing power—also declined.[9] Indeed, as measured by recorded work stoppages, "General

6. See Walter Mossberg, "Factory Boredom: How Vital an Issue?," *Wall Street Journal,* March 23, 1973, p. 13. See also, Laurence G. O'Donnell, "General Motor's Plan to Increase Efficiency Draws Ire of Unions," *Wall Street Journal,* December 6, 1972, p. 1.

7. William W. Winpisinger, a paper presented before the Industrial Relations Research Association, December 1972, at Toronto, Canada, cited in Wool, *op. cit.,* p. 48.

8. "The Real Cause of Workers' Discontent," *New York Times,* January 21, 1973, Section 3, p. 11.

9. Cited in Byron E. Balame, "Wary Labor Eyes Job Enrichment," *Wall Street Journal,* February 26, 1973, p. 17.

Work Stoppages by Selected Issues, 1964–1970*

	1964	1967	1970
Total Stoppages	3655	4595	5716
Percentage due to general			
wage changes	38%	46%	49%
Supplementary benefits	2	1	1
Plant administration†	16	15	16

* *Handbook of Labor Statistics, 1972* (Washington, D. C.: U. S. Government Printing Office, 1972), Table 157.

† Includes physical facilities, safety measures, supervision, work assignments, speed up, work rules, overtime work, discipline.

Wage Changes" increased as a percentage of all issues relating to strikes between 1964 and 1970.

Let us, then, look at some of the actual experiences that are reported, to see, first, if there is, in fact, a new configuration possessing new qualities, and, if so, do these dimensions match the presumed new work ethic; that is, are they appropriately interpreted by this formulation. It is only then that we can turn to possible explanations of new work attitudes and behavior.

1. Many blacks, minorities, and poor workers, beginning in the antipoverty period of the sixties, appear to reject various types of "dead-end" jobs, "dirty" work, domestic work, and the like; and are demanding jobs that are "meaningful," serve the community, provide training and education, respect, and the possibility for advancement.[10]

2. To take a totally different area, many teachers, government workers, and other professionals have evidenced discontent with the lack of autonomy on the job, the bureaucratization which prevents the utilization of their skills, knowledge, and training. The rapid growth of unionization of these workers is, perhaps, at least in part, a reflection of this discontent.

3. Quite a number of women appear to be rejecting their traditional work roles—e.g., housework, child care, etc.—and are de-

10. "Who Will Do the Dirty Work?," *Fortune,* LXXXIX, 1 (January 1974), pp. 132 ff.

manding much more access to, and equality in, paid work outside the home. This is evidenced, in part, by the tremendous increase of the number of women in the labor force and is reflected in the women's movement.

4. There seems to be considerable desire on the part of at least a portion of workers to resist compulsory overtime. Most prominently this has been the case in the automobile industry. At the UAW's prebargaining convention, in February 1973, voluntary overtime was the demand that received greatest delegate support.[11] Pressure for maintenance of compulsory overtime is strong in an automobile industry which has seen absenteeism doubled over the past five years, with overtime often the way to keep lines running on Fridays and Mondays when up to 15 percent of the workers are absent on late shifts. Nonetheless, the heart of the 1973 settlement at the Big 3 automobile companies involved reduction in the work demands upon both the present labor force with the restrictions upon compulsory overtime work, and those close to retirement with the instituting of a full "30-and-out" retirement plan.

5. There is also evidence reported by the American Management Association that some managers are expressing dissatisfaction with their work and the fact that they are being "robbed by computers" of their decision-making roles. In this connection, there is also the phenomenon of career change by professionals, managers, executives in their forties and fifties.[12]

6. Public opinion poll data indicate that the more educated the worker, the more he expresses dissatisfaction with regard to his job, and it is clear that the work force is becoming more educated.[13]

11. Walter Mossberg, "Compulsory Overtime Makes an Auto Worker Wealthier but Wearier," *Wall Street Journal,* March 19, 1973, p. 1. Laurence G. O'Donnell, "The UAW's Bargaining Quandary," *Wall Street Journal,* February 12, 1973, p. 17.

12. *Business Week* has noted that the "tight white-collar of job dissatisfaction is making many middle managers writhe and is pinching some of the occupants of executive row." See "GM Zeroes in on Employee Discontent," *Business Week,* May 12, 1973, p. 141.

13. Indirectly, one might also note that the large number of people involved in acquiring some kind of education (Moses estimates that there are over 120

What does stand out, then, is that there are various forms of dissatisfaction among professionals, white-collar workers, blue-collar workers, women, managers and executives, young people, blacks, and third world minorities, regarding various aspects of the work process, as well as among students and women-at-home in their work roles. Some are concerned with lack of amenities, others with boredom and autonomy, others with low wages and the length of the work day and week, others with the content and organization of the work, others with the lack of advancement opportunity, still others with overt and subtle forms of discrimination in employment and advancement. Furthermore, there are differences in their expressed wishes: some want a job that is respect-worthy, that leads to a career; others want the job to be minimally involving, not requiring too much work or time, thus allowing more leisure time that would be under their own control; still others want the job to be less time-consuming, better paying, under less autocratic control; others want more interesting work with greater autonomy, more collegiality. Equally wide ranging are the recommendations proposed, including higher wages, shorter and/or rearranged hours, more amenities, equal employment opportunities rigorously enforced, a national full employment policy and program, reorganization of the work, reallocation of workplace control, job enrichment, worker control, worker ownership, broader scope to worker organization concerns.[14]

---

million people in the learning force in the United States and in the ages eighteen to twenty-one years, 48 percent are attending college) may be seen to some extent as avoidance of the unpleasantness of work. But this, of course, is highly inferential.

14. The literature on these topics is enormous. Here we include only a sampling from the past two years. *Works in America, op. cit.*, contains an extensive bibliography, as does Sheppard and Herrick, *op. cit.* See also, Gerry Hunnius, *et al.*, *Workers' Control* (New York: Random House, 1973); Harold L. Sheppard, *et al.*, *The Political Economy of Public Service Employment* (Lexington, Mass.: Lexington Books, 1972); Alan Gartner, *et al.*, *Public Service Employment* (New York: Praeger, 1973); Zwerdling, *op. cit.*; Walton, *op. cit.*; "Workers: A Special Section," *Liberation*, XVII, 3, 4, 5 (August 1972); Walter Mossberg, "A Day's Work," *Wall Street Journal*, December 7, 1972; William Buckley, "Short Shift," *Wall Street Journal*, April 30, 1973, p. 1; "Three Day Work Week," *New York Times*, April 25, 1973; David Sirota, "Job Enrichment: Nice But No Cure-All," *New York Times*, May 6, 1973,

While we cannot readily subscribe to a well-defined new work ethic in which all the various types of discontent are focused toward the quest for greater autonomy, increased participation, and so on, there does appear to be a very wide range of work discontent taking many different forms, expressing itself in a variety of ways that might be contagious.[15] Rather than seeing work discontent as exclusively or

Section 3, p. 8; Neil Ulman, "The Workers' Voice," *Wall Street Journal,* February 24, 1973, p. 1; Janice Neipert Hedges, "New Patterns for Working Time," *Monthly Labor Review,* XCVI, 2 (February 1973), pp. 3–8; Robert Shrank, "For a Worker Exchange Program," The Ford Foundation, March 1973; David Jenkins, "Industrial Democracy," *New York Times,* May 13, 1973; Joseph Mire, "European Workers' Participation in Management," *Monthly Labor Review,* XCVI, 2 (February 1973), pp. 9–15; Wool, *op. cit.;* Staughton Lynd, "Blue-Collar Organizing," *Working Papers,* I, 1 (Spring 1973), pp. 28–34; Edward Greer and Paul Booth, "Pollution and Community Organization in Two Cities," *Social Policy,* IV, 1 (July–August 1973), pp. 42–49; Kahn, *op. cit.;* Ivar Berg, "They Won't Work," *The Columbia Forum,* II, 1 (Winter 1973), pp. 15–22; Laurence O'Donnell and Walter Mossberg, "A Day's Work," *Wall Street Journal,* December 8, 1973, p. 1; Rasmus, *op. cit.,* p. 75.

15. At a broader level, we can note the declining percentage of the average twenty-year-old working man's life spent in the labor force (adapted from Denis F. Johnston, "The Future of Work: Three Possible Alternatives," *Monthly Labor Review,* XCV, 5 [May 1972], p. 4).

	1900	1950	1968
Life expectancy (years)	42.2	48.9	49.2
Work life expectancy (years)	39.4	43.1	41.5
Retirement expectancy (years)	2.8	5.8	7.7
Percent of life in work force	93%	88%	84%

At quite another level of work force participation is the growing number of part-time workers, 12.3 million nonagricultural workers at the end of 1972, up from 8.8 million in 1962. Part-timers now make up 16 percent of the non-agricultural workers (*Manpower Report of the President, op. cit.,* Table A-24). While many of these part-time workers are those, particularly women, who moved from no paid work to part-time work, many of these new workers "simply want to work less." They often consider part-time work as an economically feasible halfway house between the "deadly rat race" and "drop-ping out" (Roger Ricklefs, "Employees, Employers Both Discover the Joys of Part-time Positions," *Wall Street Journal,* March 7, 1973, p. 1). For ex-ample, among part-time nonagricultural workers, the number of those who work part-time for "voluntary" reasons has grown from 73 percent of part-time workers in 1962 to 80 percent of such workers in 1972 (*Manpower Report of the President, op. cit.,* Tables A-34, A-25).

primarily in the old industrial sectors, we would suggest that it is a recent phenomenon there, perhaps one-sidedly spotlighted by the media.

WORK DISCONTENT AND THE SERVICE SOCIETY

At the simplest level, the discontent can be understood as reflecting a changed demographic character of the labor force—it is increasingly younger, more educated, and includes considerably more women and minorities. The discontent that these groups have reflected in national life particularly in the sixties and largely around consumer issues seems to be increasingly reflected in the work force itself. It is also most striking that these groups are disproportionately employed in service work and relatively less employed in traditional industrial goods production. Moreover, the service work force as a whole has expanded enormously and all the predictions indicate that this trend will continue. Thus, the work force as a whole is changing in the service direction and service workers more often include groups such as the young, the educated, the minorities, the women, the poor, who in different ways have already expressed considerable dissatisfaction. It is appropriate to note, also, that much of the discontent expressed at the industrial workplace comes from the younger and black workers.

As we noted earlier, service work (including the human services) has, in fact, been routinized and bureaucratized, but the intrinsic nature of human service work itself, its traditions and required preparation, call for more expression, autonomy, self-involvement, and lend themselves less easily to bureaucratization, than work on the assembly line. To some extent, we would argue, it is the model of what human service work should be like that is implicitly affecting some of the new expectations about work in general. This also produces an especially powerful and unique alienation among these workers, particularly professionals and government workers, whose educational socialization has led them to expect a more humane, less bureaucratized practice.

Service work, historically, is less hierarchically organized in contrast to the world of goods production. The latter is a world of organization "in which men are treated as 'things' because one can more easily coordinate things than men."[16] This hierarchical "thing" orientation is not entirely suited to service occupations. Fuchs points out that these service industries have operated traditionally on a much smaller scale with more self-employment.[17] It might be argued that in small-scale service enterprises where the emphasis is more on relations between people and a tradition of serving is called for, there will be somewhat less concern for the hierarchical, bureaucratic type of organization, which is likely to be more characteristic of large-scale organizations where the product is things and goods. However, as the services (including the human services) have come to be organized on a larger scale, such as in school and hospital systems, a conflict between the new hierarchical and bureaucratized practices and the old traditions of humanized relationships comes to the fore and is perhaps a key feature in the special alienation of government employees and human service workers in general.

In turning to the consumer role, we find some similar reinforcing factors. The consumer ethic, so to speak, calling forth a concern for the quality of life and a participatory, nonhierarchical life style, is perfectly compatible with the consumer role. The work role, however, especially in large settings, requires more organization and lends itself more readily to hierarchical practices and norms. While these work norms are countered to some extent by the character and traditions of service work, we suspect that the driving force behind the new work discontent—and its demand for more participatory, less hierarchical work arrangements—stems at least as much from the consumer ethos of the service society as it does from the service work model. In a sense, workers are coming to seek fulfillment of consumer ethos values at the workplace—*viz.,* intrinsic satisfaction, pleasant inter-

16. Daniel Bell, "Labor in the Post-Industrial Society," *Dissent,* XIX, 1 (Winter 1972), p. 166.
17. Victor Fuchs, *The Service Economy* (New York: Columbia University Press, 1968).

personal relations, autonomy, self-initiative, a decrease in hierarchy, lack of constraints, personal amenities, a chance for growth. The workplace becomes in this sense another product to be consumed.

An additional part of the consumer orientation stems from the role of leisure in our society. There has developed in the service society what might be called a leisure ethic, as leisure time has expanded.[18] Some of it is imposed leisure, such as that of the unemployed, but there is also the leisure acquired by large numbers of people in college in an extended period of youth, the leisure of the affluent and near affluent, of the retired, of the woman-at-home, and so on. In our consumer-oriented society, much leisure time, unbounded time so to speak, is spent quite differently than time spent in the highly structured, repetitive character of much work. And while there is ambivalence toward a leisure that is frequently unfulfilling and invaded by the mass culture,[19] there are advantages which contrast sharply with the characteristic organization of work. The unbounded time is more open to autonomous decision (or at least it can be experienced as such), is less subject to hierarchical supervisory relationships, promises the possibility of self-development, makes possible participation in self-selected volunteer activities that are not characterized by the usual work norms, calls for less direct pressure and competition (although naturally there is spillover from the competitive work world), and produces the opportunity to expand the quality of life via artistic expression.

To return to work issues, Richard E. Walton has identified three "basic societal forces" which he says feed new expectations of employees. These forces are rising levels of wealth and security; declining emphasis upon socialized obedience in schools, families, and churches; and shifting emphasis from individualism to social commitment. Walton counterposes these new employees' expectations against traditional organization forms.

18. The average adult spent 2,650 leisure hours per year. Andresen Securities Research, *The Entertainment Industries* (New York: Andresen and Company, 1973), Table 1.
19. Some 70 percent of leisure time is spent watching television or listening to the radio. *Ibid.*

New Expectations	*Traditional Forms*
Challenge, personal growth.	Work designed to minimize the skill required.
Egalitarian concerns.	Tall hierarchies, status differentials, chains of command.
Social significance of the organization, intrinsic interest and dignity of work.	Emphasis on material rewards and employment security.
"Now" orientation to careers.	Job hierarchies and career paths.
Balance of emotional and rational aspects of organization life.	No legitimization of the emotional part of organizational experience.
Preference for community versus competitive relations.	Reward systems and career patterns that emphasize competition.[20]

In summarizing the factors involved in these phenomena, we turned first to the shift in the work being done, the fact that a rapidly increasing proportion of the work force is engaged in service work. This work is characterized by people-to-people interactions in contrast to the industrial people-to-things relationship. In the human services, the fastest-growing sector of service work, there is an ethos of people-serving, an associated pattern of preparation, and some antihierarchical and antibureaucratic traditions, as well as the essential relational characters of such work.

We have also noted the growing entry into the work force of women, blacks, other minorities, and youth, just those groups from among whose members came the vanguard efforts of the 1960s; efforts, as will be discussed below, which were concerned with consumer values and quality-of-life issues. In effect, they brought these issues from the consumer arena with them into the workplace. And with their clustering in service work, these "qualitative demands" at the workplace have gained added prominence.

The sixties were characterized by consumer-oriented issues: the quality of life, the environment, community control, welfare rights,

20. Richard E. Walton, "How to Counter Alienation in the Plants," *Harvard Business Review* (November–December 1972), Exhibit I.

student participation, personal liberation, consumer boycotts, culture, and style. In the seventies, the concern seems to be drifting toward issues related to work, workers, and the workplace: worker alienation, overtime, equal pay for equal work for women. Some of the consumer demands of the sixties seem to be moving from the community to the workplace: concern for the environment is reflected in concern about health and working conditions in the factory; demands for participation are being expressed in some workers' concerns for a voice in relation to production, for example.

These consumer-based values have spilled over from the service sectors to affect the more traditional work areas.[21] In part, this has occurred through the growing employment of persons from the vanguard groups—women, blacks, and youth—in the old industrial areas. In part, the example of developments in the service sector have affected the industrial. In part, the growing importance of consumption in the increasingly extended nonwork lives of these workers has led them to transfer consumer values—fulfillment, autonomy, intrinsic direct satisfaction—to the workplace.

We have seen a shift in the work being done and those who do it. It is not surprising, then, that there are new feelings about work. This is, in part, due to the new work being done; in part, due to those who are doing it; and, in part, due to a series of new largely consumer-based values affecting not only these new workers in the new work but also older workers doing the old work. These last are affected by example from the new sectors, and the new workers there; by the new workers coming into the old work arenas; by their own new consumer roles; by "contagion" from their children, wives, and the media.

21. The demands of the UAW and the settlements with the automobile companies reflect some of this admixture of new and old. It has been the younger workers and the blacks who have been getting much of the media attention, and it was principally their pressure which led to the unlimited compulsory overtime issue. The older workers (more white, as well) have fought for some time for a full "30-and-out" retirement plan.

A Note on the Work Force

In the decade following World War II, the United States economy, according to a variety of indicators, entered a new phase. About 1950, employment figures showed that there were more service-producing than goods-producing workers.[1] During the course of that decade, there came to be more white-collar than blue-collar workers.[2] And by the end of the decade, "professional, technical and kindred" workers exceeded for the first time the number of "managers, officials, and proprietors."[3] In sum, the work done and the workers doing it had changed.

The "turning point" of the decade of the 1950s, of course, was not an isolated event but a part of an ongoing process. In terms of sector of employment, for example, goods-producing workers will move from 82 percent of the total work force in 1870 to an expected 31 percent in 1980.

By 1970, white-collar workers outnumbered blue-collar by more than five to four;[4] by 1980, it is estimated that the ratio will be five to three, with there being more white-collar workers than all other occupational categories.[5] And the traditional notions of who works

1. *The U. S. Economy in 1980,* U. S. Department of Labor Bulletin 1673 (1970).

2. Daniel Bell, *The Coming of Post-Industrial Society: A Venture in Social Forecasting* (New York: Basic Books, 1973), p. 17.

3. *Manpower Report for the President,* 1967, p. 211.

4. Bell, *op. cit.,* p. 17.

5. *Ibid.,* Table 2–5.

Sector Distribution of Employment, 1870–1968, Projected to 1980*
(in Thousands)

	1870	1900	1920	1940	1947	1968	1980
Total	12,900	29,000	41,600	49,860	51,770	80,780	99,600
Goods-producing	10,630	19,620	23,600	25,610	26,370	28,975	31,600
Service-producing	2,990	9,020	15,490	24,250	25,400	51,800	67,980

* Adapted from Bell, *op. cit.,* Table 2–1.

Sector Distribution of Employment, 1870–1968, Projected to 1980*
(Distribution by Percentages)

	1870	1900	1920	1940	1947	1968	1980
Total	100	100	100	100	100	100	100
Goods-producing	82	67	56	51	50	35	31
Service-producing	18	33	44	49	50	65	69

* Adapted from Bell, *op. cit.,* Table 2–2.

where need to be changed with 31 percent of the manufacturing work force white-collar.[6] And, as Gross points out, "The latest blue-collar worker is the official expert or politician who wears a blue-tinted shirt (or dress) just in case he (or she) may unexpectedly appear before a TV camera."[7]

It is "professional" work that has grown most rapidly. We have already noted that the number of "professional, technical and kindred" workers, the elite categories of the new work, in the late 1950s surpassed the number of "managers, officials, and proprietors," the elite categories of industrial work. The same pattern has its counterpart at a lower level on the occupational hierarchy. From 1910 to 1970, "operatives" (the semi-skilled workers who are the mainstays of mass production) were the single largest occupational category.

6. *Ibid.,* p. 133.
7. Bertram M. Gross, "America's Post-Industrial Revolution: A Selective Overview of a Transitional Society," unpublished mansucript (1967), p. 3–1.

However, by 1980 it is estimated that they will be *"third* in size ranking, outpaced by clerical, which will be the largest, and by professional and technical workers."[8]

Percentage Distribution of Selected Occupation Groups, 1900–1968,
Projected to 1980*
(Distribution by Percentages)

	1900	1910	1920	1930	1940	1950	1960	1968	1980
Professional and technical	4.3	4.7	5.4	6.8	7.5	8.6	10.8	13.6	16.3
Managers, officials, and proprietors	5.8	6.6	6.6	7.4	7.3	8.7	10.2	10.0	10.0
Clerical	3.0	5.3	8.0	8.9	9.6	12.3	14.5	16.9	18.2
Operatives	12.8	14.6	15.6	15.8	18.4	20.4	18.6	18.4	16.2

* Figures computed from *The U. S. Economy in 1980, op. cit.*

As we can see, between 1960 and 1980, at both the elite and lower levels, those in the older work ("managers, officials, and proprietors" and "operatives") were surpassed in numbers by those in the newer work ("professional and technical" and "clerical").

Overall figures mask as much as they reveal. For example, while men held 63 percent of all jobs in 1970, they held nearly 80 percent of all professional, technical, and managerial jobs. But just as most "new" jobs added to the work force between 1960 and 1970 were outside of the goods-producing sectors, so, nearly two-thirds of the new workers were women—65 percent of the 11.9 million jobs added to the work force were held by women.[9]

By 1972, 37 percent of the total labor was female, with 43 percent of all women of working age employed. The respective figures for 1960 were 32 and 37 percent, and for 1950, 28 and 33 percent.[10] Service work remained the heartland of female employment with

8. Bell, *op. cit.*, p. 136.
9. *Occupation by Industry,* Census Bureau Report PC-7C (1970).
10. *Economic Report of the President* (Washington, D. C.: U. S. Government Printing Office, 1973), Table 21.

some three-quarters of paid working women there.[11] Women made small gains in various goods-producing areas, 30.8 percent of the operatives in 1970 were women as compared with 27.3 in 1960, and their overwhelming role in some traditional female occupations slipped slightly, from 85.8 percent to 79.2 percent of the librarians, from 97.6 percent to 97.3 of the nurses, and from 72.6 percent to 69.3 of the elementary and secondary school teachers.[12]

While women held a disproportionate percentage of the lower-level jobs in the services, their percentage of higher-level jobs in the services was much greater than in the goods-producing sector, *viz.,* 40 percent of the professional and technical jobs compared with 19 percent of the managerial jobs.[13] Interestingly, this percentage has not changed substantially over the past twenty years, despite the increased percentage of women in the work force.

Women in the Work Force, Total and Professional,
Technical and Kindred, 1950–1970*

	1950	1960	1970
Total employed (in millions)	65.7	72.5	76.5
Percentage women	28%	32%	37%
Total professional, technical and			
kindred (in millions)	5.0	7.3	11.3
Percentage women	38%	36%	40%

* Adapted from Gross, *op. cit.,* Table 3–6, and updated, *Occupation by Industry, op. cit.*

In the big field of professional employment for women, the elementary and secondary schools, a disproportionately small percentage of them worked in the senior positions.

11. *Occupation by Industry, op. cit.*
12. Despite the slight decrease in percentage of these jobs held by women, the bulk of the growth in the number of librarians, nurses, and teachers, 1960 to 1970, was among women, 66 percent, 96 percent, and 63 percent respectively.
13. *Occupation by Industry, op. cit.*

**Employment in Elementary and Secondary Schools,
1970, by Sex***

	Total		Administrators	
Male	1,315,947	32%	124,074	63%
Female	2,874,010	68%	46,189	27%

* *1970 Census,* Table 8, "Detailed Occupation of Employed
Persons by Industry and Sex."

The figures are even more disproportionate in the health industry.

Employment in All Health Industries, 1970, by Sex*

	Total		Physicians	
Male	1,080,518	29%	255,105	91%
Female	3,165,669	71%	25,824	9%

* *Ibid.*

While white women made up fewer than half of the white "professional, technical and kindred" job holders, black women, who in 1970 made up 42 percent of the total black employment, made up 55 percent of the black "professional, technical and kindred" job holders.

**Non-White Employment, Total and Professional,
Technical and Kindred, 1950–1970***

	1950	1960	1970
Total nonwhite employment (in thousands)	5,600	6,629	10,297
Percent female	34%	39%	42%
Total nonwhite professional, technical and			
kindred (in thousands)	192	352	839
Percent female	56%	56%	55%

* Adapted from Gross, *op. cit.,* Table 4–6, and updated.

While these figures suggest the high place of black women as a part of the black employed population, we must note that blacks as a whole comprised only 7 percent of the total professional and technical group, up from 4 percent in 1960.[14]

What these data do suggest is both an overall shift from goods-producing to services-producing work, from blue-collar to white-collar occupations, from nonprofessional to professional categories (note that by 1960, professional, technical, and managerial occupational groups comprised half of the white-collar workers), as well as the special role of women in service-producing work, along with the key significance among blacks of those in professional, technical and kindred jobs.

Robert Heilbroner, in a perceptive and skeptical assessment of the claims that the United States has entered a new "stage" of our historical development,[15] offers data that both support and raise doubts as to the notion of a "post-industrial" society.

Percentage Distribution of Employed Workers*

	Agriculture	Industry	Services
U. S.: 1900	38	38	24
1970	4	35	61
France: 1950	35	45	20
1970	17	39	44
West Germany: 1950	24	48	28
1968	10	48	42

* *Ibid.,* p. 164.

While services employment has grown markedly in all three countries, Heilbroner makes the point that the growth has not so much been at the expense of the industrial sector but the shift has been from agriculture to services. Balancing this relative constancy of the

14. Bell, *op. cit.,* p. 145.
15. Robert L. Heilbroner, "Economic Problems of a 'Postindustrial' Society," *Dissent,* XX, 2 (Spring 1973), pp. 163–176.

percentage of those employed in industry, which is as far as Heil-broner takes the point, have been shifts both within that sector and within the services sector. We have already noted the increased "professionalization" of the industrial sector, pointing out the re-duced place of "operatives" (to be surpassed by 1980 by both "cleri-cals" and "professional and technical" workers in percentage of work force), and the growing white-collar composition of those employed in manufacturing (31 percent in 1970). Thus, the relative constancy of the percentage of the work force employed in industry, the point Heilbroner accurately makes, nonetheless masks shifts in the internal composition of that group.[16] Within the services sector, too, there have been shifts. This development can be seen in the following table of Bell's.

Distribution of Employment within the Services-Producing Sector, 1870–1971, Distribution by Percentages*

	1870	1900	1920	1940	1947	1971
Transportation and utilities	20	23	27	17	16	9
Trade, finance, real estate, insurance	28	30	31	36	42	39
Personal services	48	42	36	40	20	25
Government	4	5	6	7	22	26
Federal					7	6
State and local					15	20

* Daniel Bell, "Labor in the Post-Industrial Society," *Dissent,* XIX, 1 (Winter 1972), p. 166, and Bell, *op. cit.,* Table 2–3.

Heilbroner, too, emphasizes the variety of activities within the services sector.

16. Another aspect of the internal shift within the goods sector is

[A] decline of about 3,000,000 jobs in agriculture and mining [between 1948 and 1965 which] was counterbalanced by about 3 million new jobs in manu-facturing and construction. These [aggregate] data also obscure the fact that some regions of the country have only recently or partly entered the industrial revolution, correspondingly, in these areas the transition to services has been delayed.

Gross, *op. cit.,* p. 7–2.

[It] includes the most highly bureaucratized element of American life—the federal government—and the least bureaucratized—the individual proprietor or professional in the service trades or professions; very highly skilled tasks (surgeons) and very low skilled (filing clerks); the very highly paid (entertainers) and the very poorly paid (servants).[17]

Within the services area, it is government and nonprofit employment that has expanded the most. Between 1929 and 1960 nonprofit and government employment more than tripled, while total employment and services-producing employment each less than doubled.[18]

Furthermore, it is at the state and local levels, the place human services are actually delivered, where the greatest increases in employment have occurred.

Employment on Payrolls of Nonagricultural Establishments, 1947–1972*
(By Percent)

	Services	Total Civilian Government	Federal	State and local
1947	11%	12%	4%	8%
1967	15	17	4	13
1972	16	18	3	15

* *Manpower Report of the President* (Washington, D. C.: U. S. Department of Labor, 1973), Table C-1.

Between 1947 and 1972, the industrial division that showed the greatest growth in employment was the governmental, and, within that sector, state and local government. In 1947, government employment amounted to some 35 percent of manufacturing employment; by 1972, it was 70 percent.[19]

17. Heilbroner, *op. cit.*, p. 170.
18. Bell, *The Coming*, p. 147.
19. *Ibid.*

6 The Unique Educational Crisis

Whatever else its effects may be the exposure to prolonged education seems to encourage an expectation of careers in white collar, as opposed to blue collar, tasks; and this may indeed militate against the willingness of the "educated" population to consider many manual tasks as appropriate ways of making a livelihood, regardless of the relative incomes to be had from goods-handling, rather than paper-handling, work. Needless to say, this change in expectations accords very well with the actual displacement of labor from agricultural tasks and from the unskilled categories of industrial work, and its increasing deployment in service occupations.

In sum, there is little doubt that statistical examination of growth patterns among industrialized nations shows a steadily increasing importance of "knowledge related" inputs, and a corresponding decline in increases in brute "labor power" or sheer quantities of unchanged capital (for example, the addition of more railroad tracks).

—Robert Heilbroner, "Economic Problems of a 'Post-Industrial' Society"

What is the unique or special crisis in education today and how does it relate to the particular character of our service society? That schools fail large numbers of children both literally and figuratively is, of course, not new. Colin Greer in *The Great School Legend* documents that this has been characteristic of our society since the inception of public education.[1] In the early part of the twentieth century the older immigrants of the day, including Jews and Italians, Irish and Swedes, were at various times labeled "uneducable and incorrigible"[2] by the schools, just as the newer urban immigrants of our day, the blacks, are so labeled. Today's immigrants, of course, are only immigrating from one part of the United States to another, from the rural sectors to the urban. But the same difficulties persist and there is some evidence that these problems are actually transnational; for example, the Cultural Revolution in China was directed most sharply at overcoming the tendency of the schools to serve the poor badly.

Since all of this is, of course, not new, why this special concern? Didn't those old immigrants, after all, "make it" in the society with or without education? The problem is that it is much more difficult now to "make it" in the service society without an education or, at least, an educational credential. A major finding of the Jencks study[3] that is frequently overlooked has important bearing here. Jencks found that at each educational level, the credential was decisive in terms of future income; that is, whether or not an individual graduated from high school made a great difference in comparison with those individuals who did not graduate from high school, and similarly whether an individual graduated from college. Clearly, the credential was very important in relation to future income.

All of the old routes to economic success, the routes that existed throughout the earlier part of the twentieth century, are more or less closed now. Then, if you failed in the schools, you had some oppor-

1. Colin Greer, *The Great School Legend* (New York: Basic Books, 1972).
2. For example, in 1912, Henry Goddard, one of the major innovators in IQ testing, studied immigrants arriving at Ellis Island and found, based upon the tests, that 83 percent of Jews, 90 percent of Hungarians, 79 percent of Italians, and 87 percent of Russians were "feeble minded." Henry H. Goddard, "The Benet Tests in Relation to Immigrants," *Journal of Psychoasthenics,* XVIII (1913), p. 107. For further discussion of the past and present pernicious use of IQ tests, see the authors' "The Lingering Infatuation with IQ," *Change* (1974).
3. Christopher Jencks, *et al., Inequality: A Reassessment of the Effects of Family and Schooling in America* (New York: Basic Books, 1973).

tunity to get ahead via business and the general rapid expansion of the private sector. The chances of rising economically today through those old routes are greatly reduced. The jobs are now in the services, in government, in education, in research, in health, in the professions, in the offices, not the factories and small businesses. In all these areas, education or at least an educational credential is required, sometimes inappropriately—that is, there is too much education required to do the job or more than is needed. Nevertheless, more and more education is required to enter and advance in the expanding occupations of the society. Thus, it is not so possible to fail in the schools and still acquire mobility into those occupations and professions. The school is asked to do a bigger job than ever before and its failure to do that job is far more visible, leading to an educational crisis that is considerably beyond that experienced in the early years of the twentieth century when the schools were no more successful than they are today with the deprived.

The schools have always been relatively successful with their middle-class clientele; again, this is not unique to the present period nor to our own society. Teachers tend to teach upward or at least to prefer students who are like themselves with a school culture and a home culture that match. This is often formulated as the home reinforcing the school, but there is no reason why it could not be formulated in exactly the reverse fashion. That is, children from middle-class homes do well in school because the school reinforces the home and all the expectations that exist in the home.

Historically, what Greer suggests is that the earlier immigrants who "made it" economically in life had children who were indeed relatively successful in the schools. Here the school in essence rubber-stamped or credentialed what had occurred economically and culturally in the family, and this is as true today among middle-class blacks and minorities as it was in previous years for Jews, Italians, and the like.

It should be noted, of course, that there are other reasons in the service society for the special importance of the school. Since a larger and larger number of people are kept off the labor market for a greater period of time, what better place to spend this time than in education, which is increasingly extended. Moreover, education may enable individuals to use more fruitfully this greatly increased amount of leisure time built on the basis of a highly productive economy. Then, of course, there are all kinds of emergent factors that arise as the educational establishment itself, the professional associations, and the civil services structure develop vested interests in the maintenance of high educational requirements, even in the absence of evidence that such requirements are necessary to do the job of work.[4] The other side of this dimension is reflected in the statistics that indicate a vast increase in the population completing high school (e.g., while 6 percent of the population aged seventeen were high school graduates in 1900, nearly 80 percent had completed high school in 1970). Equally dramatic, whereas those enrolled in college in 1900 constituted only 4 percent of the population aged eighteen through twenty-one, today well over half of this group is in college.[5] Without an education, one is clearly at a disadvantage as the norm moves higher and higher.

THE ROLE OF CREDENTIALS

In recent years, there has developed a powerful critique of credentialism, that is, the requirement of academic credentials in order to obtain various positions. The argument has been put forward cogently by S. M. Miller and Ivar Berg that large numbers of positions in this society demand academic qualifications that have little to do with the job itself and in some cases may even lead to dissatisfaction in overqualified (that is, overeducated) workers. The case is made that training to do the job can be more satisfactorily provided in relation to the job specifications and should not be entangled with

4. Ivar Berg's *Education and Jobs: The Great Training Robbery* (New York: Praeger, 1970) is the best of several recent studies documenting the lack of correlation between education and job performance. Indeed, Berg cites numerous instances where the correlation is negative; that is, those with greater education perform the work less well.
5. Heilbroner, *loc. cit.*

academic qualifications. It has also been noted that highly skilled positions, for example, FAA controllers, do not even require a college degree.

The argument resonates very sharply with large numbers of poor people, blacks, and other minorities who, on the one hand, have been excluded from various positions because they lack credentials and, on the other, have been victimized by highly credentialized teachers and other human service workers who do not seem to be effective. It would appear that professional teachers, social workers, and the like have been overeducated and undertrained.

Another support for the critique of credentialism comes from state and federal agencies and their personnel departments. Reflecting the middle-class taxpayers' bias, they are more concerned with questions of economy and efficiency and feel that they are frequently paying for academic credentials which are, at best, only indirectly related to the job. As a result of various productivity and manpower studies, these agencies are restructuring tasks previously done by professionals so that many portions of them can be done by trained technicians. (This is, incidentally, leading to an incipient battle between these governmental agencies and the associations and unions representing their employees.) In a series of decisions following upon *Griggs* v. *Duke* (1971) various courts have ruled against the use of aptitude and "intelligence" tests, as well as formal education prerequisites when these cannot be shown to be directly related to job performance requirements.[6] The further argument against the continued existence of credentialism comes from some of the futurologists or social forecasters who predict that future work will be much more automated and will require less higher education.

In light of these various thrusts, one might anticipate that the age

6. The "New Human Services Newsletter," published by the New Human Services Institute, Queens College, City University of New York, has had regular reports upon these court-based challenges to credential requirements. It should be noted, however, that the challenges have not been restricted to the human services work areas; indeed, the *Duke* case involved an electrical power company.

of credentialism is dying in the service society—but we think this is unlikely to be the case. That, on the contrary, education and credentials will be more sought after than ever by an expanding proportion of people and, moreover, that the education establishment will attempt to make the credential more appropriate to job functioning, by moving toward various types of performance-based accountability. The credential instead of being debunked and deprecated will come more to reflect actual qualifications and skills.

There are a number of reasons why we believe this trend is likely to occur, but apart from the logic of the argument, there is already evidence that the various professional fields and higher education institutions are moving toward performance criteria. For example, in New York State, the Board of Higher Education is requiring that all teacher training institutions establish performance standards by 1974 for the training of their teachers. This trend is true throughout the various states, with more than half of them now involved to some extent in performance requirements for teachers. Washington, Minnesota, Texas, and Florida have been leaders in this effort. Moreover, the rapidly proliferating community colleges are much concerned with providing students with technical qualifications along with the new credential, the AA degree. Trade unions, particularly in the public service field, are developing their own colleges and/or their own career-oriented programs as upgrading for their members to acquire both skills and the credentials.[7] The "new careers" programs

7. District Council 37, American Federation of State, County and Municipal Employees, the largest district of the fastest-growing major union, has established a DC 37 "campus" of the College of New Rochelle. DC 37 and the United Federation of Teachers, the American Federation of Teachers' largest local, have incorporated in their collective bargaining agreements for paraprofessionals with the Board of Education of the City of New York a "career ladder" program with release time from the job for college attendance. More than 8,000 paraprofessionals are enrolled at the City University of New York in such a program. And the American Public Health Association, through its New Professional Section, has developed a college program for "new professional" family planning workers in collaboration with the Union for Experimenting Colleges and Universities, as part of its "University Without Walls" program.

provide new routes for a previously excluded clientele to acquire professional and semiprofessional positions via a work-study route.[8] The rapid escalation of various external degree programs[9] and all types of cooperative education programs provide a further illustration of the attempt to unite an academic credential and work-relevant training and experience. (The advent of open enrollment should be seen in this context.)

The minorities and the poor have demanded access to the credential, a credential which they want to be relevant but even if it is not entirely so, they desire it as a way into the system. They do not simply want adequate work and training to perform various professional and service jobs. They want the credential in addition to the training; they want the respect and status that it brings. It is, to use S. M. Miller's phrase, a form of "new income," not a substitute for cash income but a new desired addition. They do not want to be excluded, they do not want to be told that now that they are in the ball game, the credential is worthless, something that only a few "highfalutin" academics would want.

But there are other reasons, perhaps even more powerful ones, for the continuing of the academic credential, perhaps with some important modifications. For one thing, in the service society there is going to be a lot of leisure time, time in which to use education and time in which to get it. The productivity of the economy allows for large numbers of people to be off the labor market for great portions of their lives and thereby to be in various educational and training

8. In the mental health field, over 150 two-year college programs for mental health technicians have been developed in the past several years. Some 7,000 persons have already graduated from these programs, with an additional 10,000 graduates expected in the next three years. Perhaps the best of the "new careers" programs is the U. S. Office of Education–sponsored Career Opportunities Program (COP). Here some 8,000 low-income, largely minority group, mainly female paraprofessionals employed by public schools are enabled to obtain a baccalaureate degree and teacher's license.

9. Statewide external degree programs have been established in several states; thirty "University Without Walls" programs have been established by the member institutions of the Union for Experimenting Colleges and Universities, whose Union Graduate School, an external degree doctoral program, has received some 10,000 inquiries with only 300 slots.

programs. Of course, one could argue, and many do, that expanded education in the service society will be broad and liberal rather than professional and job-related. But while this abstract distinction is very nice, it doesn't entirely ring true in the world of reality where there has been a credential tradition that was mandatory for acquiring higher-level service and research positions. Not only is the tradition relevant, but powerful institutions, including the institutions of higher education themselves, as well as the various professional establishments, have vested interests in maintaining the connection between education and job mobility. Although the meritocracy may indeed lack merit, accountability, and relevance, it would seem to us more likely that it will correct itself, to some extent, to add increased merit and job effectiveness, along with the status-bringing features, to the existing credential rather than discarding that credential.

In essence, then, we are assuming that, for a great variety of reasons, not only will higher education remain crucial but that more specifically it will modify itself to include performance standards so that a person who is educated may also be trained and skilled, not only in indirect, nonspecific ways, but increasingly in a more specific, job-relevant fashion. In the abstract, one could imagine a society in which there are a large number of highly trained technical workers without higher education and a large number of people with a higher education that was broad and liberal but not job-relevant. We believe, however, that this separation is unlikely to occur in light of the traditions and institutional fabric, as well as consumer demand, that actually exist. We predict, instead, that the critique of credentialism will lead to the following:

1. The expansion of new routes combining various degrees of work experience and education for the receiving of higher-level professional positions;

2. The inclusion in higher education of much more job-relevant skills and work-oriented education;

3. The expansion of all types of recurrent and continuing education for use in life in general, in leisure, in relation to social change

(note the importance of the sixties where higher education institutions were the base of significant demands for social change). Much of education will be for general use, status, consumption, and leisure, but will not be completely disconnected from job mobility.

In essence, we are arguing that credentials rather than being discarded will be expanded to improve qualifications, performance-relevant skills, and what historically has been called training, as well as being an aspect of desired status.

We could conjecture that as more and more people in the society acquire more education, they will increase the demand for the creation of jobs that require education, e.g., for various types of public service and human service positions. We suspect that "Say's Law" will operate—that the demand will create the supply, that the "need" for these jobs will lead the government to produce more of them, particularly in light of an ecological and energy crisis which could be alleviated by having a greater number of service positions and fewer manufacturing positions that eat up the earth and its resources.[10]

THE AUTOMATION ARGUMENT

The automation argument is more complicated because it is true that large numbers of jobs, while they require far less hard physical labor than in past history, will not require as a counterpart a great deal of intellectual understanding or knowledge. The new jobs will be largely tending machines and supervision. But a major concomitant of the automated world will be, and is, far more leisure time or time outside the work force, and the question is what is to be done with that time. Recent history makes it quite clear that much of that time will probably be filled with schooling, not only in the early years, but with continuing education throughout life for the union worker, as

10. See Arthur Pearl, "The Human Service Society—An Ecological Perspective," in Alan Gartner, *et al.,* eds., *Public Service Employment* (New York: Praeger, 1971); also, Emile Benoit, "What Society for Spaceship Earth?," *Social Policy,* IV, 2 (September–October 1973).

well as the second-career executive. But perhaps even more important, the advanced positions in the automated service-oriented world seem to require (either in actuality or as a result of tradition) more and more education. Again, while the anticredentialist attack has made clear that some of these requirements are indeed inappropriate, we would speculate this will not lead to their removal but rather to the remedying of the educational credential to make it more functional to the requirements of the job.

It is this context which helps us to understand the tremendous significance of the educational crisis, because without education huge portions of the population seem doomed in both their work and their leisure lives in a service society. And, indeed, it is these excluded groups, the have-nots if you will, who have led the drive for the revamping and restructuring of education from preschool to graduate school with demands for open enrollment, teacher accountability, relevant work-study programs, new routes to mobility, community control, and so on.

In essence, then, the school is in crisis for two reasons: larger proportions of the population will need and want higher education, while simultaneously, the school system as presently organized (and teachers as presently trained) is not equipped to educate effectively youngsters whose parents are not already in the middle class.

A TWO-PRONGED ATTACK

There are two approaches to this crisis, some beginnings of which are already in existence although not necessarily conceptualized in this fashion. One approach is directly school-centered and endeavors to provide intensive compensatory education, including preschool approaches for the children who have not typically responded well to the middle-class-organized school system. For the most part, the strategy has had only limited effect, largely because of an emphasis which accents weaknesses and deficits of the youngsters rather than strengths.

The second prong of the strategy is directed at changing the parents, but in some surprising ways, some of which are work-related and some community-based. In the work area, it is significant that there is an increasing tendency to provide new routes for jobs and careers for the adult disadvantaged who have been excluded from the educational system. Thus, a paraprofessional can acquire a job first as a teacher aide, and use some of this experience and in-service training toward acquiring a college credential and a professional position. This strategy has two functions: one, it allows access to the system in newly created jobs (and it is extremely important that such jobs be created) without requiring the traditional school path to those positions. Thus, one could fail in the schools and still acquire a semiprofessional or professional position. Two, and perhaps more important, in relation to the point we are making, these adults who are now involved in school themselves provide very different models for their children who may have been experiencing difficulty in school. Various studies of paraprofessional programs indicate that the paraprofessionals' school know-how increases and, thus, they are better able to help their children make their way through the system. Also, the aspirations of other community members are raised as they see their neighbors doing varied work, going to and completing college. And the aspirations of the paraprofessionals themselves are increased as they progress through the program; persons who felt they could not complete college, having done so, aspire to go even further.[11] They, in a sense, become more like the traditional parent who has "made it" and values education. In addition to the paraprofessionals, of course, there are increasing numbers of people in the society among the disadvantaged who are acquiring higher education via recurrent or continuing education, external degrees, open enrollment, and so on. Apart from the potential value to the individuals themselves, there is the significance of their becoming a new kind of model for their children and thereby affecting the learning of the children even in the traditional school system (without significant modification).

11. See Alan Gartner, *Paraprofessionals and Their Performance* (New York: Praeger, 1971).

But there is another very different pathway for disadvantaged parents to at least indirectly affect their children's school performance. This is through participatory community involvement in relation to the schools, on school boards, for example. Community involvement is directed at transforming the schools and making them more educationally appropriate for the disadvantaged youngsters by changing the curriculum, the personnel, the procedures. This is their direct and manifest intention. But they have another indirect effect which should be noted in connection with the strategy we are outlining. They, in a sense, provide a new parental model, a model that says to the child that school and learning are important, that we, the parents, are tremendously involved in it, and that you are very capable of learning. This, then, in many ways, becomes quite like the middle-class counterpart in other communities where the parents are constantly concerned with school matters.

The importance of changed career patterns for adults and community involvement, of course, have powerful value in their own terms. We are simply noting a latent function that potentially has important learning benefits for the disadvantaged child functioning even in a traditional school culture.

By itself, this strategy probably will not be sufficient to overcome the school crisis we have described—although it should be noted that if there were many millions of paraprofessional positions open to the families of the poor and if community participation included a larger and larger percentage of the poor, the effect on the learning of the children might be magnified significantly even with only minimal change in the organization and functioning of the schools. Of course, this last is highly unlikely because the involvement and the changed work-study structure that we have described affect the schools, in some cases quite directly, as paraprofessional teacher aides come into the schools, and in other cases, more indirectly, as parents functioning on community boards begin to affect school practice and personnel.

We turn now to the second prong in the strategy, that is, how to affect school practice, organization, culture, and personnel, to attune it more sensitively to children who have been excluded from the school environment, treated as second-class citizens within it, expected to fail, and the like. As we have indicated, earlier, most efforts in this direction have been directed by theories that principally and explicitly stress the deficits and weaknesses of the children and propose to correct these by various compensatory approaches—preschool, Head Start programs, special reading classes, and the like. Without always directly stating as much, these approaches were guided by the implicit assumption that the schools were all right as they were and it was the children who needed to be remedied and changed. To some extent, this is surprising in light of the tremendous criticism of the schools from many groups.

The sixties demonstrated very conclusively the failure of most of these compensatory measures, at least in terms of affecting significant cognitive improvement, no matter how measured. But currently, this compensatory approach has been revamped in what might be termed an *intensive* compensatory approach; that is, a more highly organized one, zeroing in on specific reading defects and the like. There seems to be some evidence that this more intensive approach may be more beneficial than the broad-gauged compensatory approaches of the sixties. But the emphasis still is on deficits, and the message to the child is clearly that he or she is deficient and inadequate and must correct him(her)self to be more like the middle-class child to please the teacher. What is needed much more are approaches based upon the strengths of the children. Thus, for example, in Youth Tutoring Youth programs, where disadvantaged youngsters in high school who are doing poorly themselves tutor youngsters in the elementary school who are also doing poorly, the message is clearly that the high school youngsters have something to give, something to teach; their strengths are used; they are put in a helper, giving role. (See Chapter 8 for a fuller discussion.) It is no wonder, then, that in this context their learning improves dramatically and rapidly in a wide variety of areas, not only on achievement tests, not only in the reading that they are giving as part of the tutoring, but in their total educational function in the classroom, outside of it, in the number of books they read, and in their self-concept. It is this type of approach built on the strengths of the child that may be much more strategic for obtaining leaps in their learning.[12] (In this context, intensive compensatory reading approaches can be beneficial, that is, as long as the child can feel, "I know that I'm good at something, and, so, it is easier for me to accept some improvement in my weak areas.")

CONCLUSION

Higher education is crucial for functioning in a service society, where unskilled jobs as well as entrepreneurial-based mobility are declining and leisure (nonwork) time is widening. In this context, the deficiencies of the schools and colleges for educating students who do not come from a middle-class background are critical. These youngsters will need a credential—one based on real knowledge and training in order to enter the growth sectors of the society within the human services, government employment, or research.

We have outlined the beginnings of a two-pronged approach directed toward a major educational change for groups who are now educationally deprived.

12. A number of other "positive" approaches have been developed in the last decade but unfortunately have not been applied on the large scale necessary to produce major cognitive improvements in disadvantaged children; e.g., schools without walls, action learning, the contact curriculum, the street academy, and various types of alternative programs.

7   The Professional–Consumer Dialectic

We seem to be caught in a contradiction: there is something in the medical system that we want, that we cannot live without, but is there any way to get it on our own terms? When we make demands of the medical system, or of a particular health institution, just what is it that we want? Do we want just "more services"—when every one of them is loaded with a message of oppression? When these services may have little to do with our real needs, and may in fact discount our real needs or substitute medically manufactured needs?

Clearly, our demands must go beyond the merely quantitative. We want more than "more"; we want a new style, and we want a new substance of medical practice as it relates to women. And yet we must never get so hung up on the ideological niceties that we forget that "more" alone is still crucial—an issue of survival—for millions of women who still lack the most routine care and preventive services, and who cannot function fully as women until they have them.

> —Barbara Ehrenreich and Deirdre English,
> *Complaints and Disorders:*
> *The Sexual Politics of Sickness*

MAKING THE HUMAN SERVICES PRODUCTIVE: WHY IS IT IMPORTANT?

It is difficult to conceive of a service society advancing very far without a significant qualitative improvement in the character of the human services. These services, after all, are the central hub around which the service-society ethos revolves. Thus far in the emergence of the service sector, a sector that is emerging not incidentally within the framework of traditional industrial capitalism, there has been a marked increase in consciousness about the services, particularly about their inadequacies, but there has been as yet no qualitative leap in the development of the services. As a matter of fact, writers such as Illich[1] argue that the institutionalization which has characterized our society has been the main factor in retarding the creativity and development of the services, particularly in education, but also in health.

The advance in consciousness about the services may be an important and necessary condition for major changes in the human services, but clearly it is not sufficient in and of itself. Two major contradictions beset the human services and frame all their specific dimensions. The first contradiction is that between the intrinsic thrust of the services toward providing benefits for people, improving their welfare and the like, in the context of a highly individualistic, competitive, capitalist societal framework in which the services are used for all kinds of other purposes—shoring up the economy, controlling people's revolts, providing status to a professional stratum, and so on. The second contradiction, which often interweaves with the first, relates to the tremendous expansion in scope and scale of the services, an expansion which brings these highly interpersonal human-oriented activities and processes into conflict with the large-scale organization of these activities in big bureaucracies. Various bureaucratic dimensions, particularly the formalism, impersonality, and rigid rules, are particular anathema to activities that have humanistic ends and require relational interpersonal processes. Methods of organization that are suitable for the organization of production in factories, the army, and offices may be particularly unsuitable for the organization of human service practice, even when such practice has become mammoth in size.

1. Ivan Illich, *Deschooling Society* (New York: Harper & Row, 1971).

Clearly, the traditions, training, and historic experience of human service workers, which have largely been in small, relatively autonomous settings, have not prepared them for functioning in large bureaucratic contexts characterized by hierarchy and strict controls. The service workers resist in all manner of ways the industrialization of their occupations—an industrialization which attempts to organize their work along traditional lines; to measure it in these terms, as in the Gross National Product; and to improve or reorganize it by using managerial techniques and approaches that at best have relevance, even if serious limits, to nonservice occupational spheres that do not require close interpersonal sensitivity relating to human beings as the key end product. It is, of course, not surprising that as difficulties have appeared in the large-scale management of human services, there are countless attempts to impose industrial modes on the service sectors.[2] The attempt is to rationalize, "Taylorize," mechanize the services (make the human services as capital-intensive as possible by adding machinery, but not essentially to humanize them. Although it is interesting to note that the new participatory managerial concepts which are now being applied in some relatively limited areas of industry, with much fanfare, derive from psychologists who are much interested in the human factor.)

One thing is quite clear, however, and that is that we have not resolved the problem of how to organize the services on a large scale, maintaining their humaneness and increasing their efficiency. This dialectic problem is further magnified by the first contradiction, the fact that the bureaucratization is taking place in a capitalist context, characterized by much anarchy, chaos, confusion, and the manipulation of the services for various purposes that have nothing to do with serving humanity.

We shall argue in this context that we need to develop quite

2. Theodore Levitt, "Production-Line Approaches to Service," *Harvard Business Review,* L, 5 (September–October 1970). One of the more grotesque examples of this is the following comment by Dr. Phelps Trix, Vice-President, Detroit Institute of Technology: "Class size has to be tied to income and if we choose to louse it up by considering the influence of a teacher on a student, then we'll go bankrupt." *New York Times,* January 25, 1974.

different managerial perspectives that particularly emphasize the consumer-intensive character of the services and build organization and management around this theme rather than either abstract managerial principles or principles derived from the industrial sectors (see Chapter 10). Furthermore, we must develop a strategy for the human services that at least relates to the limits set by the societal contradictions in which the service society is emerging. That is to say, we cannot simply project a vision of how the services could be more efficient and serving and humanistic in the abstract, although some cross-cultural comparisons with services in different societies such as Israel, the Soviet Union, China, and Great Britain do provide interesting leads and contrasts. Rather, our orientation must be an attempt to develop service consciousness much further, to deepen the service consciousness so that people come to understand that while in the process of improving the services there is the need for major societal reorganization if the services are really to fulfill their potential. In sum, there is need to recognize that there are distinct limits on what can be achieved on a relatively small scale foreshadowing promises of the future, and raising consciousness as to what is needed in order to achieve this future.

In light of the growing environmental crises, it seems likely that increasing numbers of people will (have to) be employed in work that is not resource-depleting and polluting if we are to survive. Service work and perhaps human service work, in particular, fits this requirement. As the entire life style of people will (have to) change drastically, there will be a greater need for services that are less dependent on automobiles, airplanes, and machines.

People will be drawn to relating to other people more as a recreational form and the development of inner life, alternate states, and the like may replace the emphasis on external actions that destroy the outer environment.

This new direction provides a whole new agenda for services— both their production and consumption. It should lead to a tremendous broadening of the growth and development services—lifetime education, new forms of interpersonal recreation, new therapeutic forms, women's groups, men's groups, marriage encounters, sex therapy, new religious, mind-expanding forms, special services for the dying, the development of all kinds of groups, family planning services, day care centers, preventive health groups. The services of the future will go far beyond the traditional health, education, and welfare classification and should be far more consumer-involving.

Many constituencies are potentially involved in this potential service regeneration: college students are much interested in preparing for human service work; workers (and the population in general) who want continuing education; the large numbers who are involved in various growth and development activities—giving and receiving; the recognition of needs for greater child care, preventive health services being seen as rights with even greater recognition of new needs—such as those of the handicapped, the dying, the insomniacs, the aged.

The critical questions are: How good will these services be? How will consumers and servers relate? And, how will they be paid for?

This framework recognizes both the limitations imposed by the constraints of the society and the consequent need to develop in human service practice, training, management, and organization programs and strategies addressed to the larger political factors. We think such a framework provides a needed perspective for human service workers, consumers, and the constituents and vanguards of the service society. It is in this framework that we will attempt to make more specific diagnosis of particular human service problems in various sectors, particularly in education, and to propose some very specific strategies and approaches for both improving the services in these areas and changing the society. These issues will be the major concern of this and the following three chapters. Here we will be concerned with the character and quality of services at present, their inadequacies, and some reason why they fail. Then we will turn to consumer-professional relationships and look, for a different perspective, at the services in China, not as a model, but to see outside the particularities of the American scene how services can be organized.

(Indeed, whatever the existential accuracy of the picture of China outsiders can gain, its value to us as another view is served.)

In the following chapter, we will look to the central role of the consumer, and then turn to the training and organization of human service practice in order to maximize this consumer role.

THE INEFFECTIVENESS OF THE SERVICES

One can group the failures of the services, their ineffectiveness, and their inefficiency in four categories:

1. *Large numbers of people in need of services simply do not get them.* The catalogue of the unserved is almost as broad as the services themselves. There is the absence of care for infants which results in an infant mortality rate in the United States higher than that of seventeen countries and on a par with that of countries such as East Germany and Ireland.[3] There are the vast numbers suffering from chronic illnesses who are not treated (*viz.*, 23 millions suffering from hypertension,[4] the nearly 50 percent of diabetics who are "hidden,"[5] the nine million alcoholics[6]); and the nearly 50 percent of low-income women who are not reached by present family planning services.[7] To turn from the health field, there are seven million educationally handicapped children, fewer than half of whom are receiving appropriate special education services.[8]

3. *Demographic Yearbook, 1971* (New York: United Nations, 1972), Table 2.

4. *Heart Facts* (New York: American Heart Association, 1974).

5. U. S. Public Health Service, Bulletin No. 1168 (Washington, D. C.: U. S. Government Printing Office, 1968).

6. U. S. Department of Health, Education and Welfare, "First Special Report to the U. S. Congress on Alcohol and Health, from the Secretary of Health, Education and Welfare," (Washington, D. C.: U. S. Government Printing Office, 1971), p. viii.

7. Center for Family Planning Program Development, "Data and Analyses for 1973 Revision of DHEW Five-Year Plan for Planning Services," (New York: Planned Parenthood and World Population, 1973).

8. Edward W. Martin, "New Public Priority: Education of Handicapped Children," *Compact*, V, 4 (August 1971), p. 4.

2. *Many who receive services are not benefited by them.* The low reading (and low achievement) scores of growing numbers of school children, particularly among the minority groups and the poor, are not limited to them.[9] Dropouts and pushouts[10] are often a result of service system inadequacies. Recidivism among former prisoners is so high as to merit the label of "revolving door jails."[11] Those few addicts who are treated rarely are rehabilitated.[12]

3. *The services are poorly organized and designed.* We have, at best, a hospital-based medical care system, not a community-based health care system (with the hospital as a backup resource for the relatively rare instances where its use is warranted). The welfare system makes dependent those who could be independent (fails to provide jobs for those who need them). Efforts which would serve people better are shunned because they do not fit the professional bureaucratic model, *viz.,* self-help efforts. Practices shown to be effective on a small-scale demonstration are not expanded to a wider audience, or, when they are, they are so vulgarized and watered down, they no longer serve well. The services are generally characterized by vast waste and inefficiencies, with professional ripoffs not the least of the causes.

4. *Much of the practice is inadequate.* In all of the services, as, of course, in the society as a whole, racism and sexism are dominant factors both in terms of how consumers are treated and in the roles servers play. So, too, the services are overprofessionalized, self-serving, elite, jargon-filled, and, at best, peer accountable. The practice often ignores, when not acting counter to, the culture of the

9. U. S. Department of Health, Education and Welfare, *Digest of Educational Statistics* (Washington, D. C.: U. S. Government Printing Office, 1972), Tables 178, 182.

10. Bureau of the Census, *Current Population Reports,* Series P. 23, #42 (Washington, D. C.: U. S. Government Printing Office, 1972).

11. National Council on Crime and Delinquency, "Two-Year Follow-Up," *Uniform Parole Reports,* No. 2 (February 1973); Federal Bureau of Investigation, *Crime in the United States, 1972, Uniform Crime Reports* (Washington, D. C.: U. S. Government Printing Office, 1973).

12. Few longitudinal studies report rehabilitation rates for hard drug users above 10 percent. See Drug Abuse Survey Project, *Dealing with Drug Abuse* (New York: Praeger, 1972).

consumers. Where good practices are known, as in the relative effectiveness of various family planning techniques, nonetheless services are offered on a "cafeteria" basis with little if any positive direction given to consumers. (Of course, the absence of serious attempts to find male-affecting contraceptive techniques is another reflection of the male domination of the practice.) And the Freudian psychiatric model deprecates women, although all psychotherapy does not necessarily do so.[13]

Recognizing that the human services are ineffective in many ways leads naturally to the question of how to change and improve them, particularly in light of a societal framework, which, as we have indicated, constrains against the fullest development of these services for the benefit of people. That is, the fact that the services are used for so many purposes besides the benefit of the recipient frequently produces effects that actually interfere with their potentially humane, people-benefiting qualities. To the extent that services are used to socialize people to the status quo, to quell dissent, to divert people with passive recreational activities, to enhance the service givers' status and power, to maintain class, race, and sex differentials, to provide a source for the investment of surplus, or countless other purposes—to that extent the presumed people-benefiting quality is, to say the least, hampered.

In attempting to develop a strategy for service reform in our society, we should consider carefully the basic context in which the services function because this context sets certain limits, limits which will ultimately have to be overcome if the services are to flourish and a genuine human service society emerge. Our strategy should then include a double agenda, so to speak: on the one hand, efforts directed at both the increase in quantity and quality of the services performed; and on the other hand, strategy and tactics directed against the misuse of services for other than people-serving functions.

In developing a strategy it is also useful to develop some sort of timetable, otherwise any improvement or advance in the services may

13. Jean Baker Miller, *Women and Psychoanalysis* (New York: Penguin, 1973).

be measured against some ultimate objective, and cynicism and defeatism will set in. It is also helpful to develop a diagnosis of the problem of service deficiency in both molecular and molar terms; that is, at the molar level in terms of the larger system and what it imposes on the services, and at the atomistic level, a more specific operational analysis. We have to know in exactly what ways they are deficient, and this, of course, requires an evaluation model and a setting of specific criteria.

Professional work in the human services is designed, presumably, to serve the needs of the "consumer," that is, the student, patient, or client. "Serving the needs" would seem to have at least two characteristics. First, the manifest function of the service must be met. That is, students should learn, patients become well, clients whole. Second, in carrying out the manifest function, there should not be unnecessary "costs" (or what the economists call "externalities") to the consumer. For example, in learning the particular subject matter, the student should not be "turned off" from learning, or the patient, in being "cured," should not be made overly dependent or infantalized.

WHY DO THE SERVICES FAIL?

Apart from the larger societal context to which we have referred, there are a number of specific reasons that are offered to explain the failure of the services:

—*We do not know enough,* e.g., we do not know how to cure neuroses;

—*Our training is inadequate;* even in areas where we do know something, we do not train people well with regard to what we do know, e.g., group management principles for teachers;

—*The class and race gap between server and recipient,* e.g., most teachers are white and middle-class, and large numbers of children who are poorly served are from poor and minority groups;

—*The professional-consumer gap:* the fact that professionals have too much power, are elite, removed, defensive, and that their practice is often mystified, difficult to comprehend (the derivative side of this is the failure to involve the consumer and as we have indicated earlier the consumer is a powerful element in the advancement of the productivity of the service);

—*The service fails because it succeeds,* e.g., intelligence tests that are used to perform sorting roles succeed in doing just that, but fail in the development of children's learning;

—*The cross-pressures that operate,* for example, where the goals of communities may be very different from those of teachers although both presumably are concerned with the learning of children;

—There is considerable anarchy with regard to the organization of services; and management principles, particularly for large-scale service enterprises such as school systems, are highly inadequate;

—There is *a scarcity of resources*—if we had one teacher for every ten children, learning might be greatly improved and, of course, a similar argument could be made in the health and mental health fields;

—Finally, there is a derivative or emergent cynicism concerning the role and value of the services which is characteristic of large numbers of service givers and recipients. This works further to exacerbate difficulties.

In addition, there are the special difficulties that arise from the efforts to change the services, and the multiple goals that are involved. For example, while the expansion of community and consumer participation is crucial to the ultimate improvement of the services and to the advancement of an authentic service society, in the short run increased community involvement may not necessarily improve the reading of children. Part of the reason for this is that when the major objective is expanded political control, energies and resources are not targeted in on the specific service whether it be reading improvement, or whatever. Then, also, there are the derivative political battles which surround the entire issue and at least in the first transitional phase may divert energy away from the more narrow specific service improvement. We believe that this phenomenon was characteristic of much of the service efforts of the sixties in the community mental health field, as in Lincoln Hospital, and in education, as in Ocean Hill/Brownsville. Of course, these efforts were nonetheless very important first steps in shifting the balance of power from professionals to consumers.

This phase in the battle for the services set the stage for increased consumer involvement in the actual delivery of the services, which should in the long run lead to highly specific increases in productivity. In the short run, however, the conflict and friction that ensue during the battle make unlikely any immediate improvement on the more narrow specific indicators of service efficiency. It is important to recognize, however, that this is probably a transitional stage and there is increasing evidence in the current period that community boards are very much concerned not only with a shift in power, but the very specific improvement of the service, whether it be the learning of children or the health of the community. It is important to try to move as quickly as possible through this frictional, conflict-laden zone, to concrete advances in service functioning. But simultaneously it is also necessary to expand the battle for the services beyond the local community to the national agenda.

For all the causes of service failure listed above there are correlative proposals for courses of action. If there is a scarcity of services, there is a call to expand the service and have, for example, a lower pupil-teacher ratio or to hire more teacher aides. To reduce the race and class gap, drawing more teachers and paraprofessionals from low-income and minority groups is recommended, and if the paraprofessionals become professional teachers, this further adds to the picture. To meet the many managerial problems, a whole series of management proposals have been offered, including systems analysis, job task analysis, role reorganization, and accountability measures. A number of new training designs and proposals have been directed toward improving the training of teachers and principals, including the utilization of more careful task analysis, performance-based teacher education, simultational and role-playing designs, and closer combination of practice and theory. Efforts to increase consumer involvement range from the use of vouchers, to children teaching children, to community boards, to the hiring of community residents. Attempts to reduce the professional-consumer gap range from efforts to increase accountability, such as Competency-Based Teacher Certification, to community board control. There are widespread efforts to uncover and identify the various purposes of the services other than the explicit people-benefiting ones, such as the critique of IQ and similar tests that serve sorting functions of educational institutions. The development of alternative institutions serves as an important critic and monitor of the existing systems, and some of the developments taking place in the alternative areas do become absorbed sometimes with benefit into the mainstream systems. New funding approaches such as the voucher system in education are examples of attempts to increase consumer involvement and improve administrative efficiency. New roles have been established, such as ombudsman, expediter, troubleshooter, consumer advocate, to further cut through the difficulties imposed by large-scale systems. And George Berkley[14] suggests that an administrative revolution is taking place in which organizations are organized not on the basis of purpose or process, as has been the traditional way, but on the basis of the clientele to be served. He notes that the Children's Bureau was an important precursor of this development, where the orientation was not to fulfill certain set purposes, or to discharge certain types of functions, but rather to serve a particular group of clients, and to service them in all kinds of ways—it did not simply educate or secure housing for, or arrange medical treatment for, children; instead it cared for the whole child. Staff differentiation has also been proposed as a much more efficient way to utilize personnel and thereby to advance service efficiency. Attempts also have been made to identify key agents, such as the principal of the public school, who are thought to be instrumental in producing a basic change in atmosphere and service functioning in

14. George E. Berkley, *The Administrative Revolution* (Englewood Cliffs, N.J.: Prentice-Hall, 1972).

the institution in question. New technology or approaches are also being developed, such as the open classroom, the contact curriculum, the school without walls, as major avenues for service improvement. Certainly the trend has increasingly moved from, in William Ryan's powerful phrase, "blaming the victim"[15] (that is, the child in the case of the school system), and toward devoting increasing attention to systemic or structural change.

THE PROFESSIONAL–CONSUMER DIALECTIC

Daniel Bell suggests that the conflict between the professional and consumer will in post-industrial society replace the traditional conflict between the worker and the capitalist.[16] Like all dialectic relationships, the professional–consumer one has both a unity and struggle (of opposites). The unity stems from the fact, as we have seen earlier, that both are forces in the production of service work and that both the consumer and the professional want more and better services to exist. This potentially unites them in fighting for the expansion of services and in opposing the cutbacks imposed by the right, which always prefers the private sector over which there is much less public control.

The unity of the professional and the consumer breaks down, however, over the question of control and direction of the services. This came to the fore most strikingly in the sixties, where a variety of consumer vanguards—blacks, youth, and women—questioned the autonomy of the professional elite and directed a severe attack at professional mystique, irrelevance, and the monopoly that professionals exercise over the obtaining of credentials and the providing of services.

A more critical examination of both professional practice and the preparation for it took place and the relationship between the two

15. William Ryan, *Blaming the Victim* (New York: Pantheon, 1971).
16. Daniel Bell, *The Coming of the Post-Industrial Society* (New York: Basic Books, 1973).

came into question. The first training of human service practitioners took place at or near the practice sites—in the proprietary schools common in law and medicine[17] from late in the eighteenth century, in the normal schools in teacher education, and in the training schools that grew out of the Charity Organization Societies in social work. Within the professions, the advance in the development of knowledge and the increasing scientific nature of the field called for more rigorous preparation. At the same time, the growing number of practitioners encouraged those in the field to guard the gates in the name of raising standards.

> AMA spokesmen increasingly [after its reorganization in 1901] linked the raising of medical school standards with the reduction in the number of doctors, a philosophy which was attractive not only to the leading educators, whose search for foundation money for the schools was predicated on educational reform, but also to the struggling practitioner competing for his living in an already crowded profession.[18]

In legal education, there was also the concern to protect the bar from an influx of lawyers who were immigrants or the children of immigrants. And it is perhaps no accident that one of the consequences of the "Flexner Reform" in medical education was a sharp reduction in the number of blacks trained. And in both fields, women were noticeable by their absence.

It was not surprising that the professions in their striving to "upgrade" themselves turned to the university. In doing so, they added luster to their authority, gave credence to the argument that professional wisdom was based not only upon particular skills, but also upon generalized learning. Along with the move into the university, as part of the professionalization of the field, there was the development of state examination and licensing authorities, professional associations, and associations of professional schools. Some-

17. Although chairs of law and of medicine were set up in several universities during the colonial era, few attended the courses and little professional preparation actually occurred.
18. Rosemary Stevens, *American Medicine and the Public Interest* (New Haven: Yale University Press, 1971), p. 60.

thing of the "natural history" of professionalization can be seen in the flow of these events.[19]

	Becomes a full-time occupation	First training school	First university school	First national professional association	First state licensing law
Law	17th century	1784	1817	1878	1732
Medical school	1700	1765	1779	1847	Before 1780
Teaching	17th century	1823	1879	1857	1781
Social work	1898	1898	1904	1874	1940

Just as could be written of baseball in 1951, "The grass was green, the dirt was brown, and the ball players were white,"[20] so, in the professions the norm has been white. However, in terms of sex composition there were sharp variations—in 1970, 6 percent of the doctors and 3 percent of the lawyers were women, as were 57 percent of the social workers and 73 percent of the school teachers.[21] The effect of such sex stratification was suggested by Amitai Etzioni.

It is difficult to believe that many of the arrangements we found in the relations between doctors and nurses, social workers and their supervisors, teachers and principals, would work out if, let us say, 90% of the nurses and supervised social workers were male. . . ."[22]

Women have not only been excluded from particular professions, but they have been placed in subordinate positions where they are plentiful—few major schools of social work, schools of education, or large public school systems have been led by a woman, nor has there ever

19. Harold L. Wilensky, "The Professionalization of Everyone?," *American Journal of Sociology,* LXX, 2 (September 1964), p. 143.
20. Roger Kahn, *The Boys of Summer* (New York: Harper & Row, 1971), p. 1.
21. Cynthia F. Epstein, "Encountering the Male Establishments: Sex Status Limits on Women's Careers in the Professions," *American Journal of Sociology,* LXXV, 6 (May 1970), p. 967.
22. Amitai Etzioni, ed., *The Semi-Professions and Their Organization* (New York: The Free Press, 1969), p. viii.

been a woman Commissioner of Education, to say nothing of the significantly fewer female principals or agency heads relative to the number of female teachers or social workers. Also, in the professions where they are present, they occupy less visible, less prestigious, and less remunerative areas of activity.[23]

It is this closed community characteristic of the professions— closed by sex, race, class (at least, in the case of medicine and to a lesser extent law) and at its upper organizational echelons by religion and ethnic group—that is rarely mentioned in the vast literature concerning the nature and characteristics of the professions. The two core characteristics that are discussed, distilled from a vast array of features, are "a prolonged specialized training in a body of abstract knowledge, and a collectivity or service orientation."[24]

Implicit in these definitions is the characteristic of the professional which derives from the early meaning of the word and which involves an assertion or declaration.

> Professionals profess. They profess to know better than others the nature of certain matters, and to know better than their clients what ails them or their affairs. This is the essence of the professional idea and the professional claim.[25]

This position was summarized by Everett C. Hughes when he said, "The quack is the man who continues through time to satisfy his customers but not his colleagues."[26]

23. Epstein, *op. cit.*, p. 974.

24. William J. Goode, "Encroachment, Charlatanism, and the Emerging Profession: Psychology, Sociology, and Medicine," *American Sociological Review*, XXV, 6 (December 1960), p. 903; see also the author's "Community Within a Community: The Professions," *American Sociological Review*, XXIII, 1 (January 1957), pp. 194–200; Wilensky, *op. cit.*; Morris L. Cogan, "Toward a Definition of Professions," *Harvard Educational Review*, XXIII, 1 (January 1953), pp. 35–50; Everett C. Hughes, "Professions," *Daedalus*, XCII, 4 (Fall 1963), pp. 665–668; Louis M. Orzack, "Issues Underlying Role Dilemmas of Professionals," in A. B. Abramowitz, ed., *Emotional Factors in Public Health Nursing* (Madison: University of Wisconsin Press, 1961); Abraham Flexner, "Is Social Work a Profession?," *School and Society*, I, 26 (June 26, 1915).

25. Hughes, *op. cit.*, p. 658.

26. E. C. Hughes, *Men and Their Work* (Glencoe: The Free Press, 1958), p. 98.

This appeal for professional autonomy is based upon the public's acceptance of the characteristics of expertise which derive from long training and altruism.[27] As there has been an erosion of the public acceptance of these two characteristics, the power of the professions to maintain unfettered their autonomy came under challenge. Clients found the expertise inadequate and the altruism all too often absent.[28] Friedson suggests that changes in the public itself account for growing questioning of professional autonomy, which he characterizes as the sole criterion for distinguishing a profession.[29] It is the increasing education of the public—both absolutely and in relation to the professionals—that has taken place.

A century ago the average patient was no doubt illiterate and superstitious, and the difference between the formal education of the average man and the average professional was very great. [W]hile the average length of formal professional education has increased over the last fifty years . . . the average length of formal education of the public has increased even more. Thus, assuming that formal education means something important (and if we do not make that assumption about laymen we cannot do it for professionals), laymen are far more likely today than yesterday to be able to participate intelligently in the active evaluation and pursuit of the solutions which professionals offer to their problems.[30]

In addition to criticisms about practice and the preparation for it, there began to develop in the sixties strong criticism regarding the cost of the services, and the professional ripoff involved in any service expansion where large portions of the increased funds were used principally for improved professional salaries and more professional jobs rather than improved consumer services. The criticism addressed all the service fields, including education and higher education, health, mental health, social work, all of which seemed to be providing services in a traditional, nonvital manner. A major effect of the

27. Marie R. Haug and M. R. Sussman, "Professional Autonomy and the Revolt of the Client," *Social Problems*, XVII, 2 (Fall 1969), p. 153.
28. *Ibid.*, p. 156.
29. Eliot Friedson, *Profession of Medicine: A Study of the Sociology of Applied Knowledge* (New York: Dodd, Mead, 1970), pp. 89 ff.
30. *Ibid.*, p. 354.

sixties was to reduce the professionals' discretionary power and to sensitize them to consumer needs, whether those of community blacks, participatory students, the "vaginal politics" of women, homosexuals who are victimized by a combined societal and psychiatric stigma, or patients without rights.

Various mechanisms were utilized to shift power to consumers: consumer advocates, paraprofessionals, decentralized neighborhood service centers, community boards, voucher systems, students on boards of trustees, accountability measures such as competency or performance-based training and certification. In addition, a variety of alternative institutions emerged: community schools, free universities, people's health clinics, women's counseling centers, hot lines, radical therapy groups, growth centers, and a great, great many more.

These new institutions, strongly consumer-centered, were largely led by new and unorthodox professionals, "young Turks," some noncredentialed professionals, and, in general, professionals who were outside or critical of the mainstream. They combined with the strong consumer vanguard constituency forces of minorities, youth, and women, as well as affluents who were strongly dissatisfied with the available institutions such as the traditional schools which they felt were not likely to educate their children for the society that was emerging, the work that the youngsters were likely to do, and the leisure that they were likely to enjoy. Many of the developments arising from alternative institutions have, to some extent, been reflected back into the major institutions, e.g., Catholic marriage encounter groups, and the use of alternative states, the open classroom in the public schools, schools without walls, off-campus open education, the use of hot lines, and the like. The popularity of professionals like Laing in psychiatry and Holt, Postman, Illich, Leonard, *et al.,* in education is a reflection of the influence of these alternative institutions (also Maslow, Rogers, Schutz, Perls, Paul Goodman). Most of these writers were powerfully anti-institutional and were much concerned with deprofessionalization, deinstitutionalization, deschooling, and were oriented much more to consumer involvement and the reduction of distance between the professional and the consumer. It is striking that much of the modern agenda in all the human service fields derives from issues raised by the alternative institution leaders and the consumer vanguards.

What clearly occurred in the sixties was a break in the equilibrium in which the professional was always boss ("doctor knows best") and the consumer was the passive recipient of the service. Margaret Mead, as we have noted, expresses well the development of consumer rights and the questioning of professional expertise.

It would indeed be dangerous, however, if this led to complete rejection of what the professional potentially has to offer: knowledge, perspective, systematic practice based on theory. Moreover, the professional as ally is very important as a large number of human service workers are and will be resisting attempts at industrialization and further bureaucratization of the services. Large numbers of teachers, government employees, and health workers express via their alienation, and in various other ways, their resistance to the bureaucratization that is imposed upon them, and thus they are an important force in a progressive service society strategy. It must be remembered, however, that they are always an ambivalent force because their own narrow self-interests and desire for control are not necessarily consonant with social change or the improvement of the services.

While the potential unity between the professional and the consumer is quite tenuous, nevertheless the expansion of service productivity and the shift of resources to the service sectors is clearly dependent upon both groups—the ever-expanding professional human service work force (as well as its students) and the consumer vanguards who are concerned not only about service productivity in general, as the taxpayer might be, but who are particularly involved because the services do not serve them appropriately. That is, blacks, minorities, women, and students all have more pinpointed concerns regarding the character of the service they receive and the lack of power they have over these services. This is why they are consumer vanguards. All consumers, of course, have concerns about the services, both the ones they receive and the ones they pay for. They want to receive decent, relevant services and they don't want to waste money paying for ineffective ones. As taxpayers, however, many of them may be willing simply to reduce the services in order to save taxes and they have come to feel that cost reduction won't make much difference regarding the quality of the services. It is for this reason that it is extremely important to improve the quality of the services and to highlight this in a public manner. It is largely the consumer vanguard groups who are much more concerned about the character of the services they receive and the control over them. Their concern stems not only from their consumer role, which they have in common with all other consumers, including the old middle-class business people, but also from their disenfranchised status and the fact that they're not needed in the industrial work force. This provides unique dimensions to their service and consumer orientations.

They have an additional ally in the affluent groups who are much less willing to accept old-fashioned services that are not assisting them to function in their service work and leisure roles. Another pivotal ally is the nonmainstream deviant professional, the humanistic psychologists, the community educators, the alternative life-stylers, the new professionals described by Ronald Gross and Paul Osterman,[31] and, to some extent, the self-help movement and the paraprofessional "new professionals." Their progressive professional force is an extremely critical one because unless services can be made more effective, simply controlling them will not be sufficient.

In essence, then, we need effective professionals. We need not only a deprofessionalization, but a reprofessionalization combined with consumer involvement both in the sense of consumer control and consumer immersion in the direct production of the service, as in children teaching children.

If we are to have a real service society with a major redistribution of resources to the service sectors, these services must call forth something of a vision—they must embody an ethic and enlist a spreading participation. It is almost entirely in the alternate institu-

31. Ronald Gross and Paul Osterman, eds., *The New Professionals* (New York: Simon & Schuster, 1972).

tions that such feelings are observed—feelings related to helping, serving, sharing, joy, excitement, opening up, self-development, self-expression, autonomy, the expansion of experience and consciousness, growth, breakthroughs. These sentiments must become part of the mainstream as much as possible, while continuing to expand on the perimeters. It is also going to be necessary to evaluate carefully, with many new indices, what services do actually provide for people at many levels. This evaluation will be necessary not only as feedback for improving the service, but also to win new support to a service society.

The sixties initiated the first steps in this battle for the services, in that the professionals' sole control was reduced and a notion of community involvement regarding the amount and character of the services was put on the agenda. However, as in all dialectic change there was a battle back and forth. The professionals have regrouped and have turned back or diverted some of the consumer power in the context of the general backlash against service expenditures. But much has been gained, many new traditions and institutions have been established, professionals have been partially sensitized to the needs of the consumer vanguards, and the demands of one of the vanguard groups, the women, continue to move forward in questioning professional mystique and control. The problem is not only to regain initiative and to move out of the current ebb period, but also to move beyond the consumer–professional battle where the professional is the first-line defense of the welfare state. We have to move to control, not only locally but nationally, over the direction of service resources if we are really to develop a redistribution of national resources and not simply divert ourselves with the local battle between consumers and professionals. We need some positive models and a specific national agenda.

HUMAN SERVICES IN CHINA: A CROSS-CULTURAL LOOK

China, of course, is vastly different from the United States—far less advanced industrially, under monolithic control, with a unique cultural tradition. It is just these differences which offer an opportunity to look at service issues disentangled from the particularities of American life. We undertake this effort, this angular look, so as to view service issues from a different perspective, not, of course, to find a model that is transferrable to the United States.

Illustrative of the Chinese approach to the human services is their approach to the community mental health system.[32]

The Chinese conception of good care for mental illness is a blend, like their medicine, of old and new and individual and collective techniques, with the whole held together by the daily study of Mao Tse Tung's thought.[33]

Ruth and Victor Sidel identify seven essential components involved in the Chinese community mental health system.[34]

—*Collective help.* Patients are expected to help one another, the less sick the sicker, the older the more recent ones. Group discussions and study sessions are heavily emphasized.

—*Self-reliance.* The patients are expected to struggle against their disease, to take responsibility for their return to health, to engage in self-analysis and self-criticism.

—*Physical Therapy.* As appropriate, medicines (but not shock treatment) and acupuncture are used.

—*"Heart-to-heart" Talks.* Mental health professionals meet periodically with patients, individually and in groups, to discuss their problems and to provide guidance in their self-investigation.

—*Community Ethos.* This goes beyond the "collective help" offered within the treatment facility and includes broader family and community responsibility on both a preventative and after-care basis, for those who are mentally troubled.

—*Follow up Care.* Following discharge, regular examinations are carried out, either through the institution's out-patient department or home visits.

32. See Ruth and Victor Sidel, "The Human Services in China," *Social Policy,* II, 6 (March–April 1972), pp. 24–34.
33. *Ibid.,* p. 27.
34. *Ibid.*

—*The Teachings of Mao.* Mao's thoughts run through the entire mental health system, including inspirational slogans but also difficult philosophic essays.

The building of "community ethos" is facilitated by the organization and structure of government. At the local level, cities (a similar structure exists in rural areas) are divided into neighborhoods or "streets," the lowest level of local government, and these are further divided into "lanes," blocklike units of from 1,500 to 8,000 people.

The Revolutionary Committees are the key new device of government. They are, in effect, boards of directors whose members are chosen according to the "three-in-one combination"—that is, representatives from the army, cadres, and representatives of the "mass" drawn from all levels of the institution's workers.

The operation of this system can be seen in the area of health care. A "housewife" is in charge ("responsible member") of the lane revolutionary committee.

The responsibilities of the lane health station are treatment of minor illnesses, health education (which the Chinese call "health propaganda"), immunization, and birth control. Silvery Lane [in Hangchow] consists of 13 "blocks," and the number of health workers in each block ranged from two to seven. The health workers were all housewives, 50 percent of whom have other jobs. All were volunteers. They were trained by doctors and other health workers from the street health stations. The immunization process shows how intimately the health workers become involved in their neighborhood's activities. Every child has a card with his immunization record on it. When it is time for that child to have another inoculation, the cadre from his block and the health worker visit the family (the distances are very small) to inform them, and the child is then brought to the health center for the shot. If it is not convenient for the child to be brought to the health station, the inoculation is occasionally given by the health worker in the home. Through recruitment of health workers from each lane and through close coordination between the health workers and the lane cadre, every child's health can be attended to.[35]

Basic principles which Victor Sidel has identified as central to health practice in China include:

35. *Ibid.,* p. 30.

1. *Recruitment of health workers from among those who would otherwise waste valuable talents:* more people in the society thus have an opportunity to serve and fewer are cut off from their communities or frustrated by an inability to find productive work.
2. *Recruitment of health workers from among those who live in the community:* health workers are therefore well known to their neighbors and in turn know well their neighbors and the problems they face.
3. *Short periods of training that bring health workers just up to the level of knowledge and skill needed for the work they will do:* we observed no evidence of the frustrations of the over-trained (or under-utilized) health workers seen in other health care systems.
4. *Minimization of the social distance between primary care health workers and those they serve, one form of what has been called "deprofessionalization":* while there may be some negative aspects to deprofessionalization—for example, problems of inadequate technical quality of care—what we actually observed was positive: apparent ease of access and of communication between health worker and patient.
5. *Attempts to spread medical knowledge widely, one form of what has been called "demystification":* this principle is illustrated by the training of the Red Medical Worker and the worker doctor, in their willingness in turn to share their knowledge freely, and in the mass health education campaigns at every level of society.
6. *Structured referral patterns:* one reason the local aspects of the system work well is that there is a clear pathway for referral—with no loss of face or income—to more specialized levels of care, and then a clear referral back to the local level for continued care.
7. *Decentralized services:* not only are services placed so as to be physically convenient to those who use them, but in addition their clearly local and simple nature may remove some of the psychological barriers to access to centralized, complex health services.
8. *Self-reliance:* widely preached in China is the tenet that each person in the society has a personal responsibility to participate fully in bringing about his or her own well-being and in the provision of needed services for others in family or community, and that each local unit has the responsibility to provide as much as it can for itself without draining resources from other areas.
9. *Altruism:* the spirit of *Wei Renmin Fuwu*—"Serve the People"—is seen everywhere, not only in signs and slogans, but apparently integrated into a motivation system based less on personal reward

than on the desire to be of use, and less on competition than on cooperation.[36]

DIALECTICAL ASPECTS OF THE HUMAN SERVICES

In any society the efficiency and character of human service practice seem to represent a dialectic synthesis of the knowledge, skills, and technology available to the service system, on the one hand, with all manner of cultural, social, and institutional factors, on the other. These include the social distance between the server and the consumer; the centralization or decentralization of the services; the amount, quality, and training of the manpower providing the services; the national government's ethos and its commitment to the services; the rewards and salaries available to the service givers; the extent of public and local control of the services; the fragmentation or integration of the services; the management and organization of the services; the selection and promotion of the service givers; the vested interests of the various groups providing the services; and the traditions of the professions.

Thus, the human services in any society, whether China or the United States, are a product of these seemingly external cultural and institutional forces together with the level and body of knowledge and skills available to the service system.

In order to organize an effective human service system the cultural and structural factors must be managed so as to enhance human service delivery and constantly to limit or modify those institutions that hinder the fullest development of the services causing them to be inefficient, unutilized, and irrelevant.

To do this requires a constant struggle and frequently a swinging back and forth of the dialectic pendulum; it is to be hoped that ever-higher levels of service performance will be achieved, but this, of course, is not guaranteed. Progress is not inevitable, and any particular swing of the pendulum can lead to a weakening of the service in

36. Victor W. Sidel, "The Health Workers of the Fengsheng Neighborhood of Peking," *American Journal of Orthopsychiatry,* XLIII, 5 (October 1973), p. 742.

question. For example, in both China and the United States the recent strong emphasis on the on-the-job training might lead to a neglect of fundamental research; work-study programs devoid of conceptualization of the work experience can lead to poor training and deleterious service.

Both the United States and China, in some similar ways and some different ones, have been struggling with this human service dialectic; they have been attempting to find forms and methods that maximize the efficiency and development of the service and that contain or overcome the specific traditions and institutions that mar service delivery.

Chinese society has been struggling with the elitism of the old professionals; the protracted, seemingly unnecessarily long training periods for the acquisition of knowledge and skill; the previous existence of large-scale pathologies, such as alcoholism, drug addiction, prostitution, crime, and venereal disease. A comparative look at the way the Chinese have dealt with these problems may be very instructive for us, although, of course, it is extremely important to recognize that no simple mechanical application can be made of the approaches used in a developing, agrarian, socialist society, where a monolithic party rules directly and openly, manifesting itself in every institution. We should not repeat the post-Sputnik error of U. S. educators who attempted to imitate Soviet scientific success in an earlier period. Still there may be much to learn, many suggested hypotheses to explore, and a new perspective to be gathered from observing the way the Chinese deal with the problems related to the dialectic of the human services—that is, in their attempt to maximize the efficiency and development of the services, while curtailing those institutional forces that rob the human services of their vitality.

A number of things stand out very quickly in the reports on the human services in China. Perhaps most outstanding in this regard is the fact that Chinese society as a whole, at the deepest political level, seems powerfully committed to making human services development a high priority in its own right—not something that exists mainly to support industrial or agricultural development. The Chinese seem deeply committed to the concept of service and selflessness: serving the people is the main principle, followed closely by selflessness, and the Chinese do not seem to be concerned primarily with developing industrial efficiency at the expense of these human services. People do seem to come first, rather than machines, incentives for high production, and the competition with the outside world that has characterized Soviet society.

The Chinese are deeply concerned with avoiding the alienation stemming from the overspecialization and bureaucratization that they feel is a danger in any industrial society, not only capitalist societies. For Marx, specialization and bureaucratization were the very antitheses of Communism and a person could be fully human only when these manifestations of alienation were removed, allowing one to become an "all around" Communist person. While an economy might gain from a highly intense division of labor, it loses by creating people who are robots. The Chinese are struggling with this basic dialectic of modern society and that is why they stress generalists versus specialists, masses versus bureaucrats. John Gurley, the American economist, states the case well.

It is also possible that the "universal man" in an underdeveloped economy would provide more flexibility to the economy. If most people could perform many jobs moderately well, manual and intellectual, urban and rural, the economy might be better able to cope with sudden and large changes; it could, with little loss in efficiency, mobilize its labor force for a variety of tasks. Further, since experience in one job carries over to others, a person may be almost as productive, in the job-proficiency sense, in any one of them as he would be if he specialized on it. A peasant who has spent some months in a factory can more easily repair farm equipment and, so on. Finally, a Maoist economy may generate more useful information than a specialist one and so lead to greater creativity and productivity. When each person is a narrow specialist, communication among people is not highly meaningful: your highly specialized knowledge means little to me in my work. When, on the other hand, each person has a basic knowledge of many lines of activity, the experiences of one person enrich the potentialities of many others.[37]

37. John G. Gurley, "Capitalist and Maoist Economic Development," in Edward Friedman and Mark Selden, eds., *America's Asia: Dissenting Essays on Asian-American Relations* (New York: Vintage, 1971).

While the Chinese are obviously concerned with expanding their standard of living and apparently are doing this, although probably not at overpowering speed, they are not willing to sacrifice everything else to do it. Kitchen socialism is not the order of the day; that is, economic efficiency and growth are seen constantly in relation to the development of people. This is a particular variant of socialism, apparently quite different from the one that characterized the growth of the Soviet Union. Perhaps the difference is related to the particular way Marxism has been adapted in China, where the working-class vanguard has not been at all primary.

China was, and continues to be, principally an agrarian society, a developing country; as they say, it is not a big power. Perhaps more than anything else, this context provides a basic understanding of why the human services are so important in China; why they are given so much attention and such high priority; and how they are integrated into the very fabric of life, culture, and politics.

In China health services and education are not simply developed in order to make workers more efficient and healthy so that they can be more productive on the job; they seem to be valued in their own right. In this sense, Chinese socialism is a more spiritual, humanistic one; this leads quite naturally to a strong, participatory involvement of people performing human services at every level of society. Thus people will work part-time providing services; they will help other people in manifold ways all the way down to the local lane without receiving any pay; they will provide services while learning; and all levels of people with all types of background and education will serve. Obviously in such a context the elitism of traditional professionals is anathema: professionals are not permitted to rip off huge benefits; and the notion that a person requires long preparation before he or she can do anything to serve other people is entirely inconsistent with the basic ethos. Deprofessionalization is the order of the day—indeed, of the era.

This deprofessionalization includes the beliefs that professionals should not be more privileged than the rest of the people; that mental and physical work should not be bifurcated; that an elite caste should not be permitted to emerge. Rather, steps have been taken to prevent the continuance of an elite, including the recruitment of professionals from among the masses, the elimination of traditional selection processes, the requirement of manual labor for all professionals, the reduction of wage differentials, the shortened periods of training, and the massive use of paraprofessionals, including the "barefoot doctors," urban worker doctors, midwives, and Red Guard doctors.

At the same time, since the Chinese want to provide useful, efficient human services, there is recognition of the value of professional knowledge, science, technology, systematic thought, and study, although basic research is deemphasized at the present time in favor of direct service. There is a constant dialectic struggle between the positive aspects of professional systematic knowledge, which to some extent entails removal from direct practice with its attendant elitist dangers, and the need to have this professional practice rooted in experience, serving the people. Too much deprofessionalization risks lowering the level of professional knowledge, keeping it at a narrow technician level, leading to the failure to develop underlying conceptual principles—irrelevant theory divorced from practice.

The Chinese deal with this dialectic through political control of the human services ("Put Politics in Command"). For example, it is clear, in the health services field that, unlike the United States, *doctors are not necessarily in command.* Of course, it always depends on what politics are controlling human services—politics are in command in the United States too, and, thus, the human services are seen as secondary to capital development. And politics were put in command in the Soviet Union, where the partisanship reflected in Lysenko and others inhibited the development of scientific thought. In the early stages of scientific and professional development this may be less of an issue, particularly if a nation starts from an extremely low level of knowledge and service. In the long run, however, if "leaps" are to continue, new forms of democracy will have to emerge. Perhaps by that time Chinese society will have less need for monolithic party control. But will their leaders recognize this or be made to recognize it? This, after all, is a basic problem in the Soviet Union today—one that remains unresolved.

8   The Consumer: A Hidden Resource
for Human Service Productivity

> In the services, "the knowledge, experience, honesty and motivation of the consumer affects service productivity."
>
> —Victor Fuchs, *The Service Economy*

Effectiveness of the services is both an issue intrinsic to them and, as we have discussed previously, central to the expansion of a human service society. And it is in the consumer, the central player of the service society, that we find the hidden resource to service improvement. It is important to recognize that the criteria of effectiveness are neither self-evident nor neutral but need to be understood in terms of by whom (and how) they are set, for the benefit of whom, at whose cost, and received by whom.

Traditionally we think of productivity as a function of technology—the more machinery, the more efficient production will be. This has certainly been characteristic in the manufacturing of goods. On the other hand, the services are labor-intensive; they use a high proportion of labor or human power in contrast to machinery or capital in order to produce the service product, whether it be education, health, safety, or personal services. To make the services more efficient, it has seemed natural to try to mechanize them more; that is, to apply machinery so that they will perhaps become more like manufacturing.

Traditional notions argue that productivity in human service work cannot be increased sharply because it is not amenable to capital-intensive inputs; moreover, as it is labor-intensive, the work inputs are costly and potentially inflationary. Our point, however, is that human service work is consumer-intensive and the key to increasing productivity in this sector lies in effectively engaging and mobilizing the consumer.

We have already noted some of the broad consumer concerns regarding the services, but for the most part, the initial impact has been indirect or nonspecific. Thus, community advisory boards have been established on the assumption that such community involvement may make the service giver more responsive to the consumer. Para-professionals have been employed with the idea that they would bring a community voice into the service system, affecting agencies and professionals thereby. Voucher systems have been experimented with in order to capture some of the presumed power that the buyer of a service may possess. Decentralization has been applied in neighborhood service centers in order to reduce the distance of the client from the service.

Competency- or performance-based certification has been advocated in order to identify more closely what the practitioner is able to do. New methods of analyses of the work (e.g., job or functional task analysis) are designed to demystify the work that is done and to bring it under greater scrutiny and control. Advocates and expediters have been employed to cut through red tape and speed service delivery. Much more developed training designs have been employed, stressing simulation, in the hope that sharper, more pinpointed skills will emerge and thus the service be improved. And, of course, service modalities such as the open classroom, the community mental health center, and many, many more have been introduced on the grounds that they are more involving of the client or consumer and will therefore produce a better service. The reorganization of roles, both professional and paraprofessional, has been proposed as a major device for increasing effectiveness, and the use of new types of personnel has been proposed to represent clients better.

These approaches, as we discuss below, while they have had some specific service effects, have largely been accepted on face validity. While they are likely to make the services more consumer-relevant, they may not specifically make it better. Often, they have been accepted (as they have been advocated) because of what they are trying to do and their general philosophy, rather than based on discrete service effectiveness criteria. This is not to say, however, that individually (or collectively) they have not had some effect on service quality. Rather, it is that they have not led to any leaps in direct service quality. We believe that this is so, at least, in large part because while they are consumer-oriented, they do not directly harness the potential power of the consumer as producer.

Similarly, the broad community participation efforts have had general effects. They have upset the professional monopoly, put the system in a state of disequilibrium, and acting as an icebreaker, laid it open to change. But it is necessary to go beyond that stage of local struggle between community and professional, on the one hand, to the larger national arenas, and, on the other hand, to the specifics of practice and service effectiveness.

Both the broad community participation efforts and the discrete consumer-oriented practices steps are necessary, but neither alone nor together are they sufficient to achieve the necessary leaps in service productivity. What is additionally necessary is the involvement of the consumer as a producer.

THREE PHASES OF CONSUMER INVOLVEMENT

We can identify, in looking at consumer involvement in human service practice, at least three phases or facets.

—General consumer involvement around the services.
—Active roles in service delivery for those who have been (or are) service consumers.
—Engaging the consumer as a direct factor in service production.

This first phase is characterized by the community control (sometimes mislabeled decentralization) struggles, exemplified in education by the events related to the three[1] so-called demonstration school districts in New York City;[2] in mental health, in the struggles at Lincoln Hospital in the Bronx; and in health, in the various OEO-funded comprehensive neighborhood health centers, such as Columbia Point in Boston, Mound Bayou in Mississippi, and NENA in New York City.

What was achieved in this phase was a challenging of professional autonomy, a "peeling off," in a sense, of professional power. Lay people demanded and won the right, to some extent, at least, to a say about matters relating to the service they (or their children) were to receive. While issues of practice were important at this phase, larger political goals were also central. And, in some cases at least, these broader concerns diverted from (or, even, had negative consequences for) concern with direct practice issues. Nonetheless, issues which needed raising were raised and a necessary challenge to the professional service systems put forth. "Consumer involvement in delivery systems . . . is the first crucial step to change the form of existing services from institutional needs to patient needs."[3]

The second phase, in chronology often simultaneous with the first, includes a broad variety of consumer-related activities vis-à-vis the human services. In part, this was in response to increased pressure for services. A number of practices were used to help human service agencies respond positively to growing consumer-demand pressures, i.e., they were designed either to increase the resources or to use them more efficiently:

1. Ocean Hill–Brownsville in Brooklyn, and in Manhattan, IS 201 and Three Bridges.

2. The best discussion of the issues regarding the "demonstration districts" in New York City, and the broader community participation effort vis-à-vis the schools are those of an active participant in as well as student of these events. See Marilyn Gittell with Maurice R. Berube and others, *Local Control in Education: Three Demonstration School Districts in New York City* (New York: Praeger, 1972), and Marilyn Gittell, *Participants and Participation: A Study of School Policy in New York City* (New York: Center for Urban Education, 1967).

3. "New Manpower for Family Planning Services," *American Journal of Public Health*, LXVI, 10 (October 1973), p. 381.

1. Hiring underutilized persons such as older people, women, the poor, youths, part-time workers, and the like.

2. Taking advantage of nonfocused endeavors, for example, the opportunities for learning outside school. By capitalizing on informal programs or organized efforts such as Philadelphia's Parkway School (in which the city itself becomes the learning medium) or the college-level "University Without Walls" programs, a school can use the resources of the large community as its classroom.

3. Using consultation as a technique to expand resources. Unlike the usual consultation efforts, which are designed to deal with a specific individual's problem, consultation can be designed to multiply the existing efforts of individuals and groups.

4. Examining the precise features of work to be done (e.g., functional job analysis or job task analysis) and deploying human resources so they are used most effectively. Restructuring work as a series of discrete tasks to be performed allows greater productivity and efficiency than does the use of general job descriptions.

These practices represent effective ways of meeting present demands for services. However, if agencies are to meet the growing demand—caused not only by increased population but rising expectations and desires—two additional strategies must be developed. Of course, additional financial resources are necessary, but the experience with the Medicare and Medicaid programs, while serving large numbers of people, showed that enormous sums of money pumped into the health care system had little demonstrable effect on service organization, while providing enormous income to doctors.

First, indigenous or noncredentialed manpower must be used not merely as tools to reach those previously unserved, but to allow more effective use of professional resources and to increase the supply of new professionals. For instance, Haughton notes that while 80 percent of the traditionally trained registered nurses leave New York City hospitals within three years of graduation from nurses' training because of marriage, pregnancy, moving, new jobs, and so forth, community residents who become hospital professionals via "new careers" programs are likely to remain longer.[4] Paraprofessionals, who most often perform out-reach functions, must be used increasingly to deliver direct services, such as counseling clients, teaching children, and treating patients.[5]

Second, recipients of services can also render services—that is, the service user becomes a producer. For example, in a Harlem narcotics program, patients operate a free breakfast program for children; in another program, delinquent youths tutor underachievers. Similarly, prisoners in the Salem (Mass.) jail record books for the blind through the national Braille Press.

Teachers and others can be trained best by doing the work to be learned. At Hunter College in New York City, student teachers tutor sixth-grade children, who, in turn, tutor second-grade children.[6] Thus, the training program produces services, i.e., the tutoring of the two sets of children. The entire "new careers" program, in which a participant is hired first and receives the necessary training and education on the job, is another instance in which trainees deliver services.

Communities with problems can often help themselves more effectively by organizing to pressure outside resources into serving them than by trying to marshal their own resources. For example, the Office of Economic Opportunity (OEO) can claim that its antipoverty efforts mobilized federal, state, and local resources to a degree that was far beyond the power of the agency's budget, that is, it used its "leverage" successfully to multiply available resources. While a community's efforts to help itself by marshaling its own resources may produce only group sociotherapeutic effects, or, worse,

4. Personal communication from James Haughton, M.D., former First Deputy Commissioner, Department of Hospitals, New York, N.Y., June 1970.
5. See Alan Gartner, *Paraprofessionals and Their Performance* (New York: Praeger, 1971).
6. Elizabeth Hunter, "A Cross-Age Tutoring Program Encourages the Study of Teaching in a College Methods Course," *Journal of Teacher Education*, XIX, 4 (Winter 1968), pp. 447–451.

be an instance of asking someone to lift himself up by his own boot-straps when he does not have any, group action can be productive both in mobilizing new resources and drawing on the resources of its members. To some extent, the efforts of OEO's Community Action Program, welfare rights organizations, civil rights groups, and black, brown, and red nationalist groups are examples of such successful endeavors.

The use of consumers as service deliverers may have further effects on service utilization because different demands will be made on the system when these services deliverers again become consumers. If an individual is both a consumer and a deliverer—simultaneously, as in learning-through-teaching programs, or sequentially, as in many of the paraprofessional programs—he/she will be a more knowledge-able consumer in terms of which services are used, how much, in what manner, and to what effect. The following remark made by a child involved in a California learning-through-teaching program illustrates what can happen when a consumer who has been a server once again becomes a consumer:

When my teacher does something that I think is bad teaching, I ask myself now how would I do it. Then I make myself my own teacher and I teach myself the better way.[7]

In dealing with the issue of increased demand for services, we have thus far focused intentionally upon the human resources—how new ones can be marshaled and old ones better deployed. Another key feature in responding to such demand pressures has to do with chang-ing the structure or organization of the service—the issues of how it is delivered, as well as by whom.[8]

7. "Pint-Size Tutors Learn by Teaching," *American Education* (April 1967), p. 29.

8. Catherine Kohler Riessman, "The Impact of Experimental Programs on the Utilization of Health Services by Low-Income Groups," *Social Policy*, IV, 6 (May/June 1974), includes vast amounts of data addressed to these questions. The author marshals a powerful case for rejecting the psycho-cultural expla-nations of underutilization of health services, and makes the case in favor of socio-structural explanations. We are grateful to her for permission to use these data.

Data from a university-sponsored demonstration project [New York Hospital-Cornell Project],[9] prepaid group practice plans [Kaiser at Fontana, California; Kaiser at Portland, Oregon; Group Health of Puget Sound, Washington; and H.I.P. of New York at Suffolk County],[10] Neighborhood Health Centers,[11] and nationwide Family Planning Programs[12] all suggest that the health behavior of the poor can be radically altered within a relatively short period of time by introducing structural changes in the way the service is offered, e.g., the provision of a high quality, comprehensive service at nominal cost, geographic availability, flexible scheduling, the provision of patient transportation, and baby sitting services, etc.[13]

An aspect of this restructuring of the services can be seen in the greater use of community-based facilities for the prisoner, the mentally ill, the handicapped. In part, it seems that the move away from places of incarceration for these populations has been a function of the growing cost of institutionalization; however, the failure of such institutions seems to be central.

In addition to efforts involving new personnel and new uses of old personnel, and the structural changes described above, there have been efforts to mechanize the services and to introduce new management tools.

9. C. Goodrich, M. Olendski, and G. Reader, *Welfare Medical Care: An Experiment* (Cambridge: Harvard University Press, 1970).

10. G. Sparer and A. Anderson, "Utilization and Cost Experience of Low-Income Families in Four Prepaid Group Practice Plans, 1970–1971," a paper presented at the Annual Conference of the American Public Health Association, Atlantic City, N.J., November 1972.

11. "An Evaluation of the Neighborhood Health Center Program: Summary of Results and Methodology: Office of Planning, Research and Evaluation, Office of Economic Opportunity, May 1972; M. Straus and G. Sparer, "Basic Utilization Experience of OEO Comprehensive Health Services Projects," *Inquiry,* VIII (December 1971), pp. 36–48; S. Bellin and H. J. Geiger, "Actual Public Acceptance of the Neighborhood Health Center by the Urban Poor," *Journal of the American Medical Association,* CCXIV (1970), pp. 2147–2153.

12. Frederick Jaffe, "Family Planning, Public Policy, and Intervention Strategy," *Journal of Social Issues,* XIII (1967), pp. 159–160; Center for Family Planning Program Development, "Data and Analyses for 1973 Revision of DHEW Five-Year Plan for Planning Services" (New York: Planned Parenthood and World Population, 1973); Catherine Kohler Riessman, "Birth Control, Culture, and the Poor," *American Journal of Orthopsychiatry,* XXXVIII (1968), pp. 693–699.

13. Catherine Kohler Riessman, *op. cit.,* p. 25.

There are countless illustrations of mechanization in the service fields—teaching machines, tape recorders, multiphasic screening of patients, walkie-talkies for policemen. While some of these methods clearly have their uses, there has been no leap in the productivity or humanity of the services in the areas where they have been applied.[14]

Another approach to increasing service efficiency is seen in the introduction of a number of managerial approaches such as job task analysis, systems approaches, PPBS, and countless others, frequently borrowed from industry.[15] But the various "systems approaches" and the like do not seem to have revolutionized the services, either in terms of efficiency or the reduction of alienation; nor for that matter has the emphasis on training produced striking improvements in performance and productivity whether among policemen, teachers, psychiatrists, social workers, recreation specialists, drug education workers, or doctors.

The fact is that there are very few examples of marked advances in output in the service spheres, but fortunately there are a few, and perhaps something can be learned from a look at them.

Of course, there is the problem of definition. What, after all, is a marked improvement in service delivery, and how is it to be assessed?[16] As a working model, we would suggest the following indices:

14. See "Educational Technology, Does It Have a Future in the Classroom?," *Saturday Review of Education* (May 1963) for a critical overview of the use of hardware in the education field; in the health area, see R. R. Nelson, "Issues and Suggestions for the Study of Industrial Organizations in a Regime of Rapid Technical Change," in V. R. Fuchs, ed., *Policy Issues and Research Opportunities in Industrial Organization* (New York: National Bureau of Economic Research, 1972).

15. See Theodore Levitt, "Production Line Approach to Service," *Harvard Business Review*, L (September–October 1972) for illustrations of how managerial and industrial approaches are proposed to maximize service efficiency.

16. We need an evaluation model that employs multiple indices, each different from the other, each subject to different weaknesses and strengths that may counterbalance each other, but converging toward a similar result or assessment. In the psychological literature, this is termed *convergent* and *discriminant validity*. See Donald Campbell and Donald Fiske, "Convergent and Discriminant Validation by the Multitrait-Multimethod Matrix," *Psychological Bulletin*, LVI, 2 (March 1969), pp. 81–104.

1. An advance in output of considerable magnitude that is enduring; e.g., children's reading scores improving 20 percent or more above the norm, and remaining at the new level;

2. The rapid spread in the utilization of a service of "obvious" value; e.g., immunization of large numbers of children hitherto uninoculated;[17]

3. A strong positive subjective report by users of service where the subjective element may be said to be the decisive variable; e.g., partners reporting change in the enjoyment of sexual relations subsequent to receiving sex therapy;

4. Changes in behavior at multiple levels; in education, for example, changes in the cognitive and affective dimensions. An important variant of this point relates to the latent functions of a service. Thus, if in the process of learning to read, a child acquires a more cooperative attitude, a feeling of greater power, these added outputs (frequently emanating from the context of the service) can be seen as important reflections of its value. Contrariwise, a service that in itself may produce a positive output, e.g., a doctor's accurate prescription for a patient, can produce disastrous consequences because the whole relationship may make the patient feel highly dependent and mystified.

With these criteria in mind, some actual illustrations can be cited. One, as we have already noted, is the rapid and effective spread of family planning among segments of the population that hitherto were uninvolved in these procedures. Planned Parenthood now estimates that over 50 percent of the poor in the United States are utilizing family planning approaches.[18]

17. Obviously a cost-benefits analysis is necessary with all the criteria because if any particular level of service output requires tremendous and highly expensive inputs, the results would have to be weighed in this context.

18. See *Population Crisis* (March 1973): "About 3.2 million low income American women have used federal family planning programs during the year to July 1972. Services are available through federally subsidized Planned Parenthood, governmental, and private physician programs. The nation is halfway to the goal established by the Secretary of Health, Education, and Welfare to provide 6.2 million low income women with such help by 1975." The key element in the spread of family planning appears to be the utilization of the consumers themselves, employed as paraprofessionals, to involve other

The second area that illustrates marked change in output is where children have been utilized to teach other children. Here the older children who do the tutoring have been observed to achieve a dramatic advance in their own learning—as much as three years in reading improvement in six months' time.[19] These changes have been lasting and are typically accompanied by changes in attitude toward learning, increased self-confidence, and the like.

A third illustration can be found in various applications of the self-help movement. For example, it has been reported that the most effective approaches to weight control are the various weight watchers groups—and to a lesser extent this seems to be true for smokers, alcoholics, drug addicts, although the data are more ambiguous than in weight reduction.[20] Of added importance is the fact that these behaviors have been very resistant to change by all methods.

CONSUMER-INTENSIVE SERVICES

What these examples seem to have in common, in addition to the fact that they are inexpensive, is a special involvement of con-

consumers. The relevant concept is seeing "the consumer as server." See Alan Gartner, "Consumers as Deliverers of Service," *Social Work,* XVI (October 1971).

19. Alan Gartner, Mary Conway Kohler, and Frank Riessman, *Children Teach Children: Learning by Teaching* (New York: Harper & Row, 1971); Peggy Lippitt, "Children Can Teach Other Children," *The Instructor,* II, 6 (May 1969), pp. 10–14; Peggy Lippitt, Jeffrey Eiseman, and Ronald Lippitt, *Cross Age Helping Programs: Orientation, Training and Related Materials* (Ann Arbor: Center for Research on Utilization of Scientific Knowledge, Institute for Social Research, University of Michigan, 1969); Herbert Thelen, *Learning by Teaching* (Chicago: Stone-Brandel Center, University of Chicago, 1968); Herbert Thelen, "Tutoring by Students: What Makes It So Exciting?," *School Review,* XXVIII, 3 (September 1969), pp. 229–244; *Youth Tutoring Youth—It Worked* (New York: National Commission on Resources for Youth, January 1969); and *Final Report, In-School Neighborhood Youth Corps Project* (New York: National Commission on Resources for Youth, January 1969).

20. See, for example, Albert J. Strunkard, "The Success of TOPPS: A Self Help Group," *Postgraduate Medicine,* XL, 5 (May 1972), pp. 743–746; also, Frank Riessman, "The 'Helper Therapy' Principle," *Social Work,* X, 2 (April 1965), pp. 14–25; Edward Sagarin, *Odd Man In* (Chicago: Quadrangle Books, 1969); and Alfred Katz, "Self-Help Organizations and Volunteer Participation in Social Welfare," *Social Work,* XIV, 1 (January 1970), pp. 51–60.

sumers—patients, students, and clients—so that they become a force in the increase of the productivity of the service. The consumers are actually operative in the delivery of the service; it is not some general form of participation. And there is a definite increase in the output: learning and/or extension of the service.[21]

Victor Fuchs points out that unlike goods production, in the services "the knowledge, experience, honesty, and motivation of the consumer affects service productivity."[22]

Fuchs seems to be implying a new classification which might be termed, as Sumner Rosen suggests, "consumer intensive"—"the more the productivity of the provider depends on consumer behavior, the more consumer intensive we could call that industry or activity."[23] Rosen goes on to point out that "some services can be seen as both labor-intensive (that is, little capital) and consumer-intensive: health outside the hospitals would be one and social services another. Other services might be consumer-intensive and capital-intensive; banking and insurance, for example."[24] The human services, then, seem to be both consumer-intensive and labor-intensive.[25]

Here, then, is a decisive factor which can affect education or any other human service. If we see students, for example, not as the

21. We do not mean to suggest that the only qualitative advances in the services are a direct result of consumer involvement, although it is interesting how many interventions could be recast in this fashion, e.g., the open classroom, computerized self-instruction, biofeedback, the therapeutic community, the use of alternative states of consciousness, schools without walls, the street academies, encounter groups, affective education. Nevertheless, there are, of course, improvements in service outputs that are much more "directive," learner or professional centered; e.g., the work of Bereiter and Engelman in affecting children's cognitive functioning and the directive therapies in the mental health field.

22. Victor Fuchs, *The Service Economy* (New York: Columbia University Press, 1968), p. 17.

23. Personal communication, May 21, 1973: Rosen notes also that where the consumer was "negative," as in the welfare system, the service is abysmally inadequate.

24. *Ibid.*

25. Sumner Rosen offers the hypothesis that the more complicated the consumer choices, the stronger the consumer role. "Some of the consumer inputs, e.g., hold your head still, open wide, tell me where it hurts, are relatively uncomplicated. But others may require much more involvement, such as biofeedback, self-hypnosis, etc. . . ." *Ibid.*

passive recipients of teaching but as *workers in the production of their own learning,* then the organization of those learning activities takes on a quite different focus.[26]

What is key in efforts to increase children's learning, then, are those activities that can enlist the student as a more active and effective learner/worker. Helping students to learn will make them more effective and efficient learners in the future. Engaging students in a program where they learn through teaching other students makes most efficient use of the student/worker. If students are a key factor in the production of their own learning, then the other forces of production (teachers, equipment) must be directed toward maximizing the efficiency of the student. One of the ways to do this is to enlist the consumers (that is, the students, their families, and community) to give them a say in what is to be learned, who is to be employed, and how the learning is to be organized. If this is done, then the students are perhaps more likely to be motivated to work hard, that is, to be effective producers of their own learning.

Some Health Examples

A number of developments in the health field suggest some of the dimensions of a new human service practice, practice that is consumer-[27] not doctor-centered.

26. Some of the steps which may be taken in education can be seen by looking at designs developed for the improvement of the productivity of other types of workers. Much attention has been given recently to improving the work satisfaction and productivity of factory workers through developing teams to reduce worker isolation, organizing the work so as to give a sense of wholeness to their efforts, giving workers control of some (or all) of the operations involved so as to produce a feeling of autonomy and involvement. These same principles apply to efforts to improve the quality of work performed by students as a factor in the producing of their own learning. For example, the work (learning) must be interesting; it should be carried on so that the worker (student) can have positive relationships with coworkers (other students and teachers); there should be an apparent connection between the various parts of the work; the relationship of the particular job (item being studied) to the larger enterprise (the student's entire learning) should be real and clear; and the worker (student) should have some discretion and control over what he or she does—the order, pace and tempo, and content.

27. We intentionally did not use the word patient here, for such a term denotes a medical focus to health care, and it is just our point that such a

Illich and colleagues make the point that

The sources of human health are varied. They include at least four elements:

1. Self-activated behavior, e.g., breast feeding rather than artificial feeding; walking rather than riding; not smoking; temperate use of food and drink.
2. Communal behavior, e.g., caring by family members, neighbors, and friends; promotion of feelings of belonging by voluntary associations.
3. Environmental factors, e.g., physical factors, including sanitation, air pollution, transportation, and lead poisoning; unemployment, economic depressions, and conditions of work.
4. Therapeutic information, tools, and skills, e.g., vaccines, aspirin, scalpels, antibiotics, and knowing how to use them.[28]

Fuchs talks to the same issue when he says that the health of our society is far less dependent upon the number of doctors or professional personnel and much more dependent upon the attitudes, culture, and involvement of the users of the health services.

It is becoming increasingly evident that many health problems are related to individual behavior. In the absence of dramatic breakthroughs in medical science, the greatest potential for improving health is through changes in what people do and do not do to and for themselves.[29]

It is to the issues of affecting these actions of people that a consumer-centered practice must be directed.

The disease model of medical care is particularly harmful to women. For their visits to doctors are to a far less extent disease-related, e.g., regarding birth control, pregnancy, menopause, and,

---

focus is inappropriate. "Patient has come to mean THEM, not US [the writer is a doctor]. And a special kind of THEM to be taken care of, a THEM who, like irrational children, need to be cajoled, threatened, ordered about and chastised, a mindless THEM who need to be led to the path of right thinking." Mary Costanza, Introduction in Ellen Frankfort, *Vaginal Politics* (New York: Bantam Books, 1973), p. xviii.

28. Ivan Illich, John McKnight, and Robert Mendelsohn, "National Health Insurance and the People's Health," CIDOC, Document, I/V (1973).

29. Victor Fuchs, "Health Care and the United States Economic System," *Milbank Memorial Quarterly*, L, 2 (April 1972), p. 229.

given the common child-rearing practice, with children for "well baby" visits. But, nonetheless, they are treated in a disease-oriented system.[30] The "stirrups" position and the draping of women on the examining table (to say nothing of the air conditioning set at a temperature to accommodate the dressed doctor, not the undressed woman) may be efficient for the doctor, but has negative consequences for the patients in terms of their self-image and their self-respect—often meeting the doctor first in that position.[31] Indeed, the medical treatment model serves to isolate women, to prevent them from gaining a sense of shared experiences.

The medical system is strategic for women's liberation. It is the guardian of reproductive technology—birth control, abortion, and the means for safe childbirth. It holds the promise of freedom from hundreds of unspoken fears and complaints that have handicapped women throughout history. When we demand control over our own bodies, we are making that demand above all to the medical system. It is the keeper of the keys.

But the medical system is also strategic to women's oppression. Medical science has been one of the most powerful sources of sexist ideology in our culture. Justifications for sexual discrimination—in education, in jobs, in public life—must ultimately rest on the one thing that differentiates women from men: their bodies. Theories of male superiority ultimately rest on biology.

Medicine stands between biology and social policy, between the "mysterious" world of the laboratory and everyday life. It makes public interpretations of biological theory; it dispenses the medical fruits of scientific advances. Biology discovers hormones; doctors make public judgments on whether "hormonal imbalances" make women unfit for public office. More generally, biology traces the origins of disease: doctors pass judgment on who is sick and who is well.[32]

The professional-run system with its "doctor knows best" attitude is antithetical to a consumer-focused practice. Indeed, there appears

30. We are grateful to Amy Fine for this insight.
31. Ellen Frankfort, *op. cit.*
32. Barbara Ehrenreich and Deirdre English, *Complaints and Disorders: The Sexual Politics of Sickness* (Westbury, N. Y.: The Feminist Press, 1973), p. 6.

to be evidence that it is not effective in terms of patient well-being on standard measures. Glogow found that patients who adopt a compliant, nonquestioning attitude, in short, become what hospital staffs call "good patients," may well not be the most likely to get better more quickly. On the contrary, the patients who were less compliant, the hospital staffs' "bad patients," did improve more quickly.[33] And doctors who use medical jargon a great deal and thus fail to communicate with their patients are less successful in terms of their patients' health.[34]

In an advanced society, the major health problems are those of chronic illnesses, e.g., heart disorders, cancer, hypertension, diabetes, emphysema, mental illnesses.

Straus describes a series of steps necessary to enable those with chronic illnesses (the most rapidly increasing and most expensive to treat illnesses) to cope with them, and the concomitant crises.[35]

—The ability to read signs that portend a crisis, e.g., a diabetic being able to recognize the signs of oncoming sugar shortage or insulin shock, or an epileptic being able to recognize an oncoming convulsion. In a sense, this is a form of self-diagnosis.

—The ability to respond to the crisis of the moment. To use the two examples above, the diabetic who carries sugar or candy or insulin, or the epileptics who stuff handkerchiefs between their teeth just before convulsions.[36] This is, in a sense, a form of self-treatment. An aspect of this self-treatment is to carry it out in a manner which keeps "one's symptoms as inobtrusive as possible . . . [e.g.] emphysema sufferers learn to sit down or lean against buildings in such a fashion that they are not mistaken for drunks or loiterers."[37]

—The ability to establish and maintain a regimen. The extent to

33. Eli Glogow, "The Administrator and the Compliant 'Good' Patient," *Social Policy,* IV, 3 (November–December 1973), pp. 72–77.

34. Barbara Korsch and Virda Negreta, "Doctor-Patient Communication," *Scientific American,* CCXXVIII (August 1972), p. 43.

35. Anselm Straus, "Chronic Illness," *Society,* X, 6 (September–October 1973), p. 33.

36. *Ibid.*

37. *Ibid.,* p. 36.

which a person is able to do this depends upon his or her belief in the efficacy of the regimen, the effectiveness of the regimen without producing distressing or frightening side effects, "and the guarantee that important daily activities, either of the patient or of the people around him [*sic*], can continue relatively uninterrupted.[38]

All three of these steps—the ability to read signs that portend a crisis, the ability to respond to the crisis of the moment, the ability to establish and maintain a regimen—are central charactcristics of health care in a consumer-centered model. For these steps to be carried out, for the patient indeed to be a producer of his or her own health, he or she must be trained in matters traditionally the prerogative of the professional, must be encouraged to be an active participant in the achievement of the cure, must be "turned on" to doing so, must be convinced of the efficacy of the undertaking.[39]

Of course, there are occasions when the consumer is not able to play an active role. Szasz and Hollender have developed a threefold typology of doctor-patient relationships.[40]

1. *Activity-Passivity.* When the patient is incapable of participating (as is the case of a coma), the doctor does something to the patient.
2. *Guidance-Cooperation.* While ill, the patient is aware of what is happening and is capable of following directions. The thrust of this approach is for the patient to follow the doctor's directions.
3. *Mutual Participation.* Here the approach is one of the doctor helping the patient to help him (or her) self.[41]

38. *Ibid.,* p. 35.
39. Some of the same phenomena occur in the ever-expanding arena of biofeedback. See Gerald Jonas, *Visceral Learning: Toward a Science of Self-Control* (New York: Viking, 1973); also, Judith A. Green, "The Mind-Body Hyphen: Social Implications, *Social Policy,* IV, 4 (January–February 1974).
40. Discussed in Robert N. Wilson and Samuel W. Bloom, "Patient-Practitioner Relationships," in Howard E. Freeman, *et al.,* eds., *Handbook of Medical Sociology,* 2d ed. (Englewood Cliffs, N.J.: Prentice-Hall, 1972).
41. *Ibid.,* p. 323.

If the analogy for the first approach, activity-passivity, is the parent-infant; for the guidance-cooperation approach it is parent-child; and for the mutual cooperation approach it is adult-adult.

"The choice of a type of relationship that is inappropriate to the situation produces dysfunctional consequences."[42] This is seen, in particular, regarding chronic diseases which, as we noted above, are (along with preventative problems) the key medical problems of an advanced society. In a chronic disease, such as diabetes, where the patient can be relatively symptom-free, the maintenance of health requires "that the patient participate in the treatment of his [*sic*] disease to an unusual degree. Although treatment methods are usually effective, it is necessary for the patient to be a willing active partner in his [*sic*] own treatment."[43]

However, if instead of the mutual participation, the doctor operates under the guidance-cooperation approach, both the doctor and the patient are likely to see the treatment as doctor-imposed, as it is, and "the emphasis then is on being a good or bad patient and not on maintaining the best possible health."[44]

The mutual cooperation approach is, in effect, a consumer-involving one. It is the one appropriate to the illnesses of our time, to the need for greater lay person involvement in preventative care, and fits better the growing consumer ethos.

Even in the hospital setting the involvement of the patient is crucial. Rather than "viewing hospital patients as helpless persons, much as they may have been frequently when hospitals were used only for surgery and major illnesses,"[45] one can identify "varied undertakings that some patients can undertake at some time during their hospitalization."[46] One set of suggestions grouped these activities under the headings of services to individual patients incapable of self-help, recreational services, physical services, advisory or counsel-

42. *Ibid.,* p. 324.
43. *Ibid.*
44. *Ibid.*
45. Esther Brown, *Newer Dimensions of Patient Care* (New York: Russell Sage Foundation, 1961), p. 86.
46. *Ibid.,* p. 88.

ing services both of general sort and specifically, for example, "talking to, reassuring, and perhaps giving demonstrations to other patients about to undergo similar experiences."[47] Similarly, an aspect of "progressive patient care" includes the "self-care unit which constitutes those who are physically self-sufficient but require diagnostic or convalescent services."[48]

Some Further Illustrations

There are countless well-known examples that demonstrate how the involvement of the consumer in the service relates to its added efficiency. Jane Jacobs, for example, noted a decade ago that the safety of the community was essentially dependent upon the concern of the citizens rather than the police.[49] It is striking that as citizens have become less concerned about other citizens on the streets, the safety of the streets has declined markedly.

The Atkins Diet and many other nutritional approaches, such as Adelle Davis', have literally been eaten up by millions of consumers throughout the United States in controlling their own weight and improving their own health. The Atkins approach, in particular, calls for a special involvement of the client in making urine readings and in counting carbohydrate grams.[50]

To the extent that people come to understand the law better and are enabled to utilize decentralized legal services, the efficiency of the law may improve.[51] In the tenants' movement, a good many citizens have learned about housing and rent control laws and thus have made more efficient their own legal services, including the utilization of their tenants' lawyer more selectively.

47. *Ibid.,* p. 89.

48. Herman M. Somers and Anne R. Somers, *Doctors, Patients, and Health Insurance* (Washington, D.C.: The Brookings Institute, 1961), p. 73.

49. Jane Jacobs, *The Death and Life of Great American Cities* (New York: Vintage Books, 1961).

50. Robert C. Atkins, *Dr. Atkins' Diet Revolution* (New York: David McKay, 1972).

51. The OEO Legal Services Program functions in this manner.

The sex therapy developed by Masters and Johnson[52] illustrates that the involvement of the consumer is absolutely crucial in the effectiveness of the treatment and, of course, this is apparent in practically all mental health intervention except those of a highly directive type.

A program of "peer conducted research" used at a Portsmouth, N.H., high school has proved effective not simply as a way to do research on the behavior and attitudes of the students but as "a tool for prevention and intervention" regarding drug abuse.[53]

The involvement of the consumer can function at many levels. Thus, a community resident who receives good family planning assistance after the birth of her child may involve other citizens or neighbors in the community, and even organize small groups to discuss these issues, thus greatly adding to the family planning services available. Movements such as the youth movement and the women's movement have involved people in providing services in new consumer-involving ways that appear to add to service output: youth hot lines, feminine counselors, runaway houses, job corps. The tremendous expansion of "growth and development" activities, many of which are not deeply professionalized, greatly increases the services available in society largely coming from consumer to consumer, peer to peer, with minimal professional backup.

We are not suggesting the removal of the professional or the leader. Rather, we would propose new roles in which the professional may be the catalyst, stimulator, orchestrator, manager, supervisor, who is directing skills and know-how toward the maximum involvement of the consumer, student, client, parent, not merely for the sake of their participation and all that may mean in emotional terms, but also very specifically to improve the quality of the service, the learning, the mental health, whatever. The training and managerial skills of the professional will have to be quite different and will have to be focused outward upon the consumers, directed toward methods of

52. William H. Masters and Virginia E. Johnson, *Human Sexual Response* (Boston: Little, Brown, 1966).

53. Ernst Wenk, "Peer Conducted Research: A Novel Approach in Drug Education," a paper presented at the First International Congress on Drug Education, Geneva, October 1973.

involving them and organizing the system so that it will encourage better consumer input. Thus, in a school which plans to have all the children teach other children, there are special problems of logistics as well as issues related to preparing the children, parents, and others, for this new program. The actual process itself of children teaching children is not complicated, but the organization of it for maximal efficiency is quite another matter. (In the next chapter, we discuss the issues of training and management of consumer-centered human service practice.)

PARTICIPATION IS NOT ENOUGH

The role of community control in providing a context of an indirect kind is important to understand. If the community has a say in what is to be learned, who is to be employed, and how the learning is to be organized, then it is likely that the students will be much more involved in the school, more likely to be motivated to work hard— that it, to be effective producers in their own learning. However, while community participation is an improvement antecedent to the kind of consumer input we have been describing, it is not sufficient in and of itself. People may participate without any improvement in their learning; they may not become engaged in teaching themselves, learning how to learn, listening more carefully, or any cognitive mechanism related to a jump in performance. In many cases, the participation may be a detour; although it may be valuable on its own terms, it may fail in leading to increased productivity. Hence, it is important that we give careful attention to the mechanisms of connecting participation (or any other approach) to expanded consumer involvement in the actual performance or the function—whether it be learning, health services, or whatever. Much attention must be given to the various mechanisms whereby a consumer's involvement increases productivity—participation alone is not enough.

Most of what we are suggesting is not new, of course. Making learning self-directed, giving the students and their community a role in the school, increasing the students' motivation, are all well-known ideas. What we are suggesting is that these and similar efforts need to be recast in the context of seeing students as the key factors in their own learning. By enlisting the student as a force in the production of learning, by focusing other inputs so as to facilitate this role, the product of the work, the student's learning, will be maximized.

This approach we have outlined obviously is potentially highly economical in that it vastly expands the service resources of the system and thereby increases the productivity of the producer—that is, the teachers or other professionals and the agency. This is quite a different model, however, from the current approach to increasing productivity of teachers—for example, by having them teach more students. The danger in the latter is that the teaching may become less effective; teaching more—not teaching better.

MANY CAUTIONS

There are even more dangerous potential uses of the consumer-as-server design than its misuse as a cost-saving scheme. In a sense, the organizing of prisoners to maintain discipline in a prisoner of war camp is a form of consumer as server, and, so, too, was the use of Jews in Germany (and other prisoners of the Nazis) to organize their own extermination (*Judenrat*). Also, recent legal action here has uncovered the exploitation of mental institution patients in the guise of doing work as part of their own rehabilitation. And if the consumer is the key force in the production of service, the question of responsibility for service failure arises in a new context with the potential for a particularly insidious version of "blaming the victim" rather than the structure.

Akin to these issues is the one of the social control function of the services. We have noted, above, the social control functions of the education system, and cited Ehrenreich and English as to the role of the medical system in the control of women. Much has been written of the social control function of the mental health system, and Piven and Cloward have made clear the role of the welfare system.[54] Clearly the delivery mode is not neutral.

54. Frances Fox Piven and Richard A. Cloward, *Regulating the Poor: The Functions of Public Welfare* (New York: Pantheon, 1971).

Barbara Ehrenreich acutely makes the point that one must assess what happens to the social control function of a particular service when there is a switch from a provider-dominated to a more consumer-intensive mode of delivery. She suggests two possibilities.

1. The more consumer-intensive delivery mode simply provides a more appealing package for a service that is not selling well in the provider-dominated mode. For example, "youth tutoring youth" could become a more efficient and attractive way of selling the ideological content of public education to otherwise recalcitrant target groups, e.g., ghetto youth. In this case, the more consumer-intensive mode could be seen as a stratagem for enlisting the oppressed in their own oppression.
2. The more consumer-intensive mode may fundamentally alter and even subvert the social control functions of the service. To take youth-tutoring-youth again: This kind of participation in service production may *empower* kids to such an extent that many of the oppressive ideological messages of education are negated. On another level, it may lead the student participants to challenge tracking, grading, etc. [Emphasis in the original.][55]

Techniques, of course, are not neutral. Any can be used counter to the presumed good intentions of their designers or their potential. Ehrenreich makes the point well in regard to women's health.

Take two popular forms of women's self-help—gynecological self-help and Weight Watchers. (Self-help is the ultimate consumer-intensive delivery mode: The provider is eliminated, or so thoroughly merged with the recipient that the "provider"/"recipient" categories become meaningless.) I'm convinced that gynecological self-help effectively subverts the social control functions of conventional women's medical services. The recipient (participant) is freed from medical mystifications about her own body and learns that she is the sole expert on her body and its needs. She is empowered to face the conventional providers (which she must, because self-help is a long way from embracing comprehensive care), in an active, questioning, stance.

On the other hand, Weight Watchers seem to me to be a clear-cut case of enlisting women in their own oppression. The great majority of

55. Barbara Ehrenreich, Letter to the Editor, *Social Policy,* IV, 4 (January–February 1974).

Weight Watchers are not pathologically obese women, but ordinary women who are striving desperately to fit into socially determined norms of feminine beauty. The prime Weight Watcher tactics—ridicule and humiliation—are superbly designed to enforce the notions that (1) the "overweight" woman is despicable and unsexy, and (2) that *all* women are self-indulgent, child-like creatures.

My own feeling is that the service production mode—relatively consumer-intensive or provider-intensive—is *not* a neutral package, but that it profoundly alters the *content* of the service. Just how the content is altered is a question which needs our very serious attention in each case.[56]

It is indeed correct that a particular mode or technique constrains against or conduces toward a particular direction and what is necessary to do is to abet that tendency (or to fight against it, as necessary).

We believe that the consumer-intensive design does conduce toward a fuller and more self-determining role for the consumer, that it encourages both greater effectiveness for the consumer and when carried out *in concert with consumer participation in governance,* this effectiveness will more likely be consumer-determined and consumer-benefiting. None of this is guaranteed. All of this requires struggle, and all of it is continuingly at question.

Another set of issues concerning the consumer as producer relates to redistribution and costs. As presently considered, consumer time (like housekeeping time) bears no money cost, though, of course, there is a real cost in things forgone. As consumer-intensive designs develop, we will need a new calculus to assess these costs and to determine their effect upon equality. At question, of course, is whether differential capacities (and opportunities) to be effective consumer-intensive participants will not serve to widen inequalities.[57]

Again, the issue is not predetermined or foreclosed. While the consumer-intensive design, we believe, conduces toward greater equality, the struggle necessary is to assure that that is the case.

56. *Ibid.*
57. S. M. Miller, personal communication, December 10, 1973.

CONCLUSION

The consumer-intensive approach dovetails with the modern critique of bureaucracy. A major criticism of bureaucratic organization is that it does not serve the client but rather serves the bureaucratic system itself, producing perhaps some internal efficiency (although it has dysfunctions here as well). The basic thrust of the consumer-intensive approach is deeply antibureaucratic and antihierarchical because it rests on the assumption that the efficiency of the system comes at the point of relationship, the point of contact, between the consumer and server, *not within the service system itself,*[58] unless the changes in the latter are fundamentally related to the consumer.

Attempts at the "industrialization" and bureaucratization of the human services are doomed to failure, marked by enormous resistance from both service workers and consumers.[59] Even in the nonservice industrial spheres, traditional managerial methods of or-

58. Note the contrast with Levitt's point that "manufacturing looks for solutions inside the very tasks to be done." Levitt, *op. cit.,* p. 43.

59. Even the definitions of productivity are difficult and complex:

The traditional definition of productivity used in manufacturing industries— the number of units produced (output) divided by the manhours to produce them (input)—is not really applicable to local government, which provides specialized services but does not "produce" anything tangible. "What is a unit of safe streets?" wonders Karen Gerard, urban economist for Chase Manhattan Bank.

Just how knotty the problem is shows up in a number of the 300 indexes used to measure productivity in New York. For example, one measure reported by the city's Health & Hospital Corp. is "number of emergency room visits." "The problem with that," says John Tepper Marlin, executive director of the New York-based Council on Municipal Performance, a nonprofit group trying to measure and compare the quality of municipal services, "is that knowing how many people visited emergency rooms says nothing about the quality of treatment or the cost of service."

As Marlin implies, hard-to-measure quality of service is as much a part of productivity measurement as the "number of cases processed" or "number of violations issued," two other typical measures used in New York's program. But quantifying quality leaves most experts scratching their heads. Says Edward K. Hamilton: "You cannot measure the smell of garbage *not* in front of someone's house because it was picked up on a collection day."

("Boosting Urban Efficiency," *Business Week,* January 5, 1947, p. 39.)

ganization have increasingly come under scrutiny in recent years, in particular the bureaucratic, hierarchical emphasis along with the rationalization and minute division of labor. The classic approach to the organization of work developed by Frederick Taylor does not seem congenial to many modern workers and thus old managerial principles are undergoing serious revision. (This is not to say, of course, that some of the newer participatory managerial approaches being experimented with in industry may not have important applicability in the service areas.)

The very character of the services with their highly relational, interpersonal component somewhat constrains against this mechanization, rationalization, and "Taylorization." On the other hand, the very special role of the consumer—as a major force for increased service productivity—opens up enormous possibilities as yet largely untapped by current managerial perspectives. Consumers are more and more becoming a new force of production in the service society and their economic significance may have important political implications as well.

9   Training for Consumer-Oriented Practice

> Training, then, should involve the whole organization in an effort to reset its directions, orientations, strategies, as well as tactics. Professional as well as bureaucratic encrustations have to be overcome. We will have to be re-educating practitioners as well as retraining them, reorganizing and remolding agencies as well as adding new services to them.
>
> —S. M. Miller, "Training as Organizational and Professional Change"

We have seen the enormous potential of the consumer in improving human service practice. But to actualize this potential, the training of practitioners must prepare them for practice that is consumer-centered. One important way of doing this is to make that training itself consumer-centered, that is, built around the trainees. This serves to give them an object lesson in how to provide consumer-centered practice. Too often, programs of professional preparation focus only on the curriculum content and forget that the medium is often the message, and, thus, the form of teaching is as important as the content.

Training is, in part, a kind of socialization. And the training we propose must socialize the new professionals to understand the consumer point of view. Professional schools must not be the private preserves of their professors, just as practice agencies do not belong to the practitioners. To borrow (with slight modification) a phrase from the Chinese, we must *put the consumer in command.*

A central aspect of the content of consumer-oriented training is that it be skill-centered. The service to be performed must be carefully analyzed and the training built upon this analysis.[1] This may seem self-evident. However, in fact, much of the preparation of human service practitioners is knowledge- and process-centered, rather than *outcome*-centered. This is why we stress evaluation so much. A skill-centered training design moves more directly to that which is of direct help to the consumer and we need evaluation measures to insure that this occurs.

In law, medicine, social work, and teaching, the first organized preparation of practitioners took place near the practice situation—in the doctors' or lawyers' offices, or in proprietary schools run initially by the practitioner, or in the normal schools of Massachusetts, or the training schools associated with social work agencies. In the latter part of the nineteenth century, professional preparation moved into the university, although not always becoming an integral part of it. While the early practice-based preparation suffered from a lack of rigor, scientific knowledge, and perspective, the university-based training is too often academic, distant from practice, overly theoretical, knowledge- not skill-based. What is called for, we believe, is a *new integration of theory and practice.* The centrality of this issue leads us to devote considerable attention in this chapter to new training approaches directed toward this end.

Along with a skill focus a second central aspect of consumer-oriented training is that it be deprofessionalized, demystified, accessible to the consumer. Deprofessionalization is the first step toward reprofessionalization. Practitioners will need to learn how to contact and utilize consumers in human service practice, how to use the

1. The key here is task analysis. It must be done, however, not in the standard static manner; that is, analyzing practice as it is presently provided. The basis of the analysis of activities and tasks undertaken and the skills and knowledge necessary to carry them out should be the practice sought, not necessarily the current operational practice. It is from this consumer-involving analysis that the training should be built.

strength of consumers, how to share with them. In order to do this, the new professional must learn about the more consumer-based alternative institutions and the delivery of human services in other countries, such as China, Cuba, and Israel, which seem to give special attention to the role of the consumer in service practice.

The various new consumer-focused delivery formats, *viz.,* street academies, contact curriculum, schools without walls, free clinics, self-help groups, need to be known both for the lessons derived for the new professionals' own practice, as well as for the resource they may provide. That is, study of these new delivery modes may be desirable for incorporation into the practice of the professional-in-training, and knowledge about these modes and the institutions that use them may provide useful referral sources.

Ways to make services more accessible, how to contact and engage the consumer, *viz.,* changing the service's style and/or structure, use of indigenous workers, neighborhood service centers, and contact curriculum, should be known, and ways to incorporate them into practice learned.

Certain modalities of training are more effective for the delivery of the content outlined above, and more in keeping with consumer-centered practice. Role playing, particularly role reversals, is key. When the trainee plays the role of consumer, he or she is able both to "feel" what it is to be a consumer, and to see how particular practitioner actions affect the consumer. Role plays and simulations allow the development and testing out of particular techniques and practices.

Consonant with the emphasis upon a skill-centered preparation is a field base to it. And derivative from the field base, and other experiences of the practitioner-in-training, is the development of an inductive curriculum, that is, a curriculum built around the experience and practice of the students. The participatory simulation design which we discuss below incorporates these features.

Finally, we seek to make the preparation of practitioners isomorphic with the practice for which they are preparing. The old cliché that teachers teach as they are taught, not as they are taught to teach, has in it a large body of truth. Thus, the preparation of the new professional must itself be consumer-centered. In McLuhan's phrase, "The medium is the message."

Having looked in Chapter 7 to the wider world of professional preparation, we will here turn to details of training, giving particular attention to efforts to integrate theory and practice with the introduction of participatory simulation as a key device, and toward keying on the skills necessary for and the feelings involved in consumer-centered practice.

TRAINING: A PART OF THE SOLUTION

There are some who would make the case that training, pre- and/or in-service, is the panacea to change the services. We make no such argument. Indeed, we recognize that in many instances the call for training is a diversionary step, designed to avoid undertaking structural and institutional changes. Surely, the manpower (*sic*) policies of the past decade have most often substituted training for the needed jobs.[2]

There is little reliable data as to the actual effect upon practice, to say nothing of impact upon the consumer or the service,[3] of this or that type of professional preparation. What little evidence there is is largely restricted to the medical field. There, a few studies have found that the work environment is more important in explaining some elements of performance than is professional preparation.[4] Compar-

2. Alan Gartner, Russell A. Nixon, and Frank Riessman, eds., *Public Service Employment* (New York: Praeger, 1973); Harold L. Sheppard, Bennett Harrison, and William J. Spring, eds., *The Political Economy of Public Service Employment* (Lexington, Mass.: Lexington Books, 1972).

3. This question is at the heart of the debate around the implementation of Competency-Based Teacher Education and Performance-Based Teacher Certification. For a well-argued advocate's position, see Benjamin Rosner, *The Power of Competency-Based Teacher Education* (Boston: Allyn & Bacon, 1972).

4. See Oscar L. Peterson, *et al.,* "An Analytic Study of North Carolina General Practice," *Journal of Medical Education*, XXXI, 2 (December 1956), Part 2, pp. 1–165; Kenneth F. Clute, *The General Practitioner, A Study of Medical Education and Practice in Ontario and Nova Scotia* (Toronto: University of Toronto Press, 1963); P. B. Price, *et al.,* "The Effect of Medical Specialization

ing the effects of one training institution to those of another, as do these studies, however, may not be the appropriate way to assess the impact of professional preparation. For what they show is not that such preparation itself is effectless, but, rather, using the indices of effect employed, the differences between the effect of this or that training institution, all of which have much in common, generally, are not statistically significant.

We, then, seek neither to magnify nor to understate the role of training. In Chapter 7 we have talked of the contextual issues that affect practice; in Chapter 8, we have discussed what we believe to be the key factor in the practice itself, namely, the consumer as a force of production and the need to organize the practice (and train the practitioners) around this factor; and in Chapter 10, we will discuss issues of organizing and managing human service practice. Training, then, is a part, important but not alone, in shaping the practice and its effects. We are concerned with each of these factors. Here our attention is focused upon factors internal to the professional preparation—such as content, faculty, teaching methods, relationship of theory and practice, place of training, along with those external to it—who is admitted to the preparation,[5] at what point in their lives,[6] according to what standards; and how the training is related to professional practice as well as to larger societal developments.

---

on Physicians' Attitudes," *Journal of Health and Human Behavior,* VII (1966), pp. 128–132; Elliot Friedson, *Profession of Medicine: A Study of the Sociology of Applied Knowledge* (New York: Dodd, Mead, 1972), pp. 87–90.

5. "It would appear that the people who staff the professional training programs have far less control over the development of their trainees than most of them would like. They have even less control over their trainees' prior socialization, although it may be that it has more influence over the process of becoming a professional than we have previously considered." Rue Bucher, Joan Stilling, and Paul Dommermuth, "Differential Prior Socialization: A Comparison of Four Professional Training Programs," *Social Forces,* XLVIII, 2 (December 1969), p. 223.

6. Note that professional socialization, for the most part, takes place in the United States at the same time as "when students make the transition from adolescence to adulthood, as well as from layman [sic] to professional." The interrelationships—of mutual benefit or dissonance—between these two processes warrant further study. Virginia L. Olsen and Elvi W. Whittaker, *The Silent Dialogue* (San Francisco: Jossey-Bass, 1969), p. 9.

Theory and Practice

Preparation that is overly theoretical, academic, is too distant from the consumer, too distant from the actual needs of practice. On the other hand, preparation that is only practice-based will be far too limited, lacking in perspective and breadth. What is to be sought is an integration of the two, theory and practice, in a preparation design that is more targeted, consumer-centered, concerned with the needs of practice not of professional status.[7]

In examining current activities in the preparation of practitioners for law, medicine, social work, and teaching, one can see varying efforts to strike a new balance between theory and practice.

The amount of time devoted to field experience during the period of professional preparation is greatest in social work, with from 40 to 60 percent of the student's time spent in field placement. In undergraduate medical education, a third to a half of the last two years is spent in clinical clerkship; of course, the internship and residency are almost entirely clinical training. In education, usually a single course (often for more than normal credit) is devoted to practice teaching. In law, where it occurs, clinical experience usually consists of a course or two. The trend in at least the three fields which devote least time to field experience is to increase it.

Only in social work is the practice component of the training introduced at the beginning of the training. The norm in both medicine and education is to lay the theoretical foundation and then to provide the field experience.

In medicine, the clinical clerkship almost always takes place in the medical school's teaching hospital(s). In none of the other fields is it the case that the training institution universally operates a service institution. Laboratory schools are dwindling and those in existence

7. The following material comparing the professional preparation of doctors, lawyers, social workers, and teachers is drawn from Alan Gartner, "The Professional Preparation of Doctors, Lawyers, Social Workers, and Teachers: A Cross Sectoral Study of Efforts to Integrate Theory and Practice," unpublished manuscript (1972).

do not see themselves as primarily a resource for practice teaching. In a few instances, schools of social work (and in even fewer instances, law schools) operate service agencies. Most students in education, social work, and law undergo their field experience in an institution separate and divorced from their training school.

As a consequence of the institutional relationship between the medical school and the teaching hospital, the "field faculty" (practice teachers and supervisors) of the hospital generally have joint appointments at the medical school. As the institutional pattern of medical school and associated teaching hospital is not replicated in any of the other fields, so, too, the relationship of "field faculty" to training institution in them differs from that in medicine. Day-to-day supervision of the work of education, social work, or law students is usually left to persons on the staff of the school, agency, or office where the students are placed. In general, although least so in social work, these people have little if any relationship to the training institution. In each of the three fields, someone from the training institution has responsibility for the field placement but usually that responsibility is thin and the relationship of those bearing it tangential to the training institution.

The "field faculty" are rarely provided systematic training in their roles. It is assumed, it seems, that skill in practice or sometimes only scholarly knowledge of the field is sufficient. Some schools of social work provide (and a few require) courses in supervision for field placement supervisors; a few schools of education provide (and a bare handful require) courses for cooperating teachers; a bare handful of medical schools provide (and none require) such training for doctors who supervise the clinical clerkship; and no law school either regularly provides or requires such training for those who supervise the clinical experience.

While the joint appointment of teaching hospital and medical staff provides a form of integration of theory and practice, in fact, it is most common for the basic science courses of the first two years of medical school not to be taught by clinicians but by researchers. And in the other three fields there is not even medical education's institutional connection between the teaching faculty and the practice site's staff.

The clinical faculty of the medical school usually maintain at least a consultative practice. In the other three fields, teaching faculty usually do not practice although some social work faculty (and even fewer education school faculty) may do a limited amount of consultation but that is usually at the policy or management level and is rarely directly related to practice.

Not only do law school faculty not engage in practice activities while teaching, usually they have not engaged in general practice prior to joining the faculty.[8] This pattern of faculty coming to the professional school without prior experience in practice is growing in both schools of social work and education, but still remains less than usual. Almost all clinical professors in medical schools have practiced, although this is less true in the case of teachers of the basic sciences.

Each of the fields seeks to relate practice and theory. They rely, in part, on some of the features we have noted—institutional ties between school and practice site, individual roles of field faculty and teaching faculty, the particular temporal juxtaposition of theoretic and field work, *viz.,* in social work the simultaneity of the two and in the other fields the subsequent practice experience serves to provide illustration to the theoretic base. In addition, various other mechanisms are used to connect the two. Some are merely mechanical, such as holding the school's courses at the practice site. Others are integrative only by title, that is, a college course (or seminar) where the field experience is discussed. In yet other cases, the integration effort is more serious; perhaps the best representative is the well-run clinical rounds in a medical school, although too often that can become an exercise in quickness and memory.

---

8. Success on the law review and in clerking for an appellate court judge are the most commonly measured legal work experiences used in assessing prospective faculty for a law school. Whatever their importance, those activities have little connection to day-to-day practice.

NEW TRAINING FOR NEW SERVICES

For many contemporary critics of the professional preparation of human service practitioners a closer and better integration of theory and practice is the essence of their recommendations. We, too, favor a new relationship between theory and practice and recommend a powerful role in this regard for what we call "participatory simulation" and an experienced-based curriculum. However, we do so not from some abstract notions of learning theory, although these are relevant, but from the nature of the practice for which the practitioners are being prepared, practice which increasingly is (and needs even more to be) consumer-centered.

Because of the insistent demands and widespread dissatisfaction of consumers—and the recognition among professionals that the traditional ways are not always appropriate today—significant changes have been emerging in human services practice. In thinking about a new training design, it is important to outline these emerging changes. Then, the content, form, and style of the training can reflect the new service styles and prepare the service workers of tomorrow to handle effectively the kinds of situations they are likely to encounter.

The new services have the following three key characteristics, each with its derivative consequence for training:

The service is to be consumer-centered. If consumer-centered service-giving is crucial to drastic improvement of human services, then training must prepare human service workers for it. There must be courses and curriculum material with this focus. Even more important than talk and reading about consumer participation, the training must reflect this dimension as far as possible. This means that the training must have high trainee participation, rather than center around the trainer or focus on professional perspectives. When training is completed and the professional begins his or her work, the social worker should be responsive to the client, the teacher to the pupil, and the physician to the patient. Therefore, one must insist that in the training, the trainer be responsive to the trainees and the training responsive to the trainees' needs, including their perceptions of those needs.

The service is to be accountable and efficient. This means that the training model should be geared to developing the specific skills the trainee will require for effective service delivery.

Service should be expanded to meet pressing needs. Since demands for services are growing, the training must be as rapid as possible. New forms of education and training must be developed that will produce the new worker in much less time and in a much more relevant, task-oriented, and efficient fashion. This is also true for in-service training and staff development.

Plumbers Versus Pilots

How is training in other fields preparing workers to cope with the kinds of problems they face in today's technological society? Comparing the training of two other types of workers—plumbers and airplane pilots—provides clues to what a positive training model for workers in the human services might be like, recognizing, of course, that neither plumbers nor pilots are human service workers.

It takes four years to train a plumber but only eighteen months to train an airplane pilot. A look at the respective training designs readily shows why. Plumbers are generally trained as apprentices, and this process unnecessarily stretches the training. In contrast, airplane pilots learn to master the instruments of flight mainly by using simulators such as the Link Trainer, which is essentially a hooded cockpit on the ground. The trainee climbs into this cockpit and the instructor radios to the trainee problems of ever-increasing difficulty. The trainees in turn attempt to handle them and receive feedback on their performance. They learn to master each problem; then the instructor tests skills valuable for the next stage.

The pilot is trained in a carefully phased sequence using simulated exercises designed to develop highly complex skills. The training is directed by experienced trainers and the phases of simulated experiences are related to phases of later inflight training.

In contrast, the apprenticeship model in plumbing permits an inexperienced trainer who happens to be an able plumber to train the novice entirely on the job. Not only is the plumber untrained as a trainer, but he actually has a job that in many ways interferes with and prolongs the training he gives the apprentice. Furthermore, the specific tasks done as the apprenticeship proceeds are not sequenced so that the trainee learns the necessary skills in the order of their difficulty. Rather, the apprentice sees and hopefully learns the tasks relevant to performance of the work the plumber is doing on any one day. Ultimately, he may have the opportunity to fit the different parts together and acquire the necessary skills. The trainee performs the actual task under the watchful eye of the experienced plumber, but if he could do a comparable task in a simulated, protected setting, he would be able to try out various approaches without the hazard of damaging the plumbing system.

The training of human service workers much more closely resembles the prolonged indirect learning of the plumber than the planned program of the pilot. Most human service workers have been trained in the traditional professional model, which is not oriented to the rapid development of highly complex skills leading to efficient consumer-focused services. Friedson, Hughes, and others have noted that the professional model has emphasized accountability to peers.[9]

Most professional training grew out of an elite tradition in which the major concern was that the professional-to-be should acquire a definite point of view and perspective about the work to be done. For example, the law student is trained, not so much to do legal work as to be a lawyer. Nader described the process when he said, "Law professors take delight in crushing egos in order to acculturate the students to what they call 'legal reasoning' or 'thinking like a

9. See Eliot Friedson, *op. cit.,* and Everett Hughes, "Professions," *Daedalus,* XCII, 4 (Fall 1963), pp. 665–668.

lawyer.' "[10] There was no hurry about acquiring the necessary skills. In fact, it was part of the tradition that the professional should acquire these skills in a rather leisurely fashion from other peers through a long internship or apprenticeship.

In general, professional practice and training aim to maintain a monopoly over the necessary skills and knowledge and to limit the number of people who can acquire such skills and knowledge. Thus, restrictive licenses and expensive, prolonged training are highly appropriate, just as they are useful in maintaining the monopoly of the plumbers' union.

Since there was no hurry to train the human service workers— whether physicians, teachers, lawyers, or social workers—and no consumer demand for accountability of the tasks performed, it was easy to maintain the traditional highly stretched-out training and education, thereby protecting the semi-monopoly of the existing professional stratum.

In the present period, however, there is a whole wave of new demands initially from consumers, the poor, and the minorities, and, at least in regard to medicine, from women, who have complained bitterly about the character of the services provided by the professional. In addition, these excluded groups (here including women) are demanding entrance into the profession; that is, they want to become doctors, lawyers, teachers, and social workers, and they are not at all so sure that it should take so long to acquire the necessary skills. Both of these pressures (and, at least in the case of medicine, the high cost of practice and training) have led to the demand for evaluation of both performance and training. This is all part of the general ethos demanding accountability to the consumer on the part of practitioners, and new forms of education and training which will much more rapidly produce the new worker and produce him/her in a much more relevant, task-oriented, efficient fashion.

10. Ralph Nader, "Law Schools and Law Firms," *New Republic* (October 11, 1969), pp. 20–23.

New Core for Service Training: Participatory Simulation

Little serious thought has been given to a careful delineation of what can be best taught/learned in the classroom and what at the work site, what is achieved as a result of practice and what from theory, and how the two can best be interconnected. The one without the other is inadequate. So, too, a simple sequential pattern of first one or the other is also inadequate. What seems to be more appropriate is moving back and forth between the two, in part as the scope of concern broadens from topic to topic, and also in order to gain deeper knowledge and greater skill in a particular area. The experience of practice as well as the study of theory both offer answers and raise questions. For some students greater learning will take place in one forum or the other, or they may get into the material better via one facet or the other;[11] but for all, it would seem to be necessary that the two areas be experienced and that learning take place in both.

In the practice situation one becomes acculturated to the norms, pace, and mores of the work setting. The student experiences the reality of the practice, "learns the ropes," gains an understanding of how to relate to the various persons, places, and things of the work situation.[12] Here, skills can be tested, polished, and (to a lesser extent) learned. Individual style(s) can be tested. Patterns of relationships to peers, superiors, and clients can be experienced and developed.

But the virtue of the practice setting is at once the cause of its inadequacy in preparation of practitioners. For the primary obligation of the practice setting must be to deliver quality services to consumers. Thus, the pattern of work cannot easily be organized to suit the needs of the learner—namely, a particular set of problems or

11. See Frank Riessman, *Strategies Against Poverty* (New York: Random House, 1969), Ch. V, "The Strategy of Style."

12. Blanche Geer, *et al.,* "Learning the Ropes" in Irving Deutscher and Elizabeth Thompson, eds., *Among the People* (New York: Basic Books, 1968), p. 228.

symptoms cannot be arranged for at a given time or in a specified order; rather, they come in the flow of the work. In practice, it is not easy to find the time/space to look at a problem, to study a situation for its own sake, to repeat or to go back a step; the service demands must be met. And to the extent that the practice situation is juggled to meet these training needs (e.g., reduced and/or selected case load), then it loses some of the reality that is its uniqueness.

On the other hand, the academic arena offers the opportunity to reflect, to compare, to speculate, to (as in the meaning of the Greek root of *theory,* the same as that for *theater*) get an overview of things, to see the whole scene. Also, it offers an opportunity to develop the bases for further learning, to build patterns of inquiry and exploration, to gain different perspectives, to reflect upon the practice experience.

But, as is true of the practice setting, the academic arena, too, has its shortcomings. And it seems that the mere combining of the two is not sufficient.

If modern training of human service workers is to go beyond the limits of the academic classroom and avoid prolonged on-the-job apprenticeship, it will have to develop a new core. We see simulation—which, of course, is used in a good deal of skill training, such as that of airplane pilots—as a central feature of this training.[13]

Simulation is already becoming important in medical instruction. Computer models have been designed and are currently used in a number of medical schools. They present situations

which offer the student the opportunity to manipulate data, make mistakes, get into trouble, and get out of trouble—all without endangering patients or using up valuable hospital time.

Dr. Stephen Abrahamson and associates at the University of Southern California have developed a simulation model known as "Sim One" to facilitate clinical training in anesthesia. This life-size manikin has several functions, such as respiratory activity, skin color, and pupillary size, which are under the computer's control. Each function responds to drug

---

13. Of course, we recognize, however, that work in the human services has dimensions that make it qualitatively different from the work of a pilot, and the use of simulation, as discussed below, will be different there than for pilots.

administration as well as to other interventions used by the anesthesiologist in managing patients in surgery. This model can be used by a trainee to interact with a variety of situations that he will shortly encounter in the real-life operating room. . . .

Dr. William Harless and associates at the University of Illinois have developed a computer-sized simulation of the clinical encounter (CASE). During the interaction session, the computer assumes the role of the patient, and the student assumes the role of the practicing physician. Virtually any type of patient with any variety of health problems can be simulated.[14]

Simulation designs alone, however, do not fully fit the needs for the training of the service worker. Typical models, such as the design using the Link Trainer for pilots or the computer designs of the medical schools, present the kind of situation that demands a single correct or preferred response by the student. The training aims to teach the student to discover and carry out that preferred action. However, in the human services there may be many correct ways to handle a problem, or the correct way may not be known. Thus, the training must use a more open kind of simulation. Its goals should include developing individual styles, coordinating knowledge, and building new techniques.

A participatory training design can include these goals. Furthermore, it adds to the simulation group and peer dimensions that are especially valuable if training is to match the new participatory character of services.

—It encourages increasing use of members of different disciplines and backgrounds, working in teams or groups, to prepare trainees for service delivery in health, mental health, education, and social work.
—This group-centered interdisciplinary training tends to bring about cross-socialization of trainees and broaden their perspective.
—It also promotes the development of practitioners who find stimulating and helpful colleagues among their peers.

14. "Educational Technology for Medicine," *Journal of Medical Education* (July 1971).

—The design provides a situation conducive to learning by all who participate in the transaction. The learning process is most effective when this occurs; and, of course, a professor-centered training design deters learning by the teacher. The point of the helper being helped or the teacher learning is most evident in education in the learning-through-teaching design.[15] The process can also be seen in the "helper therapy" principle in mental health and social work.[16] Indeed, it may be true throughout the human services that the transaction between service-giver and service-recipient is most powerful when it involves reciprocal gain.

One can apply participatory simulation to all kinds of training. In training social workers, for example, situations can be set up in which a number of workers-in-training play the roles of clients and one plays the role of the social worker. Various problems are role-played or simulated. For example, some trainees may play clients acting in a hostile or aggressive manner at a group meeting, and the trainee playing the social worker practices various ways of dealing with these disruptive clients. At first, the trainee playing the social worker probably tries out fairly standard approaches. The whole group then discusses the simulation to see whether the situation could be handled differently. The group collectivizes its experience and brainstorms the problem, at first suggesting other specific approaches, then moving on to possible solutions.

The trainers may introduce new ideas or questions: Could the worker handle the problem by dealing with the client group as a whole rather than with individual members? Should the worker change the focus and try a different approach? Should all the clients discuss together problems of group order? Does the disruption perhaps indicate an inappropriate topic that is not appealing to group members? Could the worker perhaps change the atmosphere of the

15. See Alan Gartner, Mary Conway Kohler, and Frank Riessman, *Children Teach Children: Learning by Teaching* (New York: Harper & Row, 1971).

16. See Frank Riessman, "The 'Helper-Therapy' Principle," *Social Work*, X, 2 (April 1965), pp. 27–32.

meeting through an indirect approach, e.g., changing the seating arrangement?

The trainees might then try out various new approaches. They might change the seating structure of the make-believe meeting and see the different effect of having the group seated in a circle rather than in rows. Or they might move the chairs back in a larger circle or move them closer and see people's reactions. Thus, the trainees actually act out proposed solutions to problems.

In such a simulation, the trainees slowly become more aware of what can be done in a real situation, as well as gain practice in working out problems. From this, they begin to carve out and expand styles of their own. Each probably selects quite different approaches from the wide range of possibilities suggested by the group. Then each adapts the chosen suggestions to his or her style, becoming more conscious of that style as the repertoire of approaches grows.

In playing the role of the social worker, the trainees get feedback, reflecting what is effective and what is not. Trainees may take turns in playing the client and worker roles. It is possible to videotape the simulation, giving trainees a direct view of how they behave. Social workers in training or those having in-service training may move from simulated sessions to a microcounseling design in which they can practice new skills in a controlled setting with a small number of persons.[17] Like the simulated sessions, microcounseling can be videotaped. Trainees then may proceed to practice under careful supervision.

The entire training of the workers is carefully phased. Initially situations are simulated. In the next stage the workers might move into a neighborhood storefront center each morning, carefully supervised and backed up by trained, experienced workers. They come back to the simulation sessions each afternoon and discuss the prob-

17. Microcounseling is a variant of the microteaching technique developed by Dwight Allen and colleagues at Stanford University. The basic technique involves a teacher-in-training who practices a specific skill with a small number of students for a short period of time. In the counseling variant, a specific skill is practiced with a few clients for a short time.

lems confronted in the centers. Slowly they spend more time in the centers, on the job, with less intensive supervision.

In a sense, these workers are overtrained positively. They have acquired the power and skills to deal with problems more complex than they are likely to face. One is reminded of the way Vince Lombardi trained the Green Bay Packers; it was said, similarly, that the practice sessions were much more difficult than the games.

Benefits of Simulation

What are the special benefits of a participatory simulation training design? First, the use of simulation encourages the trainees to learn from each other more than does the model that presents the teacher as the sole dispenser of knowledge.

Then, this design has the dual advantage of shifting the focus, on the one hand, away from the traditional academic classroom instruction and, on the other, away from on-the-job learning through trial and error. The traditional professional training involves a deductive curriculum in which the teacher first presents basic ideas, then has the students react to them and perhaps try to deduce application for practice if they can. The teacher and his or her ideas are central to this design. In contrast, a simulation design centers around the students' experiences and problems that they consider and treat as real phenomena. The teacher has to apply basic concepts to these experiences and problems and develop an inductive curriculum around them.

Participatory simulation training moves the human service workers away from on-the-job trial and error by furnishing them with a protective, permissive setting in which they can observe and try out ways to handle various real-life problems, without incurring real-life consequences. In the agency placements of traditional training (or the traditional student teaching placement), most social workers (or teachers) do not have an opportunity in the field to experiment with different techniques, practices, and approaches. The risks are too great that an experimental procedure may produce disastrous results. Consequently, the worker (or teacher) does not even mentally explore various methods, but instead, seeks to develop quickly something that works at least at a minimal level. This tends to become the specific way that this individual deals with such a problem. The way is frozen and becomes a rigid part of the worker's (or teacher's) permanent style. On the contrary, in simulation, the social worker (or teacher) in training not only has the opportunity to see a variety of approaches, but can actually begin to use different ones, first in situations relatively easy to handle. Through dealing with these simple situations, the trainee builds up coping skills that can be applied and adapted as the situations become increasingly difficult.

The new services that are emerging and that will be further developed must respond to the presenting problem, but must also go beyond it. If the focus was exclusively on immediate problems, technical skills might be sufficient. However, since the new services stress both the immediate and deeper, long-term phenomena, those responsible for the training must be capable of moving with ease back and forth between theory and practice, so that the trainees gain insight into practice from the perspective of theory and understanding of theory from the grounding in practice. This design, therefore, demands far different and broader skills in the trainers than are needed for ruminating about their experiences or pontificating over their own or others' theories.

The simulation model with an inductive curriculum allows for the integration of skills and knowledge so that the resultant product—the human service practitioner—is not simply a skilled technician but rather a true professional. The essence of a professional is the integration of systematic knowledge and skill; either without the other is highly limited. In such a design the training is targeted upon the needs of the practice situation, the trainers are socialized as change agents, and the training is isomorphic with the type of practice desired.

Additional Features of Consumer-Centered Training

Simulation, of the participatory nature we have described, goes a long way toward providing for practitioners-to-be preparation that is focused upon a consumer-centered practice. There are additional features to make training more clearly targeted upon preparation for consumer-centered practice. In preparation for the various aspects of the practice to be desired, practitioners need both skills appropriate to the particular feature of practice and, as well, need to experience the carrying out of such practice. For example, as the practice sought involves accountability upon the part of the practitioner to the consumer, in the preparation of the practitioner-to-be, the deliverer of that preparation must be accountable to his or her students, as well as training them in skills involved in being accountable—how to set goals, establish milestones, assess progress, correct shortfalls. In other words, if the preparation of practitioners is designed to prepare them for practice that is responsive and accountable to the consumer, then that preparation must itself be responsible and accountable to its consumer.

Similarly, as the practice desired is to be productive, and a key to the productivity is engaging the consumer as a factor in the production of the service, the preparation of the practitioners must so engage its consumers, the practitioners-to-be. It must engage them both as an example and an object lesson, and, as well, teach them how to engage consumers (those whom they will serve) in the production of the service. Thus, for example, practitioners need to learn about the customs and mores of those whom they will serve, not as an exercise in exotica or as an anthropological exploration, but both because in knowing about the consumer they will be better able to enlist him or her in the production of the service (i.e., provide it in the style of the consumer), and the activity of learning about the consumer is an expression of the importance of the consumer. Of course, this means that the teacher of the practitioners must in the conduct of the preparation seek to learn about the consumers of that course. It hardly is desirable, as has been the case at a New York City university, to conduct a course in the open classroom entirely through the lecture method!

The effort to know about the consumer is a part of seeking to assess his or her experience, knowledge, values, strengths, in order to attune the practice to them.

Another aspect of training for consumer-centered practice is for the practitioner to become more aware of, reflect upon, be self-conscious about, server-client relationships. Thus, role plays, and particularly role reversals, are key training devices. The doctor-to-be must understand how the patient feels, how various doctor's actions, verbal and nonverbal, overt and manifest, affect the patient. Indeed, the very act of establishing a patient-client relationship (or any other consumer-server relationship) is critical. In addition to role plays, observations, and exercises, as ways of sensitizing practitioners-to-be to how it is and what it feels like to be a service consumer, there is, of course, the personal experience of the practitioner-to-be. Thus, in the training of teachers, one of the key resources is the experience brought to the subject of the students themselves.

Another way to encourage in practitioners greater awareness of practice issues is to engage in both cross-cultural and cross-disciplinary examination. In looking to how other cultures or disciplines address a particular issue or problem, the practitioner-to-be can gain heightened awareness of the generic issues involved, as well as gain potential insights to alternative modes and means.

A second area of benefit to be gained from using the practitioner-to-be's own experience is that it contributes, to coin a phrase, to the "decentralization of the classroom." That is, it serves to deemphasize the teacher, or other professional, as the sole source of knowledge and wisdom and to encourage a more active role upon the part of the consumer. In education, any number of activities which intrude upon the teacher focus in the self-contained classroom are ways to "decentralize" the classroom. Thus, for example, use of the library and other media sources teaches children about additional sources of knowledge. Encouragement of classroom discussion and reports, especially when the teacher does not feel it necessary to respond to or comment upon every point or item, conduces toward such "decentralization." Reliance upon community resources, television, people from outside of the classroom, all lead in this direction. And, when this is done using sources of knowledge from the child's culture, the consumer is put at the center of the practice, as well as the classroom being decentralized. To achieve this in the preparation of practitioners-to-be, that is, to enable them to be consumer-centered practitioners, again this should be the way they are trained, that is, in a nonteacher-centered classroom, and, as well, trained how to marshal and use effectively other resources.

The study of the various alternative institutions—free schools, women's health centers, self-help groups—has multiple potential benefits for practitioners-to-be. First, as these institutions are more consumer-centered, the practitioners-to-be may learn practices helpful to their own practice. Second, they may see how, in practice, a more consumer-centered approach is effected. Third, they may find among such institutions resources of potential use to their clients. Fourth, such study is yet another way to become more alert to and self-conscious about issues of the structure and organization, style and nature of practice and of the professions.

CONCLUSION

Typical professional training in the human services has been explicitly neither skill-centered nor participatory. Both these qualities are essential if services are to become markedly more efficient and more responsive to the consumer.

What, then, are the desired characteristics of the new training model? It must relate directly to a real improvement of service to the consumer; it must help change the traditional professional, whether a service provider or trainer. It must be participatory and open in character. Workers must be trained in ways they will perform.

The modern simulation-centered training design leads to much more rapid development of the trainee's skills. It is compatible with new kinds of trainees who will not tolerate a long-drawn-out apprenticeship under a professional who will slowly socialize them to traditional professional norms. It uses a skill-centered curriculum with systematic professional knowledge built around it.

Training, to be relevant and effective, has to be highly attuned to the tasks, the work, and the activities to be carried out. This requires careful task analyses so that appropriate skills can be developed. Trainers must base the curriculum on a task analysis of what trainees need to do the job and on-job descriptions of the new work. The training should not try simply to teach workers to imitate what the current professional does or is. The era is rapidly coming to an end when professional behavior is valued solely for itself. Moreover, the new trainer is a person trained as a trainer, not just a smart person who happens to do some teaching—like the able plumber who trains the apprentice but knows little or nothing about training techniques.

Traditionally, most human service workers have been given quite a bit of general education, but little skill training. Currently, the pendulum has swung the other way. But unless skills are combined with systematic professional knowledge, there is the danger that this kind of training will produce skilled technicians with narrow perspectives, rather than new professionals. Hence, it is extremely important that the simulated sessions and the experience-based curriculum lead to and focus on broader issues, rather than limit themselves simply to skills and immediate practice. In addition, of course, new systematic professional knowledge must be developed and then become a part of the total educational and training pattern.

Much professional knowledge at the present time is neither adequately related to practice and field experience nor sufficiently based on skills. A revamping of professional knowledge will, hopefully, emerge from new practice and new training designs. Rapping, sensitivity training, and the contact curriculum all have value, but they are not enough. A real leap forward in the character of the services requires sound systematic professional knowledge that is well understood and flexibly applied. Skilled technicians can improve the human services, but they will not produce the necessary leap, the reorganization, the really new and effective human services that are so needed.

10 Management of Consumer-Oriented Practice

> The Children's Bureau was not organized on either the basis of purpose or process but on the basis of the clientele it served. Its orientation was not to fulfill certain set purposes or to discharge certain types of functions but to service a particular group of clients and to service them in all kinds of ways. . . . it cared for the *whole child*. [Emphasis in the original.]
>
> —George E. Berkley, *The Administrative Revolution*

In Chapter 8 we described some of the essential characteristics of practice that is consumer-oriented, while in Chapter 9 we described training that would provide appropriate preparation for such practice. We noted there that training was but a part of the achievement of consumer-oriented practice. So, too, management has but a part, important but not alone, in providing this type of human service practice.

Some organization and management practices can be viewed as positive in terms of consumer orientation, others are negative toward such an orientation, and still others might be called neutral or likely to have effect either way depending upon how they are used.

—Consumer boards, decentralization, use of ombudsmen, expediters, indigenous workers, advocates, as well as the granting of rights to students, patients, and clients are examples of practices that are consonant with consumer-oriented rights.

—Mechanization, "Taylorization," bureaucracy, and hierarchy are inconsonant practices.

—Phasing, keying, and use of a trained cadre may be described as simple and neutral management practices, while vouchers and Program Planning and Budgeting Systems (PPBS) might be called practices that could go either way.

A Typology of Management Practices

Consonant with consumer-oriented practice	Constrain against consumer-oriented practice	Neutral simple techniques	Can go either way subject to use
Community boards	Mechanization	Phasing	Program Planning
Decentralization	Taylorization	Keying	and Budgeting
Use of indigenous	Bureaucracy	Planning	Systems (PPBS)
workers	Hierarchy	Cadre develop-	Management by Ob-
New careers	Supersystem ap-	ment	jectives
New roles such as	proach	Demonstration	Task (or Job)
expediters,		site training	Analysis
ombudsmen, ad-		bases	Vouchers
vocates		Debugging	Performance-Based
Legal (and admin-			Teacher Educa-
istrative) rights			tion (PBTE)
for consumers			Competency-Based
			Teacher Certifica-
			tion
			Evaluation systems

We will examine in more detail those organizational and management practices that are consonant with consumer-oriented practice and then look at those that can go either way. We will then examine some of the simple principles, first in an example of the spread of a good idea from limited demonstration to broader application, and then in the implementation of a particular piece of consumer-oriented practice, Youth Tutoring Youth. Finally, we will turn to the issue of evaluation as a critical matter of management, in terms most directly of feedback on what is happening, but more deeply in terms of the very practice itself—what is to be sought, and how is it to be measured.

TECHNIQUES THAT CONDUCE TOWARD CONSUMER-ORIENTED PRACTICE

George Berkley, in an unfortunately neglected book, *The Administrative Revolution,* points to the Children's Bureau as what he dubs a client-oriented administrative organization.

Traditionally, most administrative agencies are organized differently. The most common basis of organization is purpose. In this manner, police departments are organized to fight crime, fire departments are organized to fight fires, postal departments are organized to deliver mail. Another and less popular . . . basis of administrative organization is by process. An agency organized in terms of the type of work that it does. An example of such an agency is a city law department. . . .

The Children's Bureau was not organized on either the basis of purpose or process but on the basis of the clientele it served. Its orientation was not to fulfill certain set purposes or to discharge certain types of functions but to service a particular group of clients and to service them in all kinds of ways. It proudly boasted that it did not simply educate, or secure housing for, or arrange medical treatment for, children: instead, it cared for the *whole child.* [Emphasis in the original.][1]

This structural design, focusing upon the client, has been used vis-à-vis other groups at the national level—for example, DHEW's Older Americans Office—and at the local level, the Neighborhood Service Center developed by the antipoverty program for its special client population. The traditional designs begin from the perspective of the practitioners and their practice, but, as Berkley notes, while "government agencies are mono-professional . . . people are multi-problem."[2]

While structuring the entire agency around the consumer is rare, more common is the use of particular administrative or management

1. George E. Berkley, *The Administrative Revolution: Notes on the Passing of Organization Man* (Englewood Cliffs, N.J.: Prentice-Hall, 1971), p. 119.
2. *Ibid.,* p. 120.

features designed to result in (or have the potential to be used for) increased attention to the consumer. There are a great variety of such techniques.

We have already discussed various forms of community participation. These range from advisory committees to policy-making bodies. It is a rare human service agency today that does not have some form of consumer involvement. More frequently the issue is not whether there should be such involvement, but what form it should take, what power the body should have, and just who is to be represented. Clearly, there needs to be, in some fashion, involvement of all relevant players.[3] A prominent observer of health care in New York City noted, "Consumer participation plus the participation of a public funding and regulatory agency . . . are non-expendable ingredients in modern, hospital-based ambulatory care."[4] The consequences of the failure to involve all of the relevant players in the area of cost and efficiency, to say nothing of effectiveness, is described in a report on allied health personnel.

In the health-care industry, the crucial decisions about labor and its use have not been based on productivity, economy, or consumer demand. Clinicians and professionals—not administrators or consumers—have determined priorities and assigned tasks.[5]

Often confused with community participation is decentralization. Services are brought from "downtown" to the neighborhood, as with

3. The New York State Liquor Authority (SLA) has long given heed to the liquor concerns which it regulates. Recently, however, it formed an advisory committee of drinkers and nondrinkers! *Ibid.*, p. 123. This question of whose advice is to be sought has plagued regulatory agencies which frequently have been more concerned with protecting than regulating the industries involved. However, the question of who is to be represented has broader scope. For example, in the struggle around the so-called Green Amendment to the Economic Opportunity Act, there was the issue of whether the governing bodies should include (and to what extent) those to be served, those doing the serving, the other agencies (public and private, administrative and legislative) affected by the program, and those who pay for the program.

4. Lowell Bellin, a paper presented at the Annual Meeting of the American Public Health Association, October 1971.

5. Anthony Robbins, "Allied Health Manpower," *New England Journal of Medicine*, CCLXXXVI, 17 (April 1972), p. 920.

the establishment of neighborhood service centers. Or, decision-making authority is transferred (in whole or more usually in some not entirely explicit part) from "headquarters" to a more local site, *viz.,* school decentralization in New York City, Chicago, Baltimore, and many other cities.

Various matters affecting personnel can also contribute to consumer-oriented practice. We have discussed in Chapter 8 the use of indigenous workers, and earlier in this chapter worker participation in decision making. In addition to the values usually ascribed to worker participation (see Chapter 3), in the human services worker participation may well serve to set the tone, isomorphically, for consumer participation.

Another aspect of consumer-oriented management in the personnel area is the use of persons in special consumer-focused roles. These include such roles as ombudsmen, consumer advocates, child advocates (there is a jointly funded NIMH–USOE effort on this), expediters, advocate planners, and the like. Such persons serve to sensitize the system, to put consumer issues on the agenda, and to give voice and weight on the consumers' side within the agency (often an effective complement to community pressure from the outside).

Yet another feature in the personnel area is for consumers to play leadership roles in the agency. One aspect of this is developed through the "new careers" effort, where career advancement through on-the-job training and education is built into the job. To date, there are several thousand persons who are now professionals who had been paraprofessionals.[6] Another design is for consumers simply to assume major responsibilities, as in the case of tenants operating the Martin Luther King housing project in St. Louis,[7] and the establishment of the Tenant Management Corporation, a tenant group which subcontracts management and maintenance responsibilities with the Boston Housing Authority.[8]

6. The largest organized effort is the U. S. Office of Education's Career Opportunities Program.
7. Berkley, *op. cit.,* p. 126.
8. *New Human Services Newsletter,* II, 5 (Summer 1973).

The right of administrators to operate programs unfettered by external controls has been reduced in a variety of ways. We have already referred to community (including consumer) participation in policy making. Another aspect of this is seen in the line of court decisions following upon *Griggs, et al.* v. *Duke Power Company* (1971) which, in essence, require that job qualification requirements (and to a lesser extent promotional standards) must be in terms of the real requirements of the job and may not be based upon such extraneous factors as race, sex, size, and formal education, unless these can be shown to be bona fide job qualifications.[9] It would seem that employees selected using such standards are likely to be better equipped to provide quality services, to serve consumers in a more relevant and appropriate manner.

Less indirect have been the various restrictions upon the rights of administrators vis-à-vis service consumers. The rights of patients and students, research subjects, prisoners, the mentally ill, have all been the subject of court actions.[10]

In the area of students' rights, courts have held that students are allowed freedom of speech in school even when administrators find it objectionable—both the "symbolic speech" represented by wearing armbands (*Tinker* v. *Des Moines Community School District,* 1969) and regarding printed material (*Eisner* v. *Stamford Board of Education,* 1971)—although their rights here were not unlimited (*Blackwell* v. *Essaquena County Board of Education,* 1966, and *Burnside* v. *Byars,* 1966). Also, the courts have held that students have due process rights and may not be expelled, suspended, or otherwise seriously punished without adherence to such procedures. (*Madera* v. *Board of Education of New York City,* 1967, was the first of a long line of such cases.)

An arena of consumer rights that has received even greater atten-

9. Wilma Scott Heide, president of the National Organization for Women, states that there are only two jobs for which sex-based discrimination is a bona fide qualification—sperm donor and wet nurse!

10. The "New Human Services Newsletter," published by the New Human Services Institute, City University of New York, 184 Fifth Ave., New York City, regularly records legal activities affecting human service practice.

tion in the courts has been the rights of welfare clients. Suits have been brought and won regarding the rights of welfare clients concerning the bases of and procedures for determining eligibility and termination, residency, living arrangements ("man in the house" rules), requirements to work, services and grant levels to be received, rights to fair hearings, and "third party" assistance.[11]

TECHNIQUES THAT CAN GO EITHER WAY

Frequently associated with these efforts are new measures of accountability. Some of these have to do with training (as in performance-based teacher education), or the granting of credentials (as in competency-based teacher certification), or budgeting (as in Performance Planning and Budget System), or management (as in Management by Objectives). Each of these has its limits, particularly in terms of what it is that is to be measured (as well as how); we will discuss the whole issue of evaluation below. Also, each of them can be diverted and/or misused. For the most part they have an industrial, space industry, or military origin. Each of them can serve to demystify the work of the human service agency, force greater clarity as to purpose, give greater attention to issues of effectiveness. At the same time, each can be a substitution of process for substance, giving the façade of accountability but, in fact, serving only to replace the traditional professional managers with new technocratic managers.

One can appreciate the need for better teachers and yet be appalled by the Performance-Based Teacher Education (PBTE) movement. An approach borrowed from the natural sciences has been transferred to a far more complex setting in which assumptions so readily met in the natural sciences as not to need verbalization are insuperable barriers. To think that we can stipulate *the* "specific behaviors" of the

11. See Frances Fox Piven and Richard A. Cloward, *Regulating the Poor: The Function of Public Welfare* (New York: Pantheon, 1971); Charles Reich, "The New Property," *Yale Law Journal*, LXXIII, 5 (April 1964), 733–787; and Jacobus Ten Brock, ed., *The Law of the Poor* (San Francisco: Chandler Publishing Co., 1966).

competent teacher in the same way that we can specify the desired range, speed, bomb load, and other characteristics of an aircraft is not to think. To believe that "research" will provide us these specific behaviors and the means to measure them reveals ignorance of the research methodology upon which the model rests.[12]

The use of vouchers, a technique also fraught with many dangers, again offers the potential of encouraging the service systems, at least in theory, to be more responsive to consumers. Some of the most prominent supporters of the voucher idea would like to see a diminished, not enlarged, public sector, e.g., Milton Friedman. Also, the voucher system proponents frequently ignore much relevant experience. For example, they assume that demand side intervention is sufficient to change service systems, while the Medicaid experience suggests the contrary. They assume, at least some proponents do, that the private sector can effectively deliver human services while the Job Corps and JOBS experience suggest, at the least, the need for some caution. Furthermore, the voucher idea is premised upon an analogy to the private sector that is of limited substance there—namely, that buyers with resources determine product outputs—and is likely to be of even more limited validity in the service sector. Nonetheless, the voucher notion (or some variant thereof, perhaps Mario Fantini's "public schools of choice"[13]), despite its faults (actual or potential), serves, as do the other techniques discussed, to give greater attention and emphasis to the consumer. And vouchers shake up the system, produce a disequilibrium that may be a necessary precursor to significant change. Much of what we have said (both negative and positive) about vouchers applies, as well, to performance contracting, with the additional negative note here that there is a strong proclivity to "teach to the test," or whatever is the standard for payment, *viz.,* the Texarkana experience.

12. W. David Maxwell, "PBTE: A Case of the Emperor's New Clothes," *Phi Delta Kappan,* LV, 5 (January 1974), p. 311.
13. Mario Fantini, "Educational Agenda for the 1970s and Beyond," *Social Policy,* I, 4 (November–December 1970).

MANAGING AND SPREADING A DEMONSTRATION PROJECT

We can see some of the simple principles of management by look-ing at a specific piece of management and organizational activity. The problem that concerns us is how to move from the local demonstra-tion phase to a national level.

The charge is being made on many sides that schools are irrelevant —that the amount of money spent, the educational practice utilized, whether the schools are desegregated or not, the pupil-teacher ratio higher or lower, have no effect on the learning of the children. The argument has had great impact in recent years spearheaded by the ideological criticism of Ivan Illich and buttressed by the large-scale national studies of James Coleman and, more recently, Christopher Jencks.[14]

Yet, despite these data, the fact of the matter is that there are numerous studies, experiments, and demonstrations that clearly indi-cate that a particular teaching practice, or a changed teacher-student ratio, or the use of new personnel such as paraprofessionals, or a new curriculum can have a decisive and measurable effect on children's learning. But these experiments have not been carried over into the educational system on a large scale. For example, Martin Deutsch has demonstrated successfully that stimulus enrichment for disadvan-taged children in the early years has a striking effect on their cognitive development, later learning, and IQ, even when they return to the standard school setting.[15] But in the nationwide Head Start program no such results were found.[16] Alan Gartner has cited a good number of studies where the utilization of paraprofessionals in schools has led to definite improvements in learning, reading scores,

14. Ivan Illich, *Deschooling Society* (New York: Harper & Row, 1970); James Coleman, *et al.,* "Equality of Educational Opportunity," Report of the Office of Education to the Congress and the President (Washington, D. C.: U. S. Government Printing Office, 1966); Christopher Jencks *et al., Inequality: A Reassessment of the Effects of Family and Schooling in America* (New York: Basic Books, 1972).

15. Marshall A. Smith and Joan S. Bissell, "Report Analysis: The Impact of Head Start," *Harvard Educational Review,* 40 (February 1970), pp. 51–104.

16. *Ibid.*

etc., on the part of children.[17] But there is no evidence that the large-scale use of paraprofessionals in the United States as a whole has had a similar effect on the learning of children. Kenneth Clark cites a number of studies, including even those of Bereiter and Engleman, that have shown decisively improved achievement scores of children.[18] And there are countless experiments showing that the IQ can be dramatically improved in a very short period of time, in some cases, as little as three to five days, while again there is no evidence that any large-scale program has had similar effects.[19] The Urban League's Street Academy approach has been highly effective with disadvantaged youngsters. But again, this program has not been developed on a national scale. There have been some experiments demonstrating that the open classroom can be effective in improving the learning of children, and one could ask the question whether this is going to be characteristic as the program is introduced on a wide basis in many school systems. This brief catalogue of examples could be multiplied many, many times.

The issue, of course, is how can these two sets of apparently contradictory data both be true. How can it be correct, as Coleman, Jencks and others argue, that school factors, collectively and individually, have little effect upon children, while studies such as those cited above (and many others) show marked and significant results? The big factor, of course, relates to the very character of the two assessments; *viz.,* the Coleman, Jencks, and similar studies are surveys of large universes, using gross measures, able to detect only broad effects across a wide spectrum of subjects. On the other hand, the studies that have shown positive results look at specific projects, often limited in time, always circumscribed in target population; in short,

17. Alan Gartner, *Paraprofessionals and Their Performance: A Survey of Education, Health and Social Service Programs* (New York: Praeger, 1971).

18. Kenneth B. Clark, *A Possible Reality* (New York: Emerson Hall Publishers, 1972).

19. Ernest A. Haggard, "Social Status and Intelligence," *Genetic Psychology Monographs,* 49, 1954, pp. 141–186; also personal communications from Dr. Haggard. See also, Alan Gartner and Frank Riessman, "The Lingering Infatuation with I.Q.," *Change* (February 1974).

they are experiments or demonstrations of small order that typically have not been institutionalized. The need, then, is to analyze some of the reasons why the experimental and demonstration results have not been carried over into institutional change.

In some cases the results that are produced in a demonstration may be unique and not translatable easily on a national scale. This may be due to the fact that there was special powerful, charismatic leadership in the demonstration program, that it was so expensive, utilizing such a tremendous overload of personnel and other resources, that it would not be economical on a large scale, or there may be some special conditions such as the selection of "creamed" populations or exceptionally trained and involved personnel.

There are, however, features of the demonstration that may have some interesting applicability at the large-scale level. For example, typically, in a demonstration, traditional rules are modified or sus-pended or used very flexibly; there is considerable commitment, a great deal of concentration and care and keying on a particular result is emphasized; and there is sufficient funding. Later we will return to these characteristics as possible variables that must be considered in producing major visible educational reform.

Lest one believe, however, that there are only favorable aspects about new programs and demonstrations, it should be pointed out that many demonstrations essentially fail and there are many factors working against success in any new venture. For example, there is the fact that the new program is charting unknown, unfamiliar paths and there is a natural resistance to upsetting the tradition, the equilibrium, the stability, the routine. Because the demonstration or experiment is new there are also likely to be a considerable number of negative serendipitous or unanticipated consequences which, unless they are overcome, will lead to the essential failure of the demonstration. The point is that in the institutionalization of an idea that has been demonstrated, there are often advantages which the demonstration itself did not have. The demonstration, if successful, has presumably debugged some of the difficulties; the territory is no longer new and uncharted; a body of practice has been developed through the demonstration that can be applied on a larger scale; the success of the demonstration indicates that it can be done and reduces some of the resistance to the new; finally, the demonstration, because of its relative success, may have won some advocates, some support, some desire for its spread, and some trained cadres.

The transition from the demonstration to large-scale institutional change[20] raises a number of managerial issues which are typically ignored and for which the demonstration itself offers no solutions. It is often assumed that in what may be labeled the "demonstration fallacy," that the good idea or good practice will naturally spread or sometimes it is mandated by a specific edict or legislation with little consideration of the special processes that will be necessary to institute an idea on a large scale. Surprisingly, there seems little awareness that in actual practice there is a powerful tendency for the original idea to be watered down, vulgarized, applied at the level of the lowest common denominator.

From a managerial perspective, two features must be considered from the beginning:

1. While the number and range of places where the demonstration idea is applied effectively have to be increased, it must be recognized that it will not be equally applied everywhere. Special methods must be introduced to compensate for the watering-down tendency—and, if possible, to reverse this tendency.

2. A strong effort should be made greatly to improve upon the results found in the demonstration as new experience is gathered and, hopefully, codified from a variety of new situations and particularly from some model sites which can be established. Recognizing the limits of the demonstration, it should be possible to improve greatly

---

20. Demonstrations essentially have two potential functions for the systems. If they are kept isolated, narrow, and small, they can be used as showcases enabling the system, whether it be education or other, to maintain its business as usual. In some cases, the demonstration may be relatively large and a parallel system constructed, still enabling the main system to maintain its stability. The other more positive function of the demonstration is to provide a mechanism whereby a system that is in trouble can be reformed by utilizing the findings and processes of the demonstrations.

on the demonstration findings if conscious attention is directed toward this objective and the necessary practices instituted. This can provide powerful medicine for compensating and even reversing the watering-down tendency that is inherent in instituting large system change.

Some of the steps and specific practices that might be useful for applying an effective practice on a large scale include the following:

1. It is necessary to specify clearly the goals and objectives of the proposed change and to establish a *timetable* for achieving them. This will prevent both grandiosity and disillusionment and enable the change agent to assess clearly what is happening and make appropriate corrections.

2. An aspect of this is *planned phasing*—that is, moving from the experimental demonstration in carefully planned steps to ever-larger territory, rather than attempting to institute a new practice into the entire system at once. Phasing has a number of clear-cut advantages: it allows the idea to spread among those who are more receptive to it and, perhaps, more likely to institute it well. It develops experience beyond the demonstration relating to putting in place of the idea in relatively large systems—and produces a body of practice that can be useful to ever-larger systems. It enables the recruitment and development of a body of trained cadres that then can be useful to the further spread of the idea. It is more manageable and allows for easier feedback and modification of the idea in practice—modification that may lead to the idea's enrichment. It leads to the development of a constituency supporting the practice. Some relatively successful examples of this phasing in the development of what might be called a middle-level demonstration can be seen in such programs as the Office of Education's Career Opportunities Program and in the Youth Tutoring Youth Program, both of which have been instituted on a fairly small scale, if one thinks of them in terms of total systems change but large compared to the usual demonstration.

The Career Opportunities Program has been established for over 13,000 paraprofessionals in 133 school systems and the Youth Tutoring Youth Program is now in place in over 400 school systems. The same phasing idea, of course, should be utilized in introducing an idea within any school system. Thus, teachers who are interested in a new idea can self-select themselves as the first users and then the idea is spread to a larger and larger number of teachers.

3. *Model demonstration training sites* should be established to develop the educational practice and to train cadres. These demonstration training bases should be well funded and equipped to evaluate the practice, develop it more fully, and disseminate its results rapidly throughout the system via conferences, newsletters, and most important, by training workers from these other systems at the training base itself. The training base should also provide ongoing technical assistance to the projects around the country and should receive input from these projects as to what is going right and what is going wrong.

4. An *ethos* should be built up around the practice that emphasizes the importance and worthwhileness of the practice even beyond its specific presumed efficiency. For example, Youth Tutoring Youth Programs do more than improve the learning of children—they increase cooperativeness, develop the power, resourcefulness, and creativity of children, and thus have a much larger social meaning which captures attention, wins a constituency beyond the immediate users of the program, and may even gain legislative support and media attention. These elements help to give the program drive and prominence and in many ways will probably increase the motivation of the youngsters, teachers and administrators, and parents who are involved. This climate or atmospheric effect (what might be labeled "institutionalized Hawthorne effect") can help to keep the program in motion, continually growing, and provide the enthusiasm that is such an important ingredient in the experimental demonstration phase. This ethos is de-

veloped through developing a sense of mission, by media attention, by visits to the programs, conferences about them, as well as articles and books and films that are concrete and specific, along with an emphasis on the ideological, broad-range implications as well as the immediate practical results.

5. *Depth training of cadres* is an extremely important part of the implementation of a large-scale program. This training can be done at the model demonstration center, at the work site itself, in special intensive conferences where specific work problems are simulated carefully and the cadres are "overtrained" in ways of dealing with these problems and issues. It is extremely important to train school principals and administrators, as well as teachers and the specific program supervisors, along with members of community boards. In the COP program a major concern has been the training of school principals and community advisory boards. It is extremely important to involve the consumer of the service and that would be the pupils, their parents, and, to some extent, the advisory boards. The consumer is a key agent of change and a major force in the productivity of a service.

There are a number of other points that should be mentioned briefly: good administrative practice requires that there be clearly someone in charge of the program locally and on the large scale who has no other conflicting responsibilities; expediters, troubleshooters, or educational change agents should be dispatched throughout the country quickly to assess difficulties that can be corrected—to some extent this can be done through means of telephone conference calls and videotapes; a strong effort must be developed by the national leadership to fight the competitiveness and divisiveness and the role of small vested interests in hurting the program; as much as possible, benefits must be found for a great variety of groups from the program; sufficient resources, particularly discretionary funds, must be provided; powerful commitment and participation must be developed at conferences and in other ways from all the participants and their ideas fed in and accepted; a major concentration of effort is crucial so that the program is not diffused by many different dimensions; small groups or teams of change agents should be introduced at every level to insure a "critical mass" and to provide the necessary mutual reinforcement and monitoring.

BUREAUCRATIZATION VERSUS INSTITUTIONALIZATION

We have indicated above that as programs move from small-scale demonstration experiments to large-scale systemwide programs, there is the possibility that they will be diluted rather than accelerated. The Youth Tutoring Youth effort of the National Commission on Resources for Youth has developed a number of ways of preventing this atrophy by bureaucratization from occurring and insuring instead a positive, spreading institutionalization of the program. Successful implementation depends upon five basic principles utilized by YTY: (1) a carefully developed internship program as well as a refresher course for administrators, supervisors, and other personnel; (2) the development of materials for use by the supervisors, administrators, and tutors themselves; (3) the winning of a solid commitment of the administrators to the program; (4) the careful assignment of specific people who would have as their sole responsibility the carrying out of the program at the local level; (5) the encouragement of flexible modification of the YTY design to make it applicable to specific local conditions.

The general atmosphere of accountability that today is being demanded by both the community and the experts can function as a powerful countervailing force to prevent bureaucratization. In addition, it is extremely important to develop constituencies committed to the full application of new efforts such as learning through teaching. These constituencies, which can be community groups, professional groups—including teachers and administrators—and, of course, the students themselves, must receive guidelines to assist them in the general monitoring of the programs. The constituencies must not only demand the fulfillment of the program but must acquire increasing knowledge regarding possible bureaucratic distortions—for example, the ways in which the climate of the school can suffocate or divert the effort.

The constituencies must be aware of the need for careful planning, training, and management on the part of the operators of the programs. They must realize that resources are required to implement the program properly, including, possibly, initial overstaffing. They must come to understand the importance of building a positive, pervasive climate for the program and the need to involve various groups, such as children, teachers, parents, and community groups, in the planning, implementation, and evaluation of the program.

The constituencies must understand the importance of phasing in the program carefully. They must see the relevance of focusing on the learning-through-teaching design to keep it as a high priority so that other school programs are not permitted to interfere and compete. Finally, they must insist on careful follow-through, great attention to detail, and constant modification based upon flexible evaluation. In essence, some of the positive aspects of the demonstration phase must be carried over in the institutionalizing of the program.

Three Stages of Change

It may be useful to provide constituencies with a working model of the stages of change. Programs in any field go through essentially three stages:

1. The *demonstration or innovation stage,* which arises because of the inadequacies of the existing program functioning at the bureaucratization stage.

2. The *institutionalization phase,* which attempts to expand those small-scale experimental demonstrations that have had some success.

3. The *bureaucratization stage,* where the institutionalized reform has now become rigidified, not attuned to changing conditions but continuing to function because of the needs of the bureaucracy rather than because of its effectiveness as a program. This in turn leads to pressure for new innovation, and the cycle may begin again.

The bureaucratic phase will resist innovation; one of the most important forms of resistance is to encapsulate or isolate the innovation as a demonstration project, thereby preventing it from becoming institutionalized. Thus, the major strategic issue in changing the system is moving from the demonstration phase to the institutional phase, and this requires the overcoming of bureaucratic resistance in all its many forms.

Unless one distinguishes between the institutional and the bureaucratic phases, one is drawn inevitably to the cynical conclusion that all innovations are destroyed either by ultimately becoming bureaucratized or by being so effectively resisted by the bureaucratic culture that they never go beyond the embryonic demonstration point.

A major reason for the failure of positive institutionalization has to do with the way innovations are introduced into the educational system and *distorted by the administrative practices* of many of these systems. Failures relate to administrative lethargy, intransigence, overcontrol, poor management approaches, and lack of participatory inclusion of teachers, students, and parents.

A basic strategy would seem to require reducing the time spent at the bureaucratic stage, increasing the time spent at the institutional phase, and moving as rapidly as possible from innovation to institutionalization. In addition, of course, one would want the fullest development of many demonstration projects.

A successful transition to a large-scale program requires capturing and using some of the features that characterize the demonstration: esprit de corps, flexible application of rules and procedures, zeroing in on the objectives of the program to the exclusion of all the various interferences or distractions that characterize school cultures, strong leadership and the designation of specific personnel to take charge of the program rather than sliding the responsibility to people who have other responsibilities.

The moving of an idea or a program to large-scale application consists of much more than idea dissemination—it will involve organization change, system change, and the change agents responsible for it must have some understanding of organizational theory and particularly the managerial issues indicated above; otherwise, they may have the simplistic notion that merely disseminating the idea will lead to its institutionalization. Such a view, which we have labeled the "dissemination fallacy," will result in cynicism and despair very early in the game, and a continuation at the scale of national effect of little impact.

THE PROBLEM OF EVALUATION

Central, of course, both to the particular techniques discussed in the early part of the chapter and the larger-scale thrust discussed above is the issue of evaluation. We have earlier discussed evaluation (see Chapter 8) as part of the consideration of consumer-based services, particularly as related to service productivity. Here we are concerned with evaluation as a management issue, evaluation in terms both of what is to be measured and how to measure it.

The problem of evaluation of human services is enormous, perhaps even more complex than it is in the social sciences in general. Let us look at a few examples. If we use achievement or reading test scores to assess the effectiveness of teachers, we are faced with the problem that the teachers may then "teach to the test." And in extreme cases, such as in the performance contracting example in Texarkana, they may actually provide the tests in advance. If we utilize a measure of the student's self-concept as a way of evaluating some educational intervention, the question arises, Has his or her self-concept improved while cognitive performance remained the same? If we use the teacher's judgment as to what has been happening to the work of the pupils, it obviously has potential bias as the teacher may want to indicate that he or she is doing a good job, while an outside independent judge may be less capable of assessing what is going on every day and/or may obtain a restricted performance on the day of the evaluation. On and on go the limitations, whether it be of teacher performance, psychotherapy (e.g., the patient's subjective report of being better may illustrate only brainwashing by the psychiatrist), or other service.

In many cases what happens is that faced with the problems of evaluation, those engaged in practice decide simply not to do it, pleading how hard it is to do. Or, the evaluators develop such superfine instruments that they find little has, in fact, occurred (or, more precisely, little that their instruments can measure). Another alternative is that recognizing this last problem, evaluators seek out only gross and impressionistic results. None of these alternatives, we believe, is acceptable if we seek a practice which, in fact, helps people and promotes the further development of a service society.

What emerges, rather, is a need for an evaluation model which employs multiple indices, each different from the other, each having different weaknesses and strengths that may counterbalance each other, but converging toward a similar result or assessment. In the psychological literature, this is termed *convergent* or *discriminant validity*.[21] Thus, in the case of a psychotherapeutic intervention, if the patient, his or her friends, relatives, fellow employees, supervisors, psychiatrists, and perhaps an independent judge agree that he or she has progressed markedly, we may be more persuaded than if any one of them alone so indicated. If, further, there is some measure such as projective tests that also indicate progress, we are further reassured. If, in addition, there are some major behavioral changes in the patient's life, such as being able to graduate from college after failing previously, this may be further evidence that the intervention is meaningful. To repeat, no one of these indices alone would be sufficient, and, of course, we can't always have all of the indicators working uniformly in the same direction, so we would need to develop some fairly acceptable pattern of indices.

There are a number of other factors that we might want to consider in our evaluation schema. First, we will want changes to be relatively enduring and not due to any such effect as the Hawthorne. Then, we might be particularly concerned that the changes be of a large quali-

21. See Donald Campbell and Donald Fiske, "Convergent and Discriminant Validation by the Multitrait-Multimethod Matrix," *Psychological Bulletin,* LVI, 2 (March 1959), pp. 81–104.

tative type; for example, children progressing as much as three years in their reading scores in six months, as has occurred in some Youth Tutoring Youth programs.[22]

In evaluating a service, we may want to consider some of its direct effects and indirect effects, its manifest results and its latent effects. For example, the doctor treats a patient and the patient gets well, but the context of the entire relationship makes the patient feel dependent and mystified. Thus, it may be necessary to assess interventions at a number of different levels and evaluate them accordingly. Every human service intervention is imbedded in a context and has many meanings beyond its direct manifest goal. The open classroom can be assessed in terms of its improvement in the learning of children, measured by a variety of indices as suggested above. But the whole context has many other latent messages, and in many cases the open classroom is a preferred intervention, not necessarily or only because of a presumed effect on the learning of children, but because of the concomitant values it expresses. For example, it is an approach that is involving of the children, drawing on their inner abilities, encouraging independence and expression. If these values are desired, the technique may be positively valued for these reasons, as well as for its manifest role in improving learning.

Evaluation is not only a question of how to measure but also what to measure, or, in a sense, what it is the service seeks to do, how it chooses to affect the consumer(s). Thus, for example, one can see the goal(s) of a school as

—Improving children's reading levels; or
—Providing full participation in the school's activities for children (and their parents), seeing the act(s) of participation as learning experiences in and of themselves, as well as, perhaps, seeing them as means toward further learning; or
—Seeking to assure the children's affective well-being; this, again, is seen as being a desirable end in itself and, perhaps, a means

22. Alan Gartner, Mary Conway Kohler, and Frank Riessman, *Children Teach Children: Learning by Teaching* (New York: Harper & Row, 1971).

toward additional and deeper affective development, as well as, maybe, cognitive area development; or
—Seeking cognitive development in depth and across a wide range of areas; this, again, is seen as being a valuable end in itself and, perhaps, leading to further development including, maybe, the affective area as well; or
—Seeking development in both the cognitive and affective areas, looking toward multiple and different aspects of growth in both areas, expecting evidence from the divergent areas which converge. In other words, believing that significant and real growth will manifest itself both affectively and cognitively.

It is the last of these sets of alternative goals (and ideas as to the manifestation in a way useful for evaluation) that we hold as goals for schools. These are goals the achievement of which the evaluation systems we propose will make clear and obvious. It is not a case of one or two measures showing positive findings, but of a whole battery of indices, coming at different facets of development in different ways, along with some serendipitous findings that were not anticipated, that should show results. Furthermore, the results should be positive both in terms of the proximate goal(s) of the practice(s) and in terms of broader consumer benefit(s).

What we are saying, then, is that in the evaluation of any human service technique or intervention, it is important to distinguish the direct effect on improvement in learning, health, mental health, or whatever, from the more indirect consequences of the technique, the way it is presented or imbedded, the place it is provided, the associated relationship, whether it is cooperative, collegial, independent, or whatever. By confusing these dimensions, we not only fail to measure the more indirect dimension, which may have more far-reaching, long-range effects, but we often confuse the two dimensions and automatically assume that they are working in the same direction; or—and this is the more typical pattern illustrated in the various new approaches to consumer control—because the approach fits our value framework (e.g., there is consumer involvement), we automatically assume that the effectiveness of the service is thereby improved. This, of course, may be true, but it requires more direct evaluation procedures, utilizing multiple indices.

Finally, in the human services, there are special evaluation questions related to the fact that some approaches are good for some people (and some groups) and not for others; individual differences, style differences, and subgroup differences are extremely important. The open classroom may work very well for some kinds of youngsters, particularly those who already have a developed interest in learning, and yet be very inappropriate for other groups; while the contact curriculum may be a complete waste of time for youngsters who are already deeply involved. Role-playing may be a useful approach with some children and be counterindicated with others. Some teachers may use games very effectively, while others function better with a more structured lesson. This is not to say that everything works, but there are many paths to Rome, many different approaches and styles that may be effective;[23] and this adds further to the evaluation problem.

CONCLUSION

The management techniques that seem to be inimical to consumer-oriented practice are those which are overly hierarchized, bureaucratized, deny by their excessive mechanization and exfoliated (almost to the point of eutrophication) systems approach the essentially relational character of the human services. "Taylorization" with its breaking down of work to the most basic unit, seeking tasks requiring nothing but repetitive, noninvolved action on the part of the workers is exactly opposite from what is called for in human service work.[24]

23. Indeed, one of the flaws of the performance-based teacher education and the competency-based teacher certification designs is that they seem to incorporate the notion that there is only one "correct" way to carry on a teaching activity, thus taking into account neither teacher style differences nor pupil differences.

24. Some efforts to implement "new careers" programs have involved activities to "shred out" of the professionals' jobs the "nonprofessional" tasks. That is not what we mean by new careers or the use of indigenous paraprofessionals.

This is an example, at best, of the inappropriate transfer from industry of a technique (we say, at best, because, increasingly, "Taylorization" is proving ineffective in industry) to human service work. Other techniques borrowed from industry or the military, including several we have noted for their positive potential vis-à-vis consumer-oriented management (*viz.,* task analysis, PPBS, management by objectives), have these same risks.

In general, we shy away from overelaborated techniques. Instead, we favor simpler management notions such as keying on the goal, highlighting the objective(s), assuring a nondiffuse effort. So, we favor the establishment of a critical mass for change, the use of coordination and phasing. Cadre development, depth training (and "overtraining"), and use of troubleshooters and key agents are personnel steps we favor.

It is the combination of these simple management techniques, the conducing toward a positive consumer orientation of those which can go either way, along with those which are in and of themselves consonant with consumer-oriented practice (*viz.,* community boards, use of indigenous workers, decentralization), that will produce a full array of consumer-oriented organizational and management techniques. These techniques need to be combined with the consumer-oriented training designs we have discussed earlier (Chapter 9) and the structural organization of practice (see Chapter 8 for discussion of such issues as accessibility of the service). In other words, the practice itself, the training for it, and the management of it must all focus upon the consumer orientation.

To a large extent human services involve a non-routine technology as opposed to a routine technology, the latter characterizes much of the industrial sector. . . . The human service system, to a great extent, is less amenable to such organization devices as centralization, standardization, formalization, and other traditional bureaucratic features. When you have a technology which is characterized by greater complexity and a non-routine character there is a need to have greater decentralization with more options and discretionary powers permitted or given to the person providing the services, as well as . . . greater consumer involvement.[25]

25. Sol Levine, personal communication, November 30, 1973.

And the managers of human service activities must know the politics of the situation, as well as technology. They must be "technopols" who know more than the practice itself, and more than the surrounding area. They must understand the diverse pressures, multiple players, and varied goals (and measures of assessment) of human service practice.

For it is in services that increasingly the consumer is expressing the individuality of his own personal wants, where controls and planning, necessarily conducted in terms of general categories and tending towards standardised products, are peculiarly inappropriate.[26]

The consumer-oriented practices that we propose will not lead directly to increased Gross National Product, for the increased productivity will be gained through capturing the potential of the consumer who, as an unpaid worker in the production of his/her own learning or health, is not counted in GNP. Nor will these changes show in standard measures of server/client ratios which are the generally used bases for assessing service productivity. Rather, the gains will be seen in the quality of the services, in the student's learning both more and better, not in the teacher's teaching more students. There is no simple "bottom line" in human service work, and those who manage it must know that, accept it, and work from that point to meet the complex and different ends of such work.

26. Russell Lewis, *The New Service Society* (London: Longman, 1973), p. 43.

11 Limits and Potential

Reforms aim to change things within a given framework to make them function better. Structural reforms seek to achieve, simultaneously, changes that will benefit but that cannot be absorbed into the old framework. In order to accommodate a structural change, the framework must be altered. And the most important element in the change is that it is so integral to the new functioning, and its amplitude is so large, that it is irreversible.

—Roy Bennett, "Symposium on Social Change"

We have been concerned with a description and analysis of basic trends and institutions of the emerging service society, a highly significant feature being the human service institutions, particularly in the health and education fields. We have looked at the *practices* in these fields, especially their ineffectiveness and lack of consumer responsiveness. Our major concern was directed toward the fullest utilization of the consumer as a basic new source of productivity. We proposed that training and management procedures need to be actively directed toward the maximization of this objective, if the tremendous potential of consumer intensity is to be actualized toward the necessary leap in service practice.

Now we return to an overview and critique of the service society and its potential directions.

SPECIAL CONTRADICTIONS OF THE SERVICE SOCIETY

There are a number of special contradictions experienced in the service society:

—The development of large-scale bureaucracy, which in many ways is antithetical to the basic values and character of the human services.

—The emergence of new values of autonomy and creativity with little concern for how the simple routine work of the society is to be accomplished.

—The continued tremendous importance of the worker role and worker power, but the relative decline of the worker as vanguard.

—Concomitantly, the tremendous increase in consumer motion and leadership along with the limitations of consumer power.

—The fact that the positive motion in the human services seems to derive largely from the alternative institutions and various unpaid activities rather than from the more professionalized formal structures.

—The fact that many of the new values that may appear radical and directed toward system change function to prepare people for their work and leisure roles in a service society.

Illustrative of this contradiction is the role of free schools and of the new more open education within the public schools. Traditionally organized schools, with their emphasis upon discipline, rigid curricula, hierarchy, and deferral of gratification, were appropriate socialization instruments for both the work of early industrial capitalism and the appropriate consumer roles therein. However, as we move into a new stage of capitalism, with a greater role for service work and related consumption, a different form of school organization is required to socialize future workers and consumers. Here the emphasis upon self-development, the affective, a more cooperative and nonhierarchical structure—themselves positive values—may well be the appropriate modalities for socializing workers who are going to be more engaged in human service work than in factory production, who are going to play increasingly important consumer roles characterized by much leisure time. Used in this way, the radical potential of these values may well be defused. Of course, the advocates of free schools and more open education are not the handmaidens of the society's managers; but their goals may well suit the new needs of the society.

Besides these special contradictions, there is the ongoing conflict between the emerging service society and the existing industrial society, with its old majority, traditional values, and basic economic and political power.

The service dimensions of an emerging service society overlap with and are dependent upon the industrial base.[1] The service society is superimposed upon industrial capitalism. This is not an economic abstraction, but relates very powerfully to different groups of people employed in the various sectors and the respective values emanating from them. The old industrial sector still exists and is very strong, employing large numbers of industrial workers, managers, and technicians. These groups, the upper and middle portions of the working class, form the "old majority." They identify themselves with the old values of the puritan ethic: hard work, material gain, advancement, deferred gratification, and sublimation of sexual desires. They are preoccupied by a high degree of loyalty to the country and are opposed to permissiveness, pampering, and all sorts of liberation efforts. Religion, tradition, and authority are the virtues they expound. This old majority and its industrial and capitalist base have enormous power. The working-class segments of this old majority are most often employed in primary industry, relatively well paid, highly organized, with generally stable employment.

The capitalist state powerfully conditions what occurs in the

---

1. It is interesting to conjecture what principles might be said to characterize a service society that would be the counterpart of industrialism's concern for quantity, incentives, bureaucratic organization, etc. Some service principles that appear to be arising might include participation, personal growth, people-oriented planning, decentralization, recurrent education, the quality of life as a central unifying goal, a positive consumerism, work autonomy, ecological constraints, demystification, consumer-intensive work.

human service sectors. With the exception of services organized by the alternative institutions, practically all other human services are provided directly or indirectly by the state. Further, the state contributes in very important ways to the education of the human power that provides the services.

WHITHER THE SERVICE SOCIETY?

Institutional tension, subcultural conflict—where will the emerging service society go? Will the polarization between the service-consumer groups and the old majority increase? How will the battle for the state be resolved? What will happen to the tendencies toward bureaucratization and bigness?

Will the alternative institutions grow, influencing the major structures, or will they remain small experimental outlets of discontent for trying new forms and for maintaining the basic structures as they are?

What will happen to the service crisis and the related fiscal crisis in our society? How will the services be paid for? Will the services get better, leading to a real improvement in the quality of life? Will some of the fire and verve found in the alternative institutions find their way into the old services and old professions?

What will happen to all the people acquiring new credentials as a result of educational inflation? Will there be jobs for the enormous numbers obtaining college degrees?

Will the rights that were recognized in the sixties be internalized as a part of basic life and practice? Will we go beyond alienation to more positive perspectives?

What will happen to the privatism, the retreat of many of the young and the affluents? Where will the new politics go and the consumer politics of Nader, the ecology activists, the consumer boycotters? Will the new service society vanguards move toward a humanistic socialism with some new forms of egalitarianism or will they become the new elite? Will there be planning, direction, rational authority, decentralization, redistribution, controlled growth, or will anarchy, irrationality, competition—careless and unbounded growth —continue to flourish? Will the differences between male and female sex roles diminish? Will new reforms arise that begin to transform the system or will incrementalism prevail?

The direction of the emerging service society is not predetermined, it can go in an elitist or in an egalitarian, liberated direction. If the new service ethos and consumer-sensitized values are extensively to influence American society in an egalitarian direction in the 1970s, they will have to be consciously directed to the task.

The service society and its fragmented vanguards have little awareness of overall directions; thus, the new majority is slow to emerge. In fact, the service society grows in the womb of a strong (not yet dying) industrial neocapitalist base that can and might accommodate most of the new demands without revolutionary changes.

Some Predictions

In this context, we make a few predictions:

1. The service sector of the economy, particularly the human services, will continue to expand.
2. Service growth will be recognized as an appropriate form of growth to meet the environmental crisis.
3. There will be a continual expansion of people acquiring education and credentials.
4. This will produce a crisis because there will be an insufficient number of jobs, despite the expansion of the white-collar and service worlds, to employ all the new college graduates.
5. Credentialism will not die—it will, to some extent, become more performance-oriented—that is, the credential will become more relevant to the activity or task to be done.
6. The crisis in the public sector will continue around the question of who is to pay how much for the services—the working- and middle-class taxpayers or the military-industrial complex.

7. The new majority will not consist essentially of poor people below a fixed income, but rather, will include large numbers of deprived people, the youth, the women, the minorities. The deprivation, however, is not necessarily in relation to income but also in relation to status and power. Affluent consumers and professionals ("educated labor") will remain a significant ally although an ambivalent one.

8. The incompleteness, the lack of fulfillment of many of the progressive tendencies of the society, will continue, although slowly; some of these positive trends will be more reflected in the political process, at the workplace, in new forms of organization, and in the development of new ideologies which may include socialistic aspects but go beyond them; the now quiescent vanguards of the sixties, the youths and the blacks and the minorities, will increasingly use the political process, probably in new ways, and develop extended forms of organization around the workplace.

9. Consumerism will continue to expand with scrutiny of all kinds of products, all areas of life from politics (e.g., Watergate) to human service issues (e.g., nursing homes) to the private sector (e.g., the pollution-industrial complex).

10. New kinds of people-oriented services will proliferate further —sex therapy, abortion counseling, clinics for insomniacs, services for the dying, legal services for the poor.

11. Increasingly, the use of the consumer will be recognized as an important aspect in improving the productivity of the services with a marked increase of children teaching children, an enriched self-help movement that is connected to the service mainstream.

12. The service workers and consumers alike will resist attempts to industrialize, mechanize, and bureaucratize them, but the effort will continue to be made by the forces committed to it (and related to the expansion in size of the service structures).

13. The dialectic conflicts between the consumer and the profes-

sional will continue with their being united on some issues and divided on others.

14. The issue of full employment will be raised as a demand in the society with large sectors of this employment to be government-created in the public sector and in the service fields.

15. The demand for work in which the worker has a say and is less controlled bureaucratically from above will expand.

16. The conflict between the new majority groups and the old industrial forces and their allies from the middle class and the working class will continue.

17. The major developments taking place in the human service fields will probably continue to emanate from alternative institutions and consumer demand.

18. The cracks in the system, the potential points of change stemming from open, unbounded time, will *not* eventuate in a major restructuring of the society until there is a *convergence* between them and economic issues related to inflation, stagnation, etc.—in other words, unless there is a convergence of the social and economic levels.

WHAT IS TO BE DONE?

These new directions provide a whole new agenda for services—both their production and consumption. It should lead to a broadening of the growth and development services—lifetime education, new forms of interpersonal recreation, new therapeutic forms, women's groups, men's groups, marriage encounters, sex therapy, new para-religious mind-expanding forms, special services for the dying, the development of all kinds of groups. The services of the future will go considerably beyond the traditional HEW classification and should be far more consumer-involving.

Many constituencies are involved in this potential service regeneration: college students interested in preparing for human service careers; workers (and the population in general) continuing education; the large numbers who are involved in various growth and development activities—both giving and receiving. Moreover, there is the expanded recognition of the need for greater child care, preventive health services, and the recognition of new needs—such as those of the handicapped, the dying, the aged.

The critical questions are: how good will these services be, how will they be paid for, and who will control them?

There is no intrinsic or necessary reason why services should be described as less productive than goods. A meaningful service society will have to come to grips with this question, which really represents a historic lag, but one which is surely detrimental to the development of an ecologically balanced work structure. In a society in which planning and production are people-centered, the exchange of goods and services, both of which require labor power, should not be seen as unequal where the services exist on the back of the goods production. This may have been historically relevant in a less advanced industrial age, but in a developing service society, and in light of the environmental damage resulting from much goods production, it is entirely anachronistic.

For the new vanguards to achieve a genuine egalitarian society, the following seem minimally necessary:

—The narrow agenda of each of the specific groups—women, youth, and minorities—will have to be transcended; visions must be projected for the future as well as demands for the present which go considerably beyond benefits for each of the specific groups. An ideology must be put forward which goes beyond alienation, negative radicalism, and anticapitalism.

—It is clear, as Marcuse has said, that personal and social liberation must be combined with political and economic liberation, that the long march through the institutions, which is so necessary, must include the political and economic. While consumer politics has an especially important contribution to make to future politics, it will have to be integrated with electoral politics and worker tactics.

—The development of new priorities in national life will have to be undertaken, together with a continued fight for the state, for a public sector that actually serves the public.

—The new vanguard, especially the middle-class youth and women's groups, will have to accept considerable redistribution of income and wealth, and a reduction of gluttonous consumption if we are to have an ecologically balanced world and curtail the ripping off of the developing countries.

If the new consumer-rooted values are to have any significant influence in the seventies, they will have to take new forms and direction. The women's movement will have to move much more toward working-class women and women on welfare. The youth will have to raise issues in relation to work alienation, not simply issues related to the consumer-oriented quality of life. And the blacks and other minorities will have to go beyond a go-it-alone orientation and take on the basic contradictions of our society.

Only by this integration of a consumer thrust with the strength emanating from the worker's role can we have any hope of overcoming the fragmentation that has divided the potential new progressive majority of youth, blacks, women, and workers, and enabled the old, dwindling majority to be rekindled. The positive threads of the sixties, in their thrust for participation, new rights, concern for the quality of life, have to be transformed at a higher level of consciousness and integrated into the fabric of life on a much higher plane, particularly at the workplace, if we are to turn around the swing to the right which thus far characterizes the seventies and obscures the healthy trends that emerged in the sixties.

We see then four dimensions of a genuine service society:

1. An increasing consumption of services and the increasing employment of the labor force in service work;
2. A critical role of the consumer, particularly as a force in the production of services;
3. A service culture embodying new values; and,
4. A socialist mode of production that enhances service productivity.

Of course, a socialist mode is not present in the contemporary American society; indeed, its absence is a constraint upon the further development of the first three factors. While the basic service society emergents provide a tension, they do not necessarily lead to socialism, although only under some form of socialism can the service ethos that is emerging be fulfilled. Fulfillment is unlikely to occur, however, in the near future, as long as the capitalist mode of production continues to develop industrial production—essential as an underbase for the service society and any advanced society—and continues in both direct and indirect ways to develop the service forces of production, to say nothing of using them. This is why we predict the peculiar, uneven, incomplete, side-by-side development of the industrial and service sectors. The conflict will continue and can be resolved only at the *political level* through political action with the outcome dependent upon the effectiveness of the organization of the new majority and its allies, perhaps with a concomitant split in the elitists and the neutralization of the old middle class. Fundamental transformation will occur only when there is a *convergence* of the difficulties in the capitalist-industrial sectors coalescing with the new development of the service-consumer forces. The prescription for the kind of society that we desire is a service society that is socialist (in new ways), where the services and ethos connected to them (the vision) can be actualized, where there is a temporary harmony at a new level between the forces and relations of production, where the major priority is the development, production, and consumption of services (based on industrial forces, as previously industrial society was based on agricultural productivity). Some form of democratic socialism is a minimum *necessary condition* for such a society; by no means is it a sufficient condition.

We see in essence two continua: the prime course of economic development is from agriculture to industry to service with perhaps an intervening step of post-industrial or neoindustrial; the other continuum is from feudalism to capitalism to some form of socialism. The fact that socialism, historically, developed in pre-industrial societies such as the Soviet Union and China has limited what we see as the natural connection or matching stages between socialism and a service society, that is, the need for the development of industrialism in the pre-industrial nations contributed not only to the limited political forms but to the accelerated, one-sided development of industrialism to the exclusion of service forms.

To some extent, China, while still pre-industrial, has been able to borrow service society forms, technology, and methods which when combined with its socialist and some anti-industrial ethos have permitted a remarkably advanced development of the services. And because China has not been constrained in the development of these services by various profit needs, there have been some surprising developments in service organization taking place in a society that is far from being an overall advanced service society.[2]

The other side of the coin, of course, is the United States, where essentially all the economic conditions for socialism have been reached but where capitalism continues to prevail because it is still able to develop the forces of production. Here we have the incipient forms of an emerging service society which should match the socialist stage, but these developments remain as yet unfulfilled because of the continuing capitalist relations of production and the overall corporate state. In essence, a true service society exists nowhere as yet, although important dimensions exist in both the advanced economy of the capitalist West and pre-industrial China.

2. See Ruth and Victor Sidel, "Human Services in China," *Social Policy,* II, 6 (March–April 1972).

Conclusion: *All About People (and Profits)*

One of the most characteristic features of our advanced society is the fact that the work life (and the nonwork life) of large portions of the population is concerned with people and interpersonal relationships. This is the link, the linchpin, between the economic dimensions on the one side, and the new culture, the changing consciousness, on the other.

The new work life is increasingly characterized by interpersonal occupations, including sales and advertising (the occupations concerned with distributing the huge overproductivity); personal services, and government-provided services, going far beyond health, education, and welfare to include day care, family planning, mental health, rehabilitation, safety, and the new services concerned with the dying, the handicapped, sex therapy, and so on.

The interpersonal services are essentially consumer-proximate; they are either near the consumer, or highly consumer-centered, and they are typically intangible or nonmaterial. It is no wonder, then, that a kind of consumer-service world view emerges, particularly in the sixties, when the effects of the agricultural revolution are most sharply felt, via a marked decline of agricultural workers and a great increase of people in education and on welfare. In addition, it was a period where there was a considerable movement of women out of the home and into the service workplace.

Much of the nonwork life is filled by education, media-based recreation, and neighborhood and community interaction. Considerably less time is involved in industrial work, with its associated industrial discipline.

An important dimension of the new movements is their anti-industrial focus: they are less concerned with quantity of goods, and more with the quality of life; they are less concerned with material acquisition, and more interested in personal development; they are less concerned with discipline, hierarchy, and authority and more oriented to autonomy, self-determination, and participation—activities that are more fitting to service work and consumer life.

We call the groups who play the major role in propelling these new value patterns "consumer vanguards"—namely, youth, women, minorities. These groups have considerable "unbounded" consumer time and, when they are employed, it is typically in service work. Moreover, the service work that they are involved in is in the interpersonal spheres rather than the goods-supporting services. These groups were most involved in the development of the new movements, and while some of them may be relatively quiescent at the moment, practically all public opinion polls indicate that much of their basic value orientation continues; they are concerned with social change and increasing personal rights.

The assembly-line work discontent about which we hear so much in the seventies derives, we believe, from these vanguard groups, and was expressed initially in service-work areas and in consumer roles, by women who didn't like housework, students who didn't like school, minorities who didn't like meaningless dead-end jobs, and professionals who didn't like bureaucratic, stifling work.

But the service surround and the consumer life do not develop in the abstract. While both are based upon changes in the forces of production, the basic profit system determines the way the services are to be utilized and the *kind of service that will develop.*

The services are distorted by their use as mechanisms for socializing people and reducing discontent, and their effectiveness is marred by professional profit and status seeking, mystification, and the like. Attempts at reducing their costs lead to bureaucratization, efforts at mechanization, and false indicators of productivity.

Consumers are becoming a central force in the emerging service society for the following reasons:

1. They are needed in the market to buy the overproduced goods;
2. They are encouraged to be continuously *dissatisfied* with last year's products;
3. They are "exploited" via high prices and taxes;
4. They have much free time in which to engage with each other and to consider their dissatisfactions and common interests;
5. They are less socialized by the traditional industrial workplace; and
6. Finally, certain consumer groups—minorities, women, and youth—are doubly alienated and angered because they are discriminated against by racism, sexism, and adultism and restricted from access to the industrial setting and the body politic.

These groups may well fit the requirements of a vanguard— namely, that it be needed, that it hurt, and that it have potential power. The expansion of "unbounded" consumer time, filled with much dissatisfaction and alienation, spills over into considerable concern with self and relational issues, as well as political demands concerning personal liberation, self-determination, and identity, re- flected in the various value configurations of the sixties. These were not oriented to traditional economic and political issues but rather focused on a politics of everyday life, producing a behavioral and sexual revolution that has central interpersonal components. Even the new political forms (which we describe as "consumer politics") are much more interpersonal—for example, confrontation, consciousness- raising groups, and persuasion by contagion or by demonstrating an alternative institution or life style.

However, the positive, system-transforming potential of the con- sumer is always limited by the profit frame of neocapitalism and the wasteful consumerism that it fosters. Until the revolutionary potential of the new consciousness is connected to the basic economic and political contradictions of the system, societal reconstruction is unlikely to take place. Rather, we will have an uneven, largely cultural revolution that is politically defanged; at best, an attenuated revolution, one-sided and incomplete.

Index

74 75 76 77 10 9 8 7 6 5 4 3 2 1